T0183753

Lecture Notes in Artificial Intelligence   11327

Subseries of Lecture Notes in Computer Science

Series Editors

Randy Goebel
University of Alberta, Edmonton, Canada
Yuzuru Tanaka
Hokkaido University, Sapporo, Japan
Wolfgang Wahlster
DFKI and Saarland University, Saarbrücken, Germany

Founding Editor

Jörg Siekmann
DFKI and Saarland University, Saarbrücken, Germany

More information about this series at http://www.springer.com/series/1244

Marin Lujak (Ed.)

Agreement Technologies

6th International Conference, AT 2018
Bergen, Norway, December 6–7, 2018
Revised Selected Papers

 Springer

Editor
Marin Lujak
IMT Lille Douai
Douai, France

ISSN 0302-9743 ISSN 1611-3349 (electronic)
Lecture Notes in Artificial Intelligence
ISBN 978-3-030-17293-0 ISBN 978-3-030-17294-7 (eBook)
https://doi.org/10.1007/978-3-030-17294-7

LNCS Sublibrary: SL7 – Artificial Intelligence

This Springer imprint is published by the registered company Springer Nature Switzerland AG
The registered company address is: Gewerbestrasse 11, 6330 Cham, Switzerland

Preface

This volume contains revised proceedings of the 6th International Conference on Agreement Technologies (AT 2018), which was held in Bergen, Norway, during December 6–7, 2018.

AT 2018 was part of the International Conference Series on Agreement Technologies, an international forum of reference in the field based on the notion of agreement among computational agents. It followed the successful outcome of previous editions of the AT Series: AT 2012 in Dubrovnik, Croatia, AT 2013 in Beijing, China, AT 2015 in Athens, Greece, AT 2016 in Valencia, Spain, and AT 2017 in Évry, France. For the fourth year in a row, the aim was to continue promoting scientific information exchange between the EUMAS and AT community. This is why AT 2018 was co-located with the 16th European Conference on Multi-Agent Systems (EUMAS 2018) in the joint program composed of two parallel and four joint sessions.

The preceding five AT conferences engaged reputed researchers from around the world and AT 2018 continued this trend. To attract early-stage as well as experienced researchers, original preliminary and mature work was invited in the form of short and long papers. We received 28 papers by authors coming from 17 countries. After a double-blind review process with a minimum of three and an average of four reviews per paper, 11 were accepted as long papers (39.29%) and six as short ones (21.43%). Researchers from various areas of agreement technologies exchanged novel ideas, techniques, results, and open questions regarding scientific advancements in the design, implementation, and verification of next-generation open distributed systems.

I would like to sincerely thank the AT 2018 local chair, Marija Slavkovik, and the Program Committee for their work and cooperation. I also thank the invited speakers – Elizabeth Sklar from King's College London (key speaker of AT 2018) and Michael Fisher from the University of Liverpool (key speaker of EUMAS 2018) for joining us and sharing their expertise. Their enlightening talks on "Shared Decision-Making in Human–Robot Teams" and "Trustworthy Autonomy" were the key highlights of the conference. Additional thanks are owed to the authors of the submitted papers and to all the participants of AT 2018 and EUMAS 2018 who made this a successful and productive international scientific event. Sincere thanks also to Alfred Hofmann and the staff of Springer for their professional support. Finally, I would like to express my appreciation to the sponsors of the conference, University of Bergen, The Research Council of Norway, and IMT Lille Douai for their support.

February 2019   Marin Lujak

Organization

AT 2018 was organized by the University of Bergen in Norway in cooperation with IMT Lille Douai.

Organizing Committee

Conference Chair

Marin Lujak   IMT Lille Douai, France

Local Chair

Marija Slavkovik   University of Bergen, Norway

Program Committee

Giulia Andrighetto   Institute of Cognitive Sciences and Technologies
                               (ISTC CNR), Rome, Italy
Estefanía Argente   Universitat Politècnica de València, Spain
Reyhan Aydogan   TU Delft, The Netherlands and Özyeğin University,
                               Turkey
Silvana Badaloni   University of Padova, Italy
Roberto Basili   University of Rome Tor Vergata, Italy
Floris Bex   Utrecht University, The Netherlands
Holger Billhardt   University Rey Juan Carlos, Spain
Olivier Boissier   Ecole des Mines de Saint-Étienne, France
Elise Bonzon   LIPADE, Université Paris Descartes, France
Elena Cabrio   Université Côte d'Azur, Inria, CNRS, I3S, France
Carlos Carrascosa   Universitat Politècnica de València, Spain
Amedeo Cesta   Institute of Cognitive Sciences and Technologies
                               (ISTC CNR), Italy
Carlos Chesñevar   Universidad Nacional del Sur, Argentina
Stéphanie Combettes   Institut de recherche en informatique de Toulouse,
                               France
Juan M. Corchado   University of Salamanca, Spain, Osaka Institute of
                               Technology, Japan, and Universiti Malaysia
                               Kelantan, Malaysia
Arnaud Doniec   IMT Lille Douai, France
Sylvie Doutre   IRIT, University of Toulouse, France
Jürgen Dunkel   Hannover University of Applied Sciences and Arts,
                               Germany
Alberto Fernandez   Universidad Rey Juan Carlos, Spain
Nicoletta Fornara   Universitá della Svizzera Italiana, Switzerland

Marija Slavkovik	University of Bergen, Norway
Giuseppe Stecca	Institute for Systems Analysis and Computer Science Antonio Ruberti (IASI-CNR), Italy
Francesca Toni	Imperial College London, UK
Denis Trček	University of Ljubljana, Slovenia
Alessandro Umbrico	Institute of Cognitive Sciences and Technologies (ISTC CNR), Italy
Serena Villata	Université Nice Sophia Antipolis, France
George Vouros	University of Piraeus, Greece
Marin Vuković	University of Zagreb, Croatia
László Zsolt Varga	Eötvös Loránd University, Hungary

Sponsoring Institutions

The Research Council of Norway   University of Bergen   IMT Lille Douai

Contents

Coordination in Open Distributed Systems with Applications

AT Foundations and Modelling of Reasoning Agents

Towards an Approach for Modelling Uncertain Theory of Mind in Multi-Agent Systems

Ştefan Sarkadi[1], Alison R. Panisson[2(✉)], Rafael H. Bordini[2],
Peter McBurney[1], and Simon Parsons[1]

[1] Department of Informatics, King's College London, London, UK
{stefan.sarkadi,peter.mcburney,simon.parsons}@kcl.ac.uk
[2] School of Technology, PUCRS, Porto Alegre, Brazil
alison.panisson@acad.pucrs.br, rafael.bordini@pucrs.br

Abstract. Applying Theory of Mind to multi-agent systems enables agents to model and reason about other agents' minds. Recent work shows that this ability could increase the performance of agents, making them more efficient than agents that lack this ability. However, modelling others agents' minds is a difficult task, given that it involves many factors of uncertainty, e.g., the uncertainty of the communication channel, the uncertainty of reading other agents correctly, and the uncertainty of trust in other agents. In this paper, we explore how agents acquire and update Theory of Mind under conditions of uncertainty. To represent uncertain Theory of Mind, we add probability estimation on a formal semantics model for agent communication based on the BDI architecture and agent communication languages.

Keywords: Multi-agent systems · Theory of Mind · Uncertainty · Socially-aware AI

1 Introduction

It is reasonable to expect that agents could be more effective at achieving their goals during social interactions with other agents if they understand the other agents involved. However, understanding other agents requires the capability of modelling and reasoning about other agents' mental attitudes. These characteristics are intrinsic to Theory of Mind (ToM) [12].

Normally, agents operate under conditions of uncertainty due to the dynamism of the environments in which they are situated [45]. Modelling other agents' minds also involves uncertainty. ToM involves uncertainty not only due to the dynamism of other agents' mental attitudes, e.g., agents might change their beliefs constantly, but also because it involves the uncertainty of a message reaching its audience (i.e., the uncertainty of the communication channels working properly), the uncertainty of other (autonomous) agents telling/acting truly,

© Springer Nature Switzerland AG 2019
M. Lujak (Ed.): AT 2018, LNAI 11327, pp. 3–17, 2019.
https://doi.org/10.1007/978-3-030-17294-7_1

and the uncertainty of an agent reading other agents' mental attitudes correctly during interactions.

Various studies have investigated the application of ToM in Multi-Agent Systems (MAS). Among them, [8,9] investigated the advantages of using different levels of ToM in games played by agents, [33] investigated the role of ToM in modelling dishonest attitudes in MAS, and [3,15,16,27,38] show the advantages of modelling the opponent when considering strategies in argumentation-based dialogues, even though ToM is not represented explicitly. It seems that modelling other agents' minds is an important topic of research, and existing results show important contributions to MAS.

However, as described in [42], most of the work considering the modelling of other agents' minds assume such model as a given, which is an understandable assumption due to the complexity of the problem, but unrealistic. Unfortunately, the question of how to represent the uncertainty of beliefs about others' beliefs when agents acquire and update the model of other agents' minds, i.e., uncertain ToM, has not been fully investigated in the literature. We believe that agents should also to be able to reason and make decisions using ToM. Therefore, taking inspiration from others who have investigated the use of others agents' model during reasoning and decision-making, e.g., [3,8,9,15,16,27,38], we propose an approach to model ToM in software agents that reflects the uncertainty present in agent communication. We also took some inspiration from the STAPLE language. STAPLE (Social and Team Agents Programming Language) has its semantics based on joint intention theory [19]. STAPLE has the goal of reaching a fault-tolerant approach to program teamwork, in which the authors argue that a team is more than a collection of individuals working together to achieve a common goal. The agents in a team must have a shared goal as well as a shared mental state [21]. Thus, STAPLE enables agents to specify the models of other agents, as well temporal properties of actions and events, allowing them to reason about group beliefs, team intentions, and team commitments [20].[1]

Our first contribution is the proposal of an approach to model ToM that reflects the uncertainty of information that agents infer about other agents' minds through communication. To the best of our knowledge, our work is the first to propose a formal model of how agents acquire and update ToM during communication in MAS given the uncertainty of other agents' model, particularly in the practical context of a BDI based Agent-Oriented Programming Language (AOPL). This approach allows us to implement multi-agent communication that reflects some desired properties from communication and common knowledge theories [6]. For example, how agents increase the certainty of their ToM by communicating more and, consequently, how communicating more reinforces the already existing model of the mental attitudes of those agents. Our second contribution is showing how agents may use our approach to reach

---

[1] Note that our approach is more general than that, in which ToM could be used to implement similar approaches for teamwork, which is a likely research direction for our work.

(or not) shared beliefs under conditions of uncertainty, and how agents make decisions using ToM and probabilistic reasoning.

2   Background

2.1   Theory of Mind and the Problem of Other Minds

ToM is the ability of humans to ascribe elements such as beliefs, desires, and intentions, and relations between these elements to other human agents. In other words, it is the ability to form mental models of other agents [1]. There are two major theories about ToM. One theory of ToM is the Theory-Theory of Mind (henceforth TT). TT can be described as a theory based approach for assigning states to other agents. While some argue TT is nothing else but folk psychology, others say that it is a more scientific way of mindreading [13]. The other major theory is Simulation Theory of Mind (henceforth ST), which is described to be 'process-driven rather than theory-driven' [2]. In other words, ST emphasises the process of putting oneself into another's shoes. TT argues for a hypothesis testing method of model extraction, whereas ST argues for a simulation based method for model selection.

An important factor that influences the acquisition, formation, or modification of ToM is uncertainty. Inferring the beliefs of others is a notorious epistemological issue named by philosophers *The Problem of Other Minds* [17]. The problem still stands since the times of Descartes [23]. It would be unreasonable for one to assume that ToM is absolute or that ToM is a universal set of beliefs shared by all agents in a system. Therefore, we believe that a reasonable approach to model how ToM is acquired and updated by artificial agents has to be able to represent the uncertainty with which agents infer beliefs about other agents' beliefs.

2.2   Agent Communication Languages

Agent communication languages have been developed based on the speech act theory [41]. Speech act theory is concerned with the role of language as actions. Among the agent communication languages which emerged from the speech act theory, FIPA-ACL [11] and KQML [10] are the best known.

In this work, for practical reasons, we choose KQML, which is the standard communication language in the Jason platform [5], the multi-agent platform we choose to implement this work. Knowledge Query and Manipulation Language (KQML) was designed to support interaction among intelligent software agents, describing the message format and message-handling protocol to support runtime agent communication [10, 25].

In order to make KQML broadly applicable, a semantic framework for KQML was proposed in [22]. The semantics for KQML-based messages in the AgentSpeak programming language, as given in [43] and implemented in Jason [5], formalises how the locutions successively operate on the states of agents, making the references to the mental attitudes of BDI agents explicit, thus addressing some of the problems of ACLs pointed out in [44]. Based on that semantics, we put forward the idea that agents are able to infer the likely model of other agents' minds during the process of communication, i.e., agents are able to acquire and update ToM, as we describe later in this paper.

2.3 Agent Oriented Programming Languages

Among the many AOPL and platforms, such as Jason, Jadex, Jack, AgentFactory, 2APL, GOAL, Golog, and MetateM, as discussed in [4], we chose the Jason platform [5] for our work. Jason extends the AgentSpeak language, an abstract logic-based AOPL introduced by Rao [37], which is one of the best-known languages inspired by the BDI architecture.

Besides specifying agents with well-defined mental attitudes based on the BDI architecture, the Jason platform [5] has some other features that are particularly interesting for our work, for example strong negation, belief annotations, and (customisable) speech-act based communication. Strong negation helps the modelling of uncertainty, allowing the representation of propositions that the agent: (i) believes to be true, e.g., about(paper1, uncertain_tom); (ii) believes to be false, e.g., ¬about(paper2, uncertain_tom); (iii) is ignorant about, i.e., the agent has no information about whether a paper is about uncertain_tom or not. Also, Jason automatically generates annotations for all the beliefs in the agents' belief base about the source from where the belief was obtained (which can be from sensing the environment, communication with other agents, or a mental note created by the agent itself). The annotation has the following format: about(paper1, tom)[source(reviewer1)], stating that the source of the belief that paper1 is about the topic tom is reviewer1. The annotations in Jason can be easily extended to include other meta-information, for example, trust and time as used in [26,30]. Another interesting feature of Jason is the communication between agents, which is done through a predefined (internal) action. There are a number of performatives allowing rich communication between agents in Jason, as explained in detail in [5]. Further, new performatives can be easily defined (or redefined) in order to give special meaning to them[2], which is an essential characteristic for this work.

3 Running Example

As a running example, we will take the following university scenario with five agents. The first agent, *John*, plays the role of a professor in the university, and the other agents, named *Bob*, *Alice*, *Nick*, and *Ted*, play the role of students. *John* has a relation of *adviser* with the *students*. Also, *John* is responsible for distributing tasks to students, which the students can accept or refuse. *John* keeps information about the students, in order to assign tasks that the students are more likely to accept.

---

[2] For example, [31,32] propose new performatives for argumentation-based communication between Jason agents.

Our model can be formally defined as $\langle Ag, \mathcal{T}, \mathcal{A}, \mathcal{S} \rangle$, in which Ag represents the set of agents, $\mathcal{T}$ the set of tasks of the kind $\mathcal{T} \subseteq \mathcal{A} \times \mathcal{S}$, describing an action from $\mathcal{A}$, requiring knowledge about a subset of subjects from $\mathcal{S}$, that might be executed to achieve the task $\mathcal{T}$. In our example, we consider the following actions, subjects, and tasks:

- $\mathcal{A} = \{\texttt{write\_paper}, \texttt{review\_paper}, \texttt{paper\_seminar}\}$
- $\mathcal{S} = \{\texttt{mas}, \texttt{kr}, \texttt{tom}\}$
- $\mathcal{T} = \left\{ \begin{array}{l} \texttt{task(write\_paper, [mas, tom])} \\ \texttt{task(review\_paper, [kr])} \\ \texttt{task(paper\_seminar, [tom, mas])} \end{array} \right\}$

For example, the task to *write a paper with the subjects MAS and ToM*, $\texttt{task(write\_paper, [mas, tom])}$, requires competence on both subjects: $\texttt{mas}$ and $\texttt{tom}$. Thus, this task has a greater likelihood to be accepted by a student who desires to execute that particular task, or who likes to execute the action $\texttt{write\_paper}$ and believes that itself knows the necessary subjects (e.g., $\texttt{knows(mas)}$ and $\texttt{knows(tom)}$ are necessary to execute this example task). Thus the probability of an agent ag to accept a task t_i is given by the following equation:

$$P(accepts(ag, task_i)) = \begin{cases} P(Des_{ag}(task_i)) & \text{if } Des_{ag}(task_i) \in \Delta_{John} \\ P(Bel_{ag}(likes(a_i))) \times P(Bel_{ag}(knows(S'))) & \text{otherwise} \end{cases}$$

with

$$P(Bel_{ag}(knows(S'))) = \prod_{s_i \in S'} P(Bel_{ag}(knows(s_i)))$$

where $task_i = \texttt{task}(\texttt{a}_\texttt{i}, \texttt{S}')$, for $task_i \in \mathcal{T}$, $a_i \in \mathcal{A}$, and $S' \subseteq \mathcal{S}$. Δ_{John} represents *John*'s knowledge.

Thus, considering our scenario, when *John* knows that some student ag likely desires to execute a particular task $task_i$, i.e., $Des_{ag}(task_i)$, it can use this information to assign the task. Otherwise, *John* can calculate the likely acceptance for each student ag, based on the probability of each student to like executing that action, $P(Bel_{ag}(likes(a_i)))$, and the knowledge the student has about each of the required subjects $P(Bel_{ag}(knows(S')))$. Note that, while modelling the students' desires is more difficult to obtain in our scenario, the students' beliefs are easily obtained by *John*, given that *John* frequently talks to students about these subjects and tasks.

In reality, agents operate with uncertain information, especially in the cases of thinking about other agents' minds. The minds of others are considered to be some sort of black boxes that are more or less accessible depending on the given scenario. Reasoning under uncertainty is a classic case where bounded rationality acts as a major constraint on what agents can infer from their beliefs. However, even if agents are constrained by their access to information, it does not mean that the agents cannot reach reasonable conclusions about the minds of other agents [14, 23].

In our scenario, *John* will reason and make decisions based on information it has about the students' minds, i.e., information from its ToM. Thus *John* will reach conclusions based on uncertain information, given that its ToM contains information about students' minds that has been estimated through the communication *John* has had with the students. Considering that an approach to reason about uncertain information, uncertain ToM in our case, is using probabilistic reasoning, as described in [14], we have modelled *John*'s decision-making process based on the probability of each information in *John*'s ToM to be correct, considering some factors of uncertainty we will describe further in this paper.

4   Modelling ToM from Other Agents' Actions

In this paper, we are going to consider the modelling of ToM based on communication only, which can be considered a general approach for any application, based on the semantics of each speech act used. On the other hand, the semantics for other actions, e.g., actions agents execute in the environment, might have different meaning according to different application domains.

In order to describe our approach, we use the following notation: $Bel_{ag}(\psi)$ means that an agent ag believes ψ; $Des_{ag}(\psi)$ means that an agent ag desires ψ; Δ_{ag} represents the ag's knowledge base. Two distinct agents are represented using ag_i and ag_j, with ag_i, $ag_j \in Ag$, and $ag_i \neq ag_j$. We label the updates agents execute in their ToM with γ, which can be used to represent the uncertainty of that information. In Sect. 5, we propose an approach for uncertain ToM, which is a particular instance for such γ label.

The speech acts considered in this particular work and their semantics are based on our work in [29]. Messages are represented as $\langle$sender, receiver, performative, content$\rangle$, and the meaning of each message is associated with the performative used:

- $\langle ag_i, ag_j, \mathtt{tell}, \psi \rangle$ means a message sent by agent ag_i to agent ag_j, with the tell performative, and content ψ. When ag_i sends this message, it carries out the following update[3] on its ToM:

$$\Delta_{ag_i} = \Delta_{ag_i} \cup Bel_{ag_i}(\psi)_{[\gamma]} \tag{1}$$

  When ag_j receives this message, it carries out the following update on its ToM:

$$\Delta_{ag_j} = \Delta_{ag_j} \cup Bel_{ag_i}(\psi)_{[\gamma]} \tag{2}$$

- $\langle ag_i, ag_j, \mathtt{ask}, \psi \rangle$ means a message sent by agent ag_i to agent ag_j, with the ask performative, and content ψ. When ag_i sends this message, it carries out the following update on its ToM:

$$\Delta_{ag_i} = \Delta_{ag_i} \cup Bel_{ag_j}(Des_{ag_i}(\psi))_{[\gamma]} \tag{3}$$

---

[3] Note that we are ignoring any other updates agents execute in their mental attitudes, given we are interested only in the updates agents make on their ToM.

When ag_j receives this message, it carries out the following update on its ToM:

$$\Delta_{ag_j} = \Delta_{ag_j} \cup Des_{ag_i}(\psi)_{[\gamma]} \tag{4}$$

Before introducing our approach for uncertain ToM, imagine that ToM could be modelled without uncertainty, i.e., that we could ignore γ in our semantic rules. Then, based on these simple semantic rules for agent communication, we are able to show that agents can reach shared beliefs in a relatively straightforward way [29].

Definition 1 (Shared Beliefs Using ToM). *An agent ag_i will reach a state of shared beliefs with another agent ag_j when, for a belief φ, it is able to match its own belief φ with a ToM about ag_j believing φ, i.e., $\varphi \wedge Bel_{ag_j}(\varphi)$.*

Example (Shared Beliefs Without Uncertainty): Following the scenario introduced, imagine that two students, *Alice* and *Bob*, need to work together to accomplish a particular task `paper_seminar`, which requires the subjects `mas` (Multi-Agent Systems) and `tom` (Theory of Mind). Also, while *Alice* only knows the subject of `mas`, *Bob* only knows the subject of `tom`. Considering that both *Alice* and *Bob* need to know both topics in order to help each other during the paper seminar, they decide to exchange knowledge about these topics. Thus, they might reach some shared beliefs (knowledge) about both topics. Note that, in this scenario, *Alice* and *Bob* assume that both are cooperating and both are rational. Thus, *Bob* starts the dialogue telling *Alice* that *"Theory of Mind is an approach to model others' minds"*, i.e., $\langle alice, \mathtt{tell}, \mathtt{def(tom},$ "an approach to model others' mind")$\rangle$. At that moment, following the semantics for the `tell` performative (Eq. (1)), *Bob* updates its ToM with the following information $Bel_{alice}(\mathtt{def(tom)},$ "an approach to model others' minds"). After that, when *Alice* receives this message, following the semantics for the `tell` performative (Eq. (2)), *Alice* updates its belief base with the following information $\mathtt{def(tom},$ "an approach to model others' mind"), as well as *Alice* updates its ToM about *Bob* with $Bel_{bob}(\mathtt{def(tom)},$ "an approach to model others' minds"). At this moment, both *Alice* and *Bob* reach a state of shared belief about the definition of `tom`, according to Definition 1.

However, agents operate under conditions of uncertainty in a MAS, and the previous assumptions are hard to obtain; thus, agents will face uncertainty about their ToM, and consequently about their shared beliefs. For example, when an agent sends a message, it faces the uncertainty of the communication channel, i.e., the uncertainty of the message reaching the receiver. Also, when receiving a message, an agent faces the uncertainty of the truth of that statement, e.g., an agent is not able to verify if the other agents are acting maliciously [33,40], thus it needs to consider the uncertainty of information it receives for those agents based on how much it trusts them [26,34,35].

One manner to overcome the uncertainty and reach a more accurate ToM, following the literature on *common knowledge* [6], is increasing the communication between agents. Thus, an agent is able to increase the certainty on a given agent ag_j believing φ, confirming whether its ToM about agent ag_j believing φ is correct. That is, the agent is able to infer that ag_j believes φ by reinforcing this belief through communication. Henceforth we describe our model for uncertain ToM, which is compatible with that behaviour.

5 A Model of Uncertain ToM

In this section we propose an approach to model ToM that reflects the uncertainty present in MAS. In order to show our approach, we are going to consider some parameter values. The first, α, reflects the uncertainty of the communication channel when sending a message. The second, β, reflects the uncertainty of the other agents telling the truth, i.e., when an agent ag_i tells φ to agent ag_j, agent ag_j is able to model that ag_i believes on φ with a degree of certainty equal to β. For simplicity, we will assume that an agent will model its ToM about the other agents with a degree of certainty equal to the trust it has on the source[4], following the ideas introduced in [34, 35].

Definition 2. *The label γ will be instantiated with $\gamma = (\alpha, t)$ for an agent sending a message, and $\gamma = (\beta, t)$ for an agent receiving a message, where α represents the uncertainty of the message reaching the target, β the uncertainty of the sender telling the truth, and t a discrete representation of the time of the MAS in which the message was exchanged.*

Thus, following Definition 2, a trace of different updates on the ToM is constructed over time. Note that α and β reflect the uncertainty of an update at a given time. In order to execute reasoning over the ToM, agents are able to use the trace of these updates to calculate the degree of certainty on their model. Using this trace, we are able to model some desired behaviour from communication theory in agent communication, as we will describe later in this paper.

For example, considering our scenario, when *Bob* tells *Alice* that "Theory of Mind is an approach to model others' minds", considering also that *Bob* knows that the efficiency of the communication channel is 0.9, i.e., $\alpha = 0.9$, *Bob* will update its ToM, following the semantics for the `tell` performative (Eq. (1)) and Definition 2, with the information $Bel_{alice}(\mathrm{def(tom)}$, "an approach to model others' minds")$_{[(0.9,t_i)]}$, with t_i the discrete time when the communication occurred. When *Alice* receives this message, considering that the trust *Alice* has on *Bob* telling the truth is 0.8, i.e., $\beta = 0.8$, and following the semantics for the `tell` performative (Eq. (2)) and Definition 2, *Alice* updates its ToM with $Bel_{bob}(\mathrm{def(tom)}$, "an approach to model other minds")$_{[(0.8,t_j)]}$, with t_j the discrete time at which the message was received, with $t_i < t_j$. Both *Alice* and *Bob* model uncertainty of their ToM about each other believing on the definition of ToM.

Considering uncertain ToM, we need to redefine shared beliefs, in order to reflect the uncertainty of agents' models.

---

[4] In [28], the authors show that trust aggregates not only the sincerity of the source but also the expertise the source has about the information communicated.

Definition 3 (Shared Beliefs Using Uncertain ToM). *An agent ag_i will reach a state of shared beliefs with another agent ag_j when, for a belief φ, it is able to match its own belief φ with a ToM about ag_j believing φ with a predetermined degree of certainty χ, i.e., $\varphi \wedge P(Bel_{ag_j}(\varphi)) \geq \chi$, with χ a value describing the certainty necessary to consider φ a shared belief.*

Following the literature on common knowledge [6], if two individuals ag_i and ag_j can repeatedly communicate, then they can repeatedly reinforce their mental state regarding an information φ. For example, telling each other that φ is true, they should increase the certainty of each others' belief in φ. In order to model this desired behaviour in our model, we maintain the trace of all updates an agent executes in its ToM, and using this trace we are able to aggregate different pieces of evidence in order to increase the certainty on ToM. There are many different ways to model this desired behaviour on agent communication, and it could consider the particularities of each application domain. In our scenario, the information communicated by agents, e.g. a concept definition, does not change over time. Thus, for simplicity, we do not weight each information according to the time it was received and the current time of the MAS, we only consider the number of evidences about that information. Thus, we model this desired behaviour using the following equation:

$$P(Bel_{Ag}(\varphi)) = \begin{cases} f(Bel_{ag}(\varphi)) & \text{if } f(Bel_{ag}(\varphi)) <= 1 \\ 1 & \text{otherwise} \end{cases} \tag{5}$$

$$f(Bel_{ag}(\varphi)) = \frac{\sum\limits_{t_i \in \Delta T} v \mid Bel_{ag}(\varphi)_{[(v,t_i)]}}{|\Delta T|} + (\lambda \times |\Delta T|) \tag{6}$$

with ΔT the number of occurrences of $Bel_{ag}(\varphi)_{[(v,t_i)]}$ in the agent ToM, and λ the *evidence factor*, i.e., a parameter that reinforce the certainty on that information according to how often it occurs in the trace. Equation 6 calculates the average of the trace for $Bel_{ag}(\varphi)$ plus the evidence factor. Thus, following Definition 3, ag_i is able to reach a state of shared belief with another agent ag_j about a belief φ when it is able to infer $P(Bel_{ag_j}(\varphi)) \geq \chi$ from Eq. 5 with $\chi = 1$, for example.

Proposition 1 (Reaching Shared Beliefs—ToM with Uncertainty). *When λ is a positive value, agents are able to eventually reach a state of shared beliefs, even considering $\chi = 1$, provided they communicate the same information repeatedly. Also, the greater the value of λ, the faster agents will reach the state of shared beliefs.*

Example (Shared Beliefs Under Conditions of Uncertainty): Following our example, imagine that *Bob* wants to reach a state of shared beliefs with *Alice* about the definition of ToM under the conditions of uncertainty described above. Thus, after sending the previous message and updating its ToM with $Bel_{alice}(\texttt{def(tom)}$, "an approach to model others' minds")$_{[(0.9,t_i)]}$, *Bob* has two options to increase the certainty on its ToM about *Alice* believing on that definition: (i) telling *Alice* that definition more times, or (ii) asking *Alice* the definition of ToM and waiting for an answer from *Alice*, in which *Alice* tells *Bob* the definition of ToM. Considering $\lambda = 0.1$, in the first case, when *Bob* tells *Alice* about the definition of ToM one more time, following the semantics for the `tell` performative (Eq. (1)) and Definition 2, *Bob* adds $Bel_{alice}(\text{def}(\text{tom})$, "an approach to model others' minds")$_{[(0.9,t_j)]}$ to its ToM, with $t_i < t_j$. Thus, Eq. 5 returns 1, considering the average $0.9 + 0.2$ from the evidence factor, which is 0.1 multiplied by the number of evidences (Eq. (6)). Also, following the semantics for the `tell` performative (Eq. (2)) and Definition 2, *Alice* updates its ToM with $Bel_{bob}(\text{def}(\text{tom})$, "an approach to model other minds")$_{[(0.8,t_j)]}$, and Eq. (5) returns 1, considering the average $0.8 + 0.2$ from the evidence factor (Eq. (6)). Thus, they reach a state of shared belief about the definition of ToM[5], considering $\chi = 1$ in Definition 3. In the other case, *Bob* asks to *Alice* to tell him the definition of ToM, and it waits for the answer. When *Alice* tells *Bob* the definition of ToM, *Alice* and *Bob* update their ToM with $Bel_{bob}(\text{def}(\text{tom})$, "an approach to model other minds")$_{[(0.9,t_j)]}$, $Bel_{alice}(\text{def}(\text{tom})$, "an approach to model others' minds")$_{[(0.8,t_i)]}$, respectively. For both, Eq. (5) returns 1, considering the average $0.85 + 0.2$ from the evidence factor, reaching a state of shared beliefs about the definition of ToM according to Definition 3 with $\chi = 1$.

6 Decision Making Using Uncertain ToM

Apart from enabling agents to model other agents' minds and allowing them to improve their models during communicative interactions, it is also essential that agents are able to make decisions using these models. Normally, a decision-making process is associated with the application domain, i.e., it is domain dependent. Therefore, we will present the decision-making process for the task assignment problem introduced in Sect. 3.

In our scenario, during advising sessions, *John* asks students about different tasks they like to execute, as well as the different subjects the students are reading about (the subjects the students know about). Thus, *John* acquires ToM about the students, and its ToM becomes more accurate as they have more advising sessions, and consequently they communicate more with each other.

$$
John_{ToM} = \left\{
\begin{array}{l}
Bel_{alice}(\text{likes}(\text{paper\_seminar}))_{[0.8]} \\
Bel_{alice}(\text{likes}(\text{write\_paper}))_{[0.7]} \\
Bel_{bob}(\text{likes}(\text{review\_paper}))_{[0.9]} \\
Bel_{bob}(\text{likes}(\text{write\_paper}))_{[0.8]} \\
Bel_{nick}(\text{likes}(\text{review\_paper}))_{[0.6]} \\
Bel_{nick}(\text{likes}(\text{write\_paper}))_{[0.5]} \\
Bel_{ted}(\text{likes}(\text{write\_paper}))_{[0.8]} \\
Bel_{ted}(\text{likes}(\text{paper\_seminar}))_{[0.4]} \\
Bel_{ted}(\text{likes}(\text{review\_paper}))_{[0.6]}
\end{array}
\right\}
$$

---

[5] When considering $\gamma = 0.1$ and α and $\beta >= 0.8$, agents are able to reach shared beliefs communicating only 2 messages.

For example, *John* has asked (in different meetings and times) *Bob*, *Alice*, *Nick*, and *Ted* which academic tasks they like to execute, e.g., ⟨*bob*, *AskIf*, likes(T)⟩. After receiving this message, according to the semantic rule for the ask performative (Eq. (4)), each student knows that *John* desires to know which task they like to execute. Based on this knowledge, each student has answered to *John* the tasks they like to execute, *John* has received these messages and updated its ToM as shown in $John_{ToM}$ [6].

Continuing with the example, during a meeting *Alice* asks *John* if there is any scheduled paper seminar about ToM and MAS, i.e., ⟨john, *AskIf*, task(paper_seminar, [tom, mas])⟩. Thus, based on the semantic rule for the ask performative (Eq. (4)), *John* models that *Alice* is likely to desire that task, i.e., $Des_{alice}(\text{task}(\text{paper\_seminar}, [\text{tom}, \text{mas}]))_{[0.7]}$, answering positively. Also, imagine that *John* has asked the students which subject they have knowledge about, resulting in the following additional information to *John*'s ToM:

$$John_{ToM} = \begin{cases} Bel_{alice}(\text{knows}(\text{tom}))_{[0.8]} & Bel_{bob}(\text{knows}(\text{mas}))_{[0.8]} \\ Bel_{alice}(\text{knows}(\text{mas}))_{[0.9]} & Bel_{bob}(\text{knows}(\text{kr}))_{[0.9]} \\ Bel_{nick}(\text{knows}(\text{kr}))_{[0.8]} & Bel_{ted}(\text{knows}(\text{tom}))_{[0.8]} \\ Bel_{nick}(\text{knows}(\text{mas}))_{[0.7]} & Bel_{ted}(\text{knows}(\text{kr}))_{[0.5]} \\ Bel_{nick}(\text{knows}(\text{tom}))_{[0.8]} & Bel_{ted}(\text{knows}(\text{mas}))_{[0.8]} \end{cases}$$

Using its ToM, *John* executes the probabilistic reasoning described in Sect. 3, which computes the likelihood for each student to accept each task as shown in Table 1. Note that the likelihood of *Alice* accepting the task paper_seminar

Table 1. Likelihood calculation for task assignment

Student	Task	Likelihood
Alice	task(write_paper, [mas, tom])	0.5
Alice	task(review_paper, [kr])	0.0
Alice	task(paper_seminar, [tom, mas])	**0.7**
Bob	task(write_paper, [mas, tom])	0.0
Bob	task(review_paper, [kr])	**0.8**
Bob	task(paper_seminar, [tom, mas])	0.0
Nick	task(write_paper, [mas, tom])	0.3
Nick	task(review_paper, [kr])	**0.5**
Nick	task(paper_seminar, [tom, mas])	0.0
Ted	task(write_paper, [mas, tom])	**0.5**
Ted	task(review_paper, [kr])	0.2
Ted	task(paper_seminar, [tom, mas])	0.1

---

[6] We do not represent the time at which the messages were communicated, but since they were communicated at different times we introduced different values for γ.

is based on the information $Des_{alice}(\text{task}(\text{paper\_seminar}, [\text{tom}, \text{mas}]))_{[0.7]}$ in *John*'s ToM, while the other results are based on the likelihood of the students liking a particular task and knowing the subjects related to that task. Thus, *John* concludes that it is possible to increase the probability of each task to be accepted by the students by offering the task $\text{task}(\text{paper\_seminar}, [\text{tom}, \text{mas}])$ to *Alice*, offering $\text{task}(\text{review\_paper}, [\text{kr}])$ to *Bob*, and offering $\text{task}(\text{write\_paper}, [\text{mas}, \text{tom}])$ to *Ted*.

7   Future Work

Uncertainty does not only arise from noisy communication channels or levels of trust between agents. As future work, we plan to add an environment to our model in order to represent how agents infer ToM from the observation of actions performed by other agents in that environment. The modelling of ToM based on these aspects faces complex issues such as the ones mentioned in [7]: *"the slamming of a door communicates the slammer's anger only when the intended observer of that act realises that the slammer wanted both to slam the door in his face and for the observer to believe that to be his intention"*. This means that there is both uncertainty about the slammer's intentions and uncertainty about the act of slamming the door, which could be caused by an accidental shove or by natural means, hence not represent a communicative act. Therefore, observing such an event occur should not cause the observer to make any inference about the slammer's mental state. That being said, modelling ToM based on environment observations requires more than only representing both intended and non-intended acts of communication. The slammer might very well not intend to communicate when slamming the door, but that does not stop the observer from reading a message when observing the slamming of the door. These complex issues arise with the inclusion of ToM because agents are able to project beliefs in the minds of other agents they share an environment, or even just a communication channel, with. Therefore, the agents that project beliefs can be subject to what is known as the *Mind Projection Fallacy* [18]. An agent commits this fallacy using ToM when the agent incorrectly assigns beliefs to another agent's mind[7]. In our future work, we hope to improve our model in order to be able to represent complex phenomena such as the mind projection fallacy.

8   Conclusions

We have proposed an approach for agents to acquire and update their ToM during communication whilst reflecting on the uncertainty of this process. To the best of our knowledge, our work is the first to explicitly address acquisition and update of uncertain ToM in MAS. In order to show how our approach allows us to model desired properties from communication and common knowledge

---

[7] It is similar to committing a type I error in a statistical analysis.

theories [6], we have proposed a model for uncertain ToM. Using our approach, agents are able to reach accurate ToM and, consequently, accurate shared beliefs by reinforcing their mental attitudes through communication. Furthermore, in this work, we have shown not only how agents acquire and update ToM based on agent communication, but also how agents reason and make decisions using ToM.

The modelling of ToM in MAS under the condition of uncertainty is an important step towards obtaining more realistic and more socially aware artificial agents. We argue that the approach we used to model ToM in MAS is in tune with what we believe to be an upcoming discipline in the field of AI, namely the study of machine behaviour as proposed by [36]. Thus, modelling ToM is relevant to both the AI community and to multi-disciplinary research groups because it offers the possibility to study how agents reach agreements with [24], cooperate with [39], or even behave dishonestly towards [33,40] other agents using more realistic models of social interactions.

Acknowledgements. We gratefully acknowledge the partial support from CAPES and CNPq. Special thanks to Francesca Mosca for the support and for the feedback on this paper.

References

1. Apperly, I.A.: What is theory of mind? concepts, cognitive processes and individual differences. Q. J. Exp. Psychol. **65**(5), 825–839 (2012)
2. Barlassina, L., Gordon, R.M.: Folk psychology as mental simulation. In: Zalta, E.N. (ed.) The Stanford Encyclopedia of Philosophy. Metaphysics Research Lab, Stanford University, summer 2017 edn. (2017)
3. Black, E., Atkinson, K.: Choosing persuasive arguments for action. In: The 10th International Conference on Autonomous Agents and Multiagent Systems, pp. 905–912 (2011)
4. El Fallah Seghrouchni, A., Dix, J., Dastani, M., Bordini, R.H. (eds.): Multi-Agent Programming. Springer, Boston, MA (2009). https://doi.org/10.1007/978-0-387-89299-3
5. Bordini, R.H., Hübner, J.F., Wooldridge, M.: Programming Multi-Agent Systems in AgentSpeak using Jason (Wiley Series in Agent Technology). Wiley, Hoboken (2007)
6. Chwe, M.S.Y.: Rational Ritual. Culture, Coordination, and Common Knowledge. Princeton University Press, Princeton (2001)
7. Cohen, P.R., Perrault, C.R.: Elements of a plan-based theory of speech acts. In: Readings in Distributed Artificial Intelligence, pp. 169–186. Elsevier (1988)
8. de Weerd, H., Verheij, B.: The advantage of higher-order theory of mind in the game of limited bidding. In: Proceedings of the Workshop on Reasoning About Other Minds, CEUR Workshop Proceedings, vol. 751, pp. 149–164 (2011)
9. de Weerd, H., Verbrugge, R., Verheij, B.: Higher-order social cognition in rock-paper-scissors: a simulation study. In: Proceedings of the 11th International Conference on Autonomous Agents and Multiagent Systems, pp. 1195–1196 (2012)
10. Finin, T., Fritzson, R., McKay, D., McEntire, R.: KQML as an agent communication language. In: Proceedings of the 3rd international conference on Information and knowledge management, pp. 456–463. ACM (1994)

11. FIPA, T.: FIPA communicative act library specification. Foundation for Intelligent Physical Agents (15.02.2018) (2008). http://www.fipa.org/specs/fipa00037/SC00037J.html
12. Goldman, A.I.: Theory of mind. In: The Oxford Handbook of Philosophy of Cognitive Science, 2012 edn. vol. 1, Oxford Handbooks Online (2012)
13. Gopnik, A., Glymour, C., Sobel, D.M., Schulz, L.E., Kushnir, T., Danks, D.: A theory of causal learning in children: causal maps and bayes nets. Psychol. Rev. **111**(1), 3 (2004)
14. Gopnik, A., Wellman, H.M.: Reconstructing constructivism: causal models, Bayesian learning mechanisms, and the theory theory. Psychol. Bull. **138**(6), 1085 (2012)
15. Hadidi, N., Dimopoulos, Y., Moraitis, P., et al.: Tactics and concessions for argumentation-based negotiation. In: COMMA, pp. 285–296 (2012)
16. Hadjinikolis, C., Siantos, Y., Modgil, S., Black, E., McBurney, P.: Opponent modelling in persuasion dialogues. In: International Joint Conference on Artificial Intelligence, pp. 164–170 (2013)
17. Hyslop, A.: Other minds. In: Zalta, E.N. (ed.) The Stanford Encyclopedia of Philosophy. Metaphysics Research Lab, Stanford University, spring 2016 edn. (2016)
18. Jaynes, E.T.: Probability theory as logic. In: Fougère, P.F. (ed.) Maximum Entropy and Bayesian Methods. Springer, Dordrecht (1990). https://doi.org/10.1007/978-94-009-0683-9_1
19. Kumar, S., Cohen, P.R.: STAPLE: an agent programming language based on the joint intention theory. In: Proceedings of the 3rd International Joint Conference on Autonomous Agents and Multiagent Systems, pp. 1390–1391 (2004)
20. Kumar, S., Cohen, P.R., Huber, M.J.: Direct execution of team specifications in STAPLE. In: Proceedings of the 1st International Joint Conference on Autonomous Agents and Multiagent Systems, pp. 567–568 (2002)
21. Kumar, S., Cohen, P.R., Levesque, H.J.: The adaptive agent architecture: achieving fault-tolerance using persistent broker teams. In: Proceedings of Fourth International Conference on MultiAgent Systems, pp. 159–166 (2000)
22. Labrou, Y., Finin, T.: A semantics approach for KQML - a general purpose communication language for software agents. In: Proceedings of the Third International Conference on Information and knowledge Management, pp. 447–455. ACM (1994)
23. Leudar, I., Costall, A.: On the persistence of the problem of other minds in psychology: chomsky, grice and theory of mind. Theory Psychol. **14**(5), 601–621 (2004)
24. Luck, M., McBurney, P.: Computing as interaction: agent and agreement technologies. In: IEEE International Conference on Distributed Human-machine Systems. IEEE Press, Citeseer (2008)
25. Mayfield, J., Labrou, Y., Finin, T.: Evaluation of KQML as an agent communication language. In: Wooldridge, M., Müller, J.P., Tambe, M. (eds.) ATAL 1995. LNCS, vol. 1037, pp. 347–360. Springer, Heidelberg (1996). https://doi.org/10.1007/3540608052_77
26. Melo, V.S., Panisson, A.R., Bordini, R.H.: Argumentation-based reasoning using preferences over sources of information. In: 15th International Conference on Autonomous Agents and Multiagent Systems (2016)
27. Oren, N., Norman, T.J.: Arguing using opponent models. In: McBurney, P., Rahwan, I., Parsons, S., Maudet, N. (eds.) ArgMAS 2009. LNCS (LNAI), vol. 6057, pp. 160–174. Springer, Heidelberg (2010). https://doi.org/10.1007/978-3-642-12805-9_10

28. Paglieri, F., Castelfranchi, C., da Costa Pereira, C., Falcone, R., Tettamanzi, A., Villata, S.: Trusting the messenger because of the message: feedback dynamics from information quality to source evaluation. Comput. Math. Organ. Theory **20**(2), 176–194 (2014)
29. Panisson, A.R., Sarkadi, S., McBurney, P., Parsons, S., Bordini, R.H.: On the formal semantics of theory of mind in agent communication. In: 6th International Conference on Agreement Technologies (2018)
30. Panisson, A.R., Melo, V.S., Bordini, R.H.: Using preferences over sources of information in argumentation-based reasoning. In: 5th Brazilian Conference on Intelligent Systems, pp. 31–26 (2016)
31. Panisson, A.R., Meneguzzi, F., Fagundes, M., Vieira, R., Bordini, R.H.: Formal semantics of speech acts for argumentative dialogues. In: 13th International Conference on Autonomous Agents and Multiagent Systems, pp. 1437–1438 (2014)
32. Panisson, A.R., Meneguzzi, F., Vieira, R., Bordini, R.H.: Towards practical argumentation in multi-agent systems. In: Brazilian Conference on Intelligent Systems (2015)
33. Panisson, A.R., Sarkadi, S., McBurney, P., Parsons, S., Bordini, R.H.: Lies, bullshit, and deception in agent-oriented programming languages. In: Proceedings of the 20th International Trust Workshop, pp. 50–61 (2018)
34. Parsons, S., Sklar, E., McBurney, P.: Using argumentation to reason with and about trust. In: McBurney, P., Parsons, S., Rahwan, I. (eds.) ArgMAS 2011. LNCS (LNAI), vol. 7543, pp. 194–212. Springer, Heidelberg (2012). https://doi.org/10.1007/978-3-642-33152-7_12
35. Parsons, S., Tang, Y., Sklar, E., McBurney, P., Cai, K.: Argumentation-based reasoning in agents with varying degrees of trust. In: The 10th International Conference on Autonomous Agents and Multiagent Systems, pp. 879–886 (2011)
36. Rahwan, I., Cebrian, M.: Machine behavior needs to be an academic discipline (2018). http://nautil.us/issue/58/self/machine-behavior-needs-to-be-an-academic-discipline
37. Rao, A.S.: AgentSpeak(L): BDI agents speak out in a logical computable language. In: Van de Velde, W., Perram, J.W. (eds.) MAAMAW 1996. LNCS, vol. 1038, pp. 42–55. Springer, Heidelberg (1996). https://doi.org/10.1007/BFb0031845
38. Rienstra, T., Thimm, M., Oren, N.: Opponent models with uncertainty for strategic argumentation. In: International Joint Conference on Artificial Intelligence, pp. 332–338 (2013)
39. Rosenschein, J.S.: Rational interaction: cooperation among intelligent agents (1986)
40. Sarkadi, S.: Deception. In: IJCAI, pp. 5781–5782 (2018)
41. Searle, J.R.: Speech Acts: An Essay in the Philosophy of Language. Cambridge University Press, Cambridge (1969)
42. Thimm, M.: Strategic argumentation in multi-agent systems. KI-Künstliche Intelligenz **28**(3), 159–168 (2014)
43. Vieira, R., Moreira, A., Wooldridge, M., Bordini, R.H.: On the formal semantics of speech-act based communication in an agent-oriented programming language. J. Artif. Int. Res. **29**(1), 221–267 (2007)
44. Wooldridge, M.: Semantic issues in the verification of agent communication languages. Auton. Agent. Multi-Agent Syst. **3**(1), 9–31 (2000)
45. Wooldridge, M.: An Introduction to Multiagent Systems. Wiley, Hoboken (2009)

On the Formal Semantics of Theory of Mind in Agent Communication

Alison R. Panisson[1]([⊠]), Ştefan Sarkadi[2], Peter McBurney[2],
Simon Parsons[2], and Rafael H. Bordini[1]

[1] School of Technology, PUCRS, Porto Alegre, Brazil
alison.panisson@acad.pucrs.br, rafael.bordini@pucrs.br
[2] Department of Informatics, King's College London, London, UK
{stefan.sarkadi,peter.mcburney,simon.parsons}@kcl.ac.uk

Abstract. Recent studies have shown that applying Theory of Mind
to agent technologies enables agents to model and reason about other
agents' minds, making them more efficient than agents that do not have
this ability or agents that have a more limited ability of modelling others'
minds. Apart from the interesting results of combining Theory of Mind
and agent technologies, an important premise has not been yet fully
investigated in the AI literature: how do agents acquire and update their
models of others' minds? In the context of multi-agent systems, one
of the most natural ways in which agents can acquire models of other
agents' mental attitudes is through communication. In this work, we
propose an operational semantics for agents to update Theory of Mind
through communication. We not only make our formalisation broadly
applicable by defining a formal semantics based on components from
the BDI architecture, but we also implement our approach in an agent-
oriented programming language that is based on that architecture.

Keywords: Multi-Agent Systems · Theory of Mind ·
Agent-Oriented Programming Languages

1 Introduction

It seems reasonable to assume that agents will be more effective at achieving
their goals during interactions if they understand the other entities involved.
Understanding others requires the capability of modelling and reasoning about
other agents' minds. These characteristics are intrinsic to Theory of Mind (ToM)
[10]. ToM is the ability of humans to ascribe elements such as beliefs, desires,
and intentions, and relations between these elements to other human agents. In
other words, it is the ability to form mental models of other agents.

The Multi-Agent Systems (MAS) community is showing increased interest
in ToM [6,7,24]. One reason for this interest might be that ToM could boost
the quality of communication between agents that need to exchange information
in order to make decisions and reach meaningful agreements. By meaningful

© Springer Nature Switzerland AG 2019
M. Lujak (Ed.): AT 2018, LNAI 11327, pp. 18–32, 2019.
https://doi.org/10.1007/978-3-030-17294-7_2

agreements we mean agreements that result from a mutual understanding. We consider mutual understanding to be represented by a certain set of shared beliefs reached through communication.

Various studies have investigated the use of ToM in MAS. Among them, [6,7] investigated the advantages of using different levels of ToM in games played by agents, and [1,11,12,20,29], even though ToM is not mentioned, show the advantages of modelling the opponent when considering strategies in argumentation-based dialogues. All that work shows that modelling other agents' minds is an important topic of research, and the results are important contributions to the MAS literature. However, as described in [32], most of the work on modelling other agents' minds assume ToM as given. This is an understandable assumption, but it is nevertheless unrealistic given that there are no readily-available, practical techniques for developing such agents. Also, as a result of relying on such unrealistic assumption, the question of how agents acquire the model of other agents' minds has not been fully investigated. In this work, we propose a formal semantics for updates that agents can effect to their ToM based on the communication that they have with other agents, thus allowing them to acquire a ToM.

Communication plays an important role in MAS [34], and takes places on multiple levels. Communicating content is only one part of the process of communication. It also includes forming the message in a way that will make the sender's purpose of communication clear to the receivers [8]. In order to make the sender's purpose clear, agent communication languages, such as FIPA-ACL [9] and KQML [8], have been proposed based on speech act theory. Both languages format message to include *performatives* in such a way that the sender's purpose will be clear to the agent that is receiving the communication, facilitating the correct interpretation of the content of that communication. In this work we show that, based on the semantics of the agent communication languages, agents are able to infer the likely model of other agents' minds, i.e., ToM, considering the meaning of each communication exchange. Using ToM acquired from communication, agents are able to reason and make decisions using other agents' models.

The main contributions of this paper are: (i) an operational semantics, formally defined, for updates that agents carry out on their ToM during communication—to the best of our knowledge, our work is the first to propose a formal model of how agents acquire and update ToM during communication in multi-agent systems, particularly in the practical context of an Agent-Oriented Programming Language (AOPL) based on the BDI architecture; (ii) an approach for agent reasoning and decision making, and, in particular, we show how agents can reach shared beliefs more efficiently than when they are not able to model ToM.

2 Background

2.1 Agent Communication Languages

Agent communication languages have been developed based on speech act theory [30]. Speech act theory is concerned with the role of language as actions. In speech act theory, a speech act is composed by (i) a *locution*, which represents the physical utterance; (ii) an *illocution*, which provides the speaker intentions to the hearer; and (iii) the *perlocution*, which describes the actions that occur as a result of the illocution. For example, *"I order you to shut the door"* is a *locution* with an *illocution* of a command to shut the door, and the *perlocution* may be that the hearer shuts the door. Thus, an illocution is considered to have two parts, the illocutionary force and a proposition (content). The illocutionary force describes the type speech act used, e.g., *assertive, directive, commissive, declarative, expressive*.

Among the agent communication languages which emerged based on speech act theory, FIPA-ACL [9] and KQML [8] are the best known. In this work, for practical reasons, we choose KQML, which is the standard communication language in the Jason Platform [3], the multi-agent platform we choose to implement this work.

The Knowledge Query and Manipulation Language (KQML) was designed to support interaction among intelligent software agents, describing the message format and message-handling protocol to support run-time agent communication [8,17]. In order to make KQML broadly applicable, in [16] a semantic framework for KQML was proposed. Considering the speech act semantics, they argue that it is necessary to consider the cognitive state of the agents that use these speech acts. Defining the semantics, the authors provided an unambiguous interpretation of (i) how the agents' states change after sending and/or receiving a KQML performative, as well as (ii) the criteria under which the illocutionary point of the performative is satisfied (i.e., the communication was effective).

2.2 Agent Oriented Programming Languages

Among the many AOPLs and platforms, such as Jason, Jadex, Jack, AgentFactory, 2APL, GOAL, Golog, and MetateM, as discussed in [2], we chose the Jason platform [3] for our work. Jason extends the AgentSpeak language, an abstract logic-based AOPL introduced by Rao [28], which is one of the best-known languages inspired by the BDI architecture.

Besides specifying BDI agents with well-defined mental attitudes, the Jason platform [3] has some other features that are particularly interesting for our work, for example, strong negation, belief annotations, and (customisable) speech-act based communication. Strong negation helps the modelling of uncertainty, allowing the representation of things that the agent: (i) believes to be true, e.g., about(paper1, tom); (ii) believes to be false, e.g., ¬about(paper2, tom); (iii) is ignorant about, i.e., the agent has no information about whether a paper is about tom or not. Also, Jason automatically generates annotations for all the beliefs in the agents' belief base about the source from where the belief was obtained (which can be from sensing the environment, communication with other agents, or a mental note created by the agent itself). The annotation has the following format: about(paper1, tom)[source(reviewer1)], stating that the source of the belief that paper1 is about the topic tom is reviewer1. The annotations in Jason can be easily extended to include other meta-information, for example, trust and time as used in [19,21]. Another interesting feature of Jason is the communication between agents, which is done through a predefined (internal) action. There are a number of performatives allowing rich communication between agents in Jason, as explained in detail in [3]. Furthermore, new performatives can be easily defined (or redefined) in order to give special meaning to them[1], which is an essential characteristic for this work.

3   Running Example

As a running example, we will consider a scenario with five agents in a university. The first agent, named *John*, plays the role of a professor in the university, and the other agents, named *Bob, Alice, Nick,* and *Ted*, play the role of students. *John* has a relation of *supervisor* to the *students*. Also, *John* is responsible for distributing some tasks to the students. In order to distribute the tasks, *John* maintains information about the students, so as to distribute tasks to students that have the required knowledge for each task.

Our model can be described as $\langle Ag, \mathcal{T}, \mathcal{A}, \mathcal{S} \rangle$, in which Ag represents the set of agents, $\mathcal{T}$ the set of tasks of the kind $\mathcal{T} \subseteq \mathcal{A} \times \mathcal{S}$, representing an action from $\mathcal{A}$, requiring knowledge about a subset of subjects from $\mathcal{S}$, that might be executed to achieve the task $\mathcal{T}$. In our example, we consider the following actions, subjects, and tasks:

- $\mathcal{A} = \{\texttt{write\_paper}, \texttt{review\_paper}, \texttt{paper\_seminar}\}$
- $\mathcal{S} = \{\texttt{mas}, \texttt{kr}, \texttt{tom}\}$
- $\mathcal{T} = \left\{ \begin{array}{l} \texttt{task}(\texttt{write\_paper}, [\texttt{mas}, \texttt{tom}]) \\ \texttt{task}(\texttt{review\_paper}, [\texttt{kr}]) \\ \texttt{task}(\texttt{paper\_seminar}, [\texttt{tom}, \texttt{mas}]) \end{array} \right\}$

For example, the task for *writing a paper on the subjects multi-agent systems and theory of mind*, task(write_paper, [mas, tom]), requires competence on both subjects (mas and tom). Thus, this task should be assigned to a student (or a group of students) who knows both subjects.

4   Semantics for ToM in Agent Communication

4.1   The Basis for the Operational Semantics

To define the semantics for the updates agents execute in their ToM, we extend the original operational semantics of AgentSpeak [33], which is based on a widely

---

[1] For example, [22,23] propose new performatives for argumentation-based communication between Jason agents.

used method for giving semantics to programming languages [27]. It is important to mention that we are interested in the operational semantics for the updates agents execute in their ToM, which considers the performatives (locutions) as computational instructions that operate successively on the states of agents [18]. The operational semantics is given by a set of inference rules. These inference rules define a transition relation between configurations represented by the tuple $\langle ag, C, M, T, s \rangle$, originally defined in [33], as follows:

- ag is a set of beliefs bs, a set of plans ps, and a set of theories of minds ToM.
- An agent's circumstance C is a tuple $\langle I, E, A \rangle$ where:
  - I is a set of *intentions* $\{i, i', \ldots\}$. Each intention i is a stack of partially instantiated plans.
  - E is a set of *events* $\{(te, i), (te', i'), \ldots\}$. Each event is a pair (te, i), where te is a triggering event and i is an intention—a stack of plans in case of an internal event, or the empty intention $\top$ in case of an external event. An example is when the belief revision function (which is not part of the AgentSpeak interpreter but rather of the agent's overall architecture), updates the belief base, the associated events—i.e., additions and deletions of beliefs—are included in this set. These are called *external* events; internal events are generated by additions or deletions of goals from plans currently executing.
  - A is a set of *actions* to be performed in the environment.
- M is a tuple $\langle In, Out \rangle$ whose components characterise the following aspects of communicating agents (note that communication is typically asynchronous):
  - In is the mail inbox: the multi-agent system runtime infrastructure includes all messages addressed to this agent in this set. Elements of this set have the form $\langle mid, id, ilf, cnt \rangle$, where mid is a message identifier, id identifies the sender of the message, ilf is the illocutionary force of the message, and cnt its content: a (possibly singleton) set of AgentSpeak predicates or plans, depending on the illocutionary force of the message.
  - Out is where the agent posts messages it wishes to send; it is assumed that some underlying communication infrastructure handles the delivery of such messages. Messages in this set have exactly the same format as above, except that here id refers to the agent to which the message is to be sent.
- When giving semantics to an AgentSpeak agent's reasoning cycle, it is useful to have a structure which keeps track of temporary information that may be subsequently required within a reasoning cycle. In this particular work, we consider only T_ι, which records a particular intention being considered along the execution of one reasoning cycle.
- The current step within an agent's reasoning cycle is symbolically annotated by $s \in \{\mathsf{ProcMsg}, \mathsf{SelEv}, \mathsf{RelPl}, \mathsf{ApplPl}, \mathsf{SelAppl}, \mathsf{AddIM}, \mathsf{SelInt}, \mathsf{ExecInt}, \mathsf{ClrInt}\}$. These labels stand for, respectively: processing a message from the agent's mail inbox, selecting an event from the set of events, retrieving all relevant plans, checking which of those are applicable, selecting one particular applicable plan (the intended means), adding the new intended means to the set of

intentions, selecting an intention, executing the selected intention, and clearing an intention or intended means that may have finished in the previous step.

- The semantics of AgentSpeak makes use of "selection functions" which allow for user-defined components of the agent architecture. We use here only the S_M function, as originally defined in [33]; the *select message* function is used to select one message from an agent's mail inbox.

In the interests of readability, we adopt the following notation in the semantics rules:

- If C is an AgentSpeak agent circumstance, we write C_E to make reference to the E component of C, and similarly for other components of the multi-agent system and of the configuration of each agent.
- We write $b[s(id)]$ to identify the origin of a belief, where id is an agent identifier (s refers to *source*)

4.2   Tell Performative

It is important to note that when we consider agents that are able to model other agents' minds during communication, both sides, sender and receiver, execute updates in their ToM. The sender will be able to infer the likely model of the receiver's mind after receiving the message, and the receiver will be able to infer the likely model of the sender based on the message received. In the semantics presented in [33], there are separate semantic rules for sending and receiving a message. We follow the same approach here.

Considering the *Tell* performative, when the sender agent sends a message to a receiver agent sid with the content φ, first the sender checks if the receiver will believe that information $Bel_{sid}(\varphi)$, using a function *func_send* (which we assume as given and is domain dependent), based on ToM it already has about the receiver ag_{ToM} and the relevant beliefs in its belief base ag_{bs}. The sender will also annotate this ToM belief with a label γ that represents, for example, the likelihood of the belief (i.e., a certainty on the expected state of mind). Note that γ represents an estimation of the uncertainty given that no absolute inference is possible in regards to an agent's private state of mind.

$$\frac{T_\iota = i[head \leftarrow \mathsf{.send}(sid, Tell, \varphi);h]}{\langle ag, C, M, T, \mathsf{ExecInt}\rangle \longrightarrow \langle ag', C', M', T, \mathsf{ProcMsg}\rangle} \quad (\textsc{SndTell})$$

where:
$$M'_{Out} = M_{Out} \cup \{\langle mid, sid, Tell, \varphi\rangle\}$$
$$\text{with } mid \text{ a new message identifier;}$$
$$C'_I = (C_I \setminus \{T_\iota\}) \cup \{i[head \leftarrow h]\}$$
$$ag'_{ToM} = ag_{ToM} + Bel_{sid}(\varphi)_{[\gamma]}$$
$$C'_E = C_E \cup \{\langle +Bel_{sid}(\varphi)_{[\gamma]}, \mathsf{T}\rangle\}$$

After the agent updates its mail outbox M_{Out} with the message, it updates its current intention to $i[head \leftarrow h]$ (considering the action $\mathsf{.send}(sid, Tell, \varphi)$

that has already been executed), then it updates its ToM with the prediction of a belief $Bel_{sid}(\varphi)_{[\gamma]}$, creating an event $\langle +Bel_{sid}(\varphi)_{[\gamma]}, \mathsf{T}\rangle$ that may be treated in a later reasoning cycle, possibly forming a new goal for the agent based on this new information.

Conversely, when a receiver agent receives a *Tell* message from an agent *sid*, first it checks whether the sender believes φ based on its previous ToM about the sender and the relevant information in its belief base. This expectation of a state of mind results from function *func_rec*. A label γ is used to annotate relevant information such as the confidence on the projected state of mind.

$$\frac{\begin{array}{c}S_M(M_{In}) = \langle mid, sid, Tell, \varphi\rangle \\ func\_rec(\varphi, ag_{ToM}, ag_{bs}) = Bel_{sid}(\varphi)_{[\gamma]}\end{array}}{\langle ag, C, M, T, \mathsf{ProcMsg}\rangle \longrightarrow \langle ag', C', M', T, \mathsf{ExecInt}\rangle} \quad (\textsc{Tell})$$

where:
$$
\begin{aligned}
M'_{In} &= M_{In} \setminus \{\langle mid, sid, Tell, \varphi\rangle\} \\
ag'_{bs} &= ag_{bs} + \varphi[s(sid)] \\
ag'_{ToM} &= ag_{ToM} + Bel_{sid}(\varphi)_{[\gamma]} \\
C'_E &= C_E \cup \{\langle +\varphi[s(sid)], \mathsf{T}\rangle\} \cup \{\langle +Bel_{sid}(\varphi)_{[\gamma]}, \mathsf{T}\rangle\}
\end{aligned}
$$

After that, the agent updates its mail inbox M_{In}, its belief base ag_{bs} with this new information $\varphi[s(sid)]$ (following the original semantics of AgentSpeak [33]), and it updates its ToM about the sender with $Bel_{sid}(\varphi)_{[\gamma]}$. Both of these updates (on the ToM and the belief base) generate events to which the agent is able to react.

Note that the predictions resulting from *func_send* and *func_rec* can be different from the actual state of mind of the other agents. Therefore, a good prediction model, considering both the ToM and relevant information from the agents' belief base, plays an important role when modelling ToM based on agent communication. Such models might consider the uncertainty present in agent communication, agents' autonomy and self interest, trust relations, reliability, etc. Thus, there are many different ways to instantiate such a model, and our approach allows different models to be implemented through the user-defined *func_send* and *func_rec* functions. Proposing a particular model for uncertainty on ToM is out of the scope of this work. Therefore, we will omit γ in our examples. A model for uncertain ToM can be found in our work presented in [31].

Example: Considering the scenario introduced in Sect. 3, imagine that *John* meets his students every week in order to supervise their work. In a particular meeting with *Alice*, *Alice* asks *John* about the definition of ToM, and *John* responds *Alice* with the following message: $\langle alice, \mathtt{tell}, \mathtt{definition}(\mathtt{tom}, $ "an approach to model others' minds"$)\rangle$. At that moment, *John* is able to model that *Alice* believes the definition of Theory of Mind as "*an approach to model others' minds*", i.e., *John* models $Bel_{Alice}\mathtt{definition}(\mathtt{tom},$ "an approach to model others' minds")) according to the SNDTELL semantic rule. Also, when *Alice* receives the message, *Alice* is able to model that *John* believes on that definition for ToM, i.e., *Alice* models Bel_{John} definition(tom, "an approach to model others' minds")) according to the TELL semantic rule.

4.3 Achieve Performative

Considering the *Achieve* performative, when a sender agent sends a message with the content φ, it expects that the receiver agent will likely desire φ. It can predict this result using its previous ToM about the receiver, ag_{ToM}, and the relevant information in its belief base, ag_{bs}, resulting in $Des_{sid}(\varphi)_{[\gamma]}$ (where again γ is an estimation of how likely the receiver is to adopt that goal).

$$\frac{T_\iota = i[head \leftarrow .\textsf{send}(sid, Achieve, \varphi);h]}{\langle ag, C, M, T, \textsf{ExecInt}\rangle \longrightarrow \langle ag', C', M', T, \textsf{ProcMsg}\rangle} \quad \text{(SNDACHIEVE)}$$

> *where:*
> $M'_{Out} = M_{Out} \cup \{\langle mid, sid, Achieve, \varphi\rangle\}$
> with *mid* a new message identifier;
> $C'_I = (C_I \setminus \{T_\iota\}) \cup \{i[head \leftarrow h]\}$
> $ag'_{ToM} = ag_{ToM} + Des_{sid}(\varphi)_{[\gamma]}$
> $C'_E = C_E \cup \{\langle +Des_{sid}(\varphi)_{[\gamma]}, \top\rangle\}$

The sender agent updates its mail outbox M_{Out}, its current intention, its ToM about the receiver with the prediction $Des_{sid}(\varphi)_{[\gamma]}$, and an event is generated from the update in its ToM.

On the other hand, when a receiver agent receives an *Achieve* message, it can safely conclude that the sender desire φ itself, using its previous ToM about the sender and the relevant information from its belief base.

$$\frac{S_M(M_{In}) = \langle mid, sid, Achieve, \varphi\rangle}{\langle ag, C, M, T, \textsf{ProcMsg}\rangle \longrightarrow \langle ag', C', M', T, \textsf{ExecInt}\rangle} \quad \text{(ACHIEVE)}$$

> *where:*
> $M'_{In} = M_{In} \setminus \{\langle mid, sid, Achieve, \varphi\rangle\}$
> $ag'_{ToM} = ag_{ToM} + Des_{sid}(\varphi)_{[\gamma]}$
> $C'_E = C_E \cup \{\langle +!\varphi, \top\rangle\} \cup \{\langle +Des_{sid}(\varphi)_{[\gamma]}, \top\rangle\}$

The receiver agent updates its mail inbox M_{In} and its ToM about the sender, which generates an event $\langle +Des_{sid}(\varphi)_{[\gamma]}, \top\rangle$. Also, another event $+!\varphi$ is generated, and the agent is able to autonomously decide whether to achieve φ or not. In case it decides to achieve φ, then the agent will look for a plan that achieves φ and make that plan one of its intentions.

Example: Continuing our scenario, imagine that during a meeting with *Bob*, *John* realises that it could be interesting for *Bob* to read a paper about multi-agent systems, so *John* sends the following message to *Bob*: $\langle bob, \textsf{achieve}, \textsf{read}(\textsf{bob}, \textsf{paper\_mas})\rangle$. At that time, *John* is able to model that *Bob* desires to read the paper, i.e., $Des_{Bob}(\mathtt{read(bob, paper\_mas)})$ according to the SNDACHIEVE semantic rule. Also, *Bob* is able to model that *John* desires that *Bob* reads the paper, i.e., $Des_{John}(\mathtt{read(bob, paper\_mas)})$ according to the ACHIEVE semantic rule. *Bob* is able to react to the event $+!\mathtt{read(bob, paper\_mas)}$, searching for a plan to achieve that goal and turning the plan into one of *Bob's* intentions. A simple plan, written in Jason, that *Bob* could use to achieve this goal is shown below:

```
+!read(Ag,Paper)
  : .my_name(Ag) & desires(Sup,read(Ag,Paper)) & supervisor(Sup,Ag)
  <- read(Paper).
```

The plan above says that, when an event of the type `+!read(Ag,Paper)` is generated, then if `Ag` unifies with the name of the agent executing this plan (obtained with `.my_name(Ag)`), and if the agent believes that its supervisor desires that it reads that paper (`desires(Sup,read(Ag,Paper))` and `supervisor(Sup,Ag)`), then the agent will proceed to execute the action `read(Paper)`. Note that the ACHIEVE semantic rule provides the context (precondition) necessary for *Bob* to execute this plan, considering the unification $\{\mathtt{Ag} \mapsto \mathtt{bob},\ \mathtt{Paper} \mapsto \mathtt{paper\_mas},\ \mathtt{Sup} \mapsto \mathtt{john}\}$ and that `desires(john,read(bob,paper_mas))` is the code representation for $Des_{John}(\mathtt{read(bob, paper\_mas)})$.

4.4   Ask-If Performative

Considering the *AskIf* performative, when the sender agent sends a message with the content φ, the only inference the agent can make is that the other agent will believe that the sender desires to know φ, i.e., $Bel_{sid}(Des_{ag}(\varphi))_{[\gamma]}$.

$$\frac{T_{\iota} = i[head \leftarrow .\mathbf{send}(sid, AskIf, \varphi); h]}{\langle ag, C, M, T, \mathsf{ExecInt} \rangle \longrightarrow \langle ag', C', M', T, \mathsf{ProcMsg} \rangle} \quad \text{(SNDASKIF)}$$

$$\frac{func\_send(\varphi, ag_{ToM}, ag_{bs}) = Bel_{sid}(Des_{ag}(\varphi))_{[\gamma]}}{}$$

$$\begin{aligned}
\textit{where:} \\
M'_{Out} &= M_{Out} \cup \{\langle mid, sid, AskIf, \varphi \rangle\} \\
&\quad \text{with } mid \text{ a new message identifier;} \\
C'_I &= (C_I \setminus \{T_\iota\}) \cup \{i[head \leftarrow h]\} \\
ag'_{ToM} &= ag_{ToM} + Bel_{sid}(Des_{ag}(\varphi))_{[\gamma]} \\
C'_E &= C_E \cup \{\langle +Bel_{sid}(Des_{ag}(\varphi))_{[\gamma]}, \top \rangle\}
\end{aligned}$$

The sender agent updates its mail outbox M_{Out}, its current intention and its ToM about the receiver with the prediction $Bel_{sid}(Des_{ag}(\varphi))_{[\gamma]}$, thus an event is generated from the update in its ToM. Conversely, when a receiver agent receives the message, it is able to infer that the sender desires to know φ. After that, in both cases the agent updates its mental state similarly to the other semantic rules.

$$S_M(M_{In}) = \langle mid, sid, AskIf, \varphi \rangle$$
$$\frac{func\_rec(\varphi, ag_{ToM}, ag_{bs}) = Des_{sid}(\varphi)_{[\gamma]}}{\langle ag, C, M, T, \mathsf{ProcMsg} \rangle \longrightarrow \langle ag', C', M', T, \mathsf{ExecInt} \rangle} \quad \text{(AskIf)}$$

$where:$
$$M'_{In} = M_{In} \setminus \{\langle mid, sid, AskIf, \varphi \rangle\}$$
$$ag'_{ToM} = ag_{ToM} + Des_{sid}(\varphi)_{[\gamma]}$$
$$C'_E = C_E \cup \{\langle +Des_{sid}(\varphi)_{[\gamma]}, \mathsf{T} \rangle\}$$

Example: Continuing our scenario, imagine that during a group meeting, *John* asks all students if they like paper seminars, using the following message: $\langle \{bob, alice, nick, tom\}, \mathtt{AskIf}, \mathtt{like(Ag, paper\_seminar))} \rangle$. At that moment *John* considers that all students believe that *John* desires to know who likes paper seminars, $Bel_{Alice}(Des_{John}(\mathtt{like(Ag, paper\_seminar)}))$, according to the SNDASKIF semantic rule. Also, all students think that *John* desires to know who likes paper seminars, $Des_{John}(\mathtt{like(Ag, paper\_seminar)})$, according to the ASKIF semantic rule. Two simple plans, written in Jason, that students could use to react the event generated by adding $Des_{John}(\mathtt{like(Ag, paper\_seminar)})$ to their ToM is shown below:

```
+!desires(Sup,like(Ag,Task))
  :  .my_name(Me) & like(Me,Task) & supervisor(Sup,Me)
  <- .send(Sup,tell,like(Me,Task)).

+!desires(Sup,like(Ag,Task))
  :  .my_name(Me) & ¬like(Me,Task) & supervisor(Sup,Me)
  <- .send(Sup,tell,¬like(Me,Task)).
```

The plans above say that an agent will tell *John* that it likes a particular task if it likes the task. Otherwise, an agent will tell *John* that it does not like that task. For example, *Alice* likes paper seminars, answering *John* with the following message: $\langle john, \mathtt{tell}, \mathtt{like(alice, paper\_seminar)} \rangle$. In this case, *John* will update its ToM stating that *Alice* likes paper seminars, and *Alice* will update its ToM stating that *John* believes that she likes paper seminars $Bel_{john}(\mathtt{like(alice, paper\_seminar)})$, according to the TELL and SNDTELL semantic rules. In the future, as *John* has this information, it would be able to allocate a task to a student who likes that task.

5 Reaching Shared Beliefs Using ToM

In [33], the authors showed how agents are able to reach shared beliefs. That approach for agents reaching shared beliefs starts with an agent ag_i, which believes in φ, sending to another agent ag_j a `tell` message with the content it desires to became a shared belief, i.e., $\langle ag_j, \mathtt{tell}, \varphi \rangle$. Thus, following the semantics in [33], agent ag_j will receive the message and update its belief base with $\varphi[\mathtt{source(ag_i)}]$. Then, agent ag_i needs to send a message to agent ag_j to achieve that shared belief, i.e., $\langle ag_j, \texttt{achieve}, \varphi \rangle$, thus the agent ag_j is able to execute the same procedure, sending a tell message to the agent ag_i with φ, i.e., $\langle ag_i, \texttt{tell}, \varphi \rangle$. Finally, agent ag_i receives this message and updates its belief base to $\varphi[\texttt{source}(\texttt{itself}), \texttt{source}(\texttt{ag}_j)]$, reaching the state of shared beliefs.

Definition 1 (Shared Beliefs [33]). *An agent ag_i will reach a state of shared beliefs with another agent ag_j when, for a belief $\varphi[S]$ with S the different sources of φ, both itself and ag_j are sources of φ, i.e., $\texttt{source}(\texttt{self})$, $\texttt{source}(\texttt{ag}_j) \in S$.*

Considering agents that are able to model ToM, we are able to redefine the idea of shared beliefs, including the model of other agents' minds, i.e., a ToM.

Definition 2 (Shared Beliefs using ToM). *An agent ag_i will reach a state of shared beliefs with another agent ag_j when, for a belief φ, it is able to match its own belief φ with a ToM about ag_j believing φ, i.e., $\varphi \wedge Bel_{ag_j}(\varphi)_{[\gamma]}$, with γ the parameter describing, for example, the certainty on ToM required to consider φ a shared belief.*

When we assume that agents are cooperative, they trust each other, and the network infrastructure guarantees that messages will reach their intended receivers, we also are able to assume that there is no uncertainty of the ToM agents model about each other. Thus, we are able to ignore the label γ, which aims to model uncertainty of ToM.

Proposition 1 (Reaching Shared beliefs—ToM without Uncertainty). *Without uncertainty of ToM, agents able to model ToM are able to reach a state of shared beliefs faster (with fewer messages) than agents without this ability.*

Proof (sketch). Following the semantic rule SndTell, when an agent ag_i believes in φ and it is able to model ToM, then it is able to reach a state of a shared belief φ with another agent ag_j communicating a single message $\langle ag_j, \texttt{tell}, \varphi \rangle$ to ag_j. When the agent ag_i sends this message, it updates its ToM with $Bel_{ag_j}(\varphi)$, reaching the state of shared beliefs according to the Definition 2. Agents that are not able to model ToM will need at least two messages, i.e., a $\texttt{tell}$ message each, according to the semantics from [33] and Definition 1.

Example: Following the scenario introduced in Sect. 3, imagine that during the meetings *John* has had with his students, the students tell *John* which subjects they know more about, and *John* has the following information of his students, according to the TELL semantic rule:

$$\left\{ \begin{array}{ll} \texttt{knows(alice, tom)} & \texttt{knows(bob, mas)} \\ \texttt{believes(alice, knows(alice, tom))} & \texttt{believes(bob, knows(bob, mas))} \\ \texttt{knows(nick, kr)} & \texttt{knows(ted)} \\ \texttt{believes(nick, knows(nick, kr))} & \texttt{believes(ted, knows(tom, [tom, mas]))} \end{array} \right\}$$

Given this knowledge and the tasks *John* wants to allocate to his students, *John* decides to assign the tasks as follows: $\texttt{task(write\_paper, [mas, tom])}$

to *Ted*, who knows about both subjects needed for completing that task, task(review_paper, [kr]) to *Nick*, who is the only student able to execute that task, and grouping *Alice* and *Bob* for the task task(paper_seminar, [tom, mas]). If *Bob* only knows mas and *Alice* only knows tom, then they need to share their knowledge in order to successfully perform the task.

Reaching Shared Beliefs: *Alice* and *Bob* need to work together to accomplish this particular task, which requires the subjects mas (Multi-Agent Systems) and tom (Theory of Mind). *Bob* only knows the subject of mas and *Alice* only knows the subject of tom. Considering that together *Alice* and *Bob* know both topics in order to help each other during the paper seminar, they decide to exchange knowledge about these topics. Thus, they might reach some shared beliefs (knowledge) about both topics. Note that, in this scenario, *Alice* and *Bob* assume that both are cooperating and both are rational. Thus, *Alice* starts the dialogue telling *Bob* that *"Theory of Mind is an approach to model others' minds"*, i.e., ⟨*bob*, tell, def(tom, "an approach to model others' minds")⟩. At that moment, following the semantic rule SNDTELL, *Alice* updates its ToM with the following information Bel_{bob}(def(tom, "an approach to model others' minds")). When *Bob* receives this message, following the semantic rule TELL, *Bob* updates its belief base with the following information def(tom, "an approach to model others' minds"), as well as its ToM about *Alice* with Bel_{alice}(def(tom, "an approach to model other minds")). By now, both *Alice* and *Bob* have reached a state of shared belief about the definition of tom, according to Definition 2. They proceed sharing the relevant information about each topic until they both feel confident about both topics. Reaching shared beliefs (knowledge) is important for this particular task, in which, when the audience asks them questions about the topics tom and mas, both *Alice* and *Bob* are able to answer the questions because they both have sufficient knowledge about the topics.

6 Future Work

The relation of trust between agents [19, 25, 26] is an interesting property agents could consider in a model for uncertain ToM. Our approach allows us to model uncertainty through the functions *func_rec*() and *func_send*(), labelling the uncertainty of that information using γ. Even though our approach allows us to model ToM that reflects uncertainty, we believe that the modelling of uncertain ToM is a task that falls beyond the scope of this particular paper and we thus leave it as future work.

Another aspect of ToM to be considered in future work is that ToM can also be inferred by agents from the environment by observing other agents' actions. The modelling of ToM based on these aspects is part of our ongoing research and it faces some more complex issues such as the ones mentioned in [5]: *"the slamming of a door communicates the slammer's anger only when the intended observer of that act realises that the slammer wanted both to slam the door in his face and for the observer to believe that to be his intention"*. This means that there is both uncertainty about the slammer's intentions and uncertainty about the act of slamming the door, which could be caused either by an accidental shove or by natural means, which would not represent a communicative act and, therefore, observing such an event occur should not cause the observer to make any inference about the slammer's mental state.

7   Related Work and Conclusions

As mentioned before, to the best of our knowledge, there is no work that explicitly and formally describes how agents acquire and update ToM during communication. However, our work is inspired by others who have investigated agents that use models of other agents in reasoning and decision making, e.g., [1,6,7,11,12,20,29]. Also, we took some inspiration from the STAPLE language, that seems to have ceased to be used. The STAPLE (Social and Team Agents Programming Language) language has its logic semantics based on joint intention theory [13]. STAPLE has the goal of reaching a fault-tolerant approach to programming teamwork, in which the authors argue that a team is more than a collection of individuals working together to achieve a common goal. The agents in a team must have shared goals as well as a shared mental state [15]. Thus, STAPLE enables agents to specify the models of other agents, as well as temporal properties of actions and events, allowing them to reason about group beliefs, team intentions, and team commitments [14]. Note that our approach is more general than that, in which ToM could be used to implement similar approaches to teamwork and scalable cooperation, which is a likely research direction for our work.

In this paper, we have defined the formal semantics for updates agents execute on their ToM during communication. The formal semantics uses components based on the BDI model and it is, therefore, broadly applicable to any BDI based AOPL. To the best of our knowledge, our work is the first to address a formal model for ToM in agent communication. We have showed not only how agents acquire and update ToM based on agent communication, but we have also shown how agents reason and make decisions using ToM through an illustrative scenario. The modelling, the implementation and the study of agents that are able to model other agents' minds (i.e., ToM) goes beyond the current interests of the AI community, in which the main research scope is to implement rational and efficient software agents that are able to reason and make decisions in order to simulate and study the social behaviour of intelligent entities [24]. ToM is also regarded as important by other research communities that engage in the interdisciplinary study of communication, negotiation, social behaviour, and developmental psychology [4]. We consider that it would be very useful for these interdisciplinary communities to have the possibility to use AOPLs in order to study ToM or any other problems in which ToM plays a significant role.

Acknowledgements. We gratefully acknowledge the partial support from CAPES and CNPq.

References

1. Black, E., Atkinson, K.: Choosing persuasive arguments for action. In: The 10th International Conference on Autonomous Agents and Multiagent Systems, pp. 905–912 (2011)
2. El Fallah Seghrouchni, A., Dix, J., Dastani, M., Bordini, R.H. (eds.): Multi-Agent Programming: Languages, Tools and Applications, 1st edn. Springer, Boston (2009). https://doi.org/10.1007/978-0-387-89299-3
3. Bordini, R.H., Hübner, J.F., Wooldridge, M.: Programming Multi-Agent Systems in AgentSpeak Using Jason. Wiley Series in Agent Technology. Wiley, Chichester (2007)
4. Carr, A., Slade, L., Yuill, N., Sullivan, S., Ruffman, T.: Minding the children: a longitudinal study of mental state talk, theory of mind, and behavioural adjustment from the age of 3 to 10. Soc. Dev. **27**(4), 826–840 (2018)
5. Cohen, P.R., Perrault, C.R.: Elements of a plan-based theory of speech acts. In: Readings in Distributed Artificial Intelligence, pp. 169–186. Elsevier (1988)
6. de Weerd, H., Verheij, B.: The advantage of higher-order theory of mind in the game of limited bidding. In: Proceedings of the Workshop Reasoning About Other Minds, CEUR Workshop Proceedings. vol. 751, pp. 149–164 (2011)
7. de Weerd, H., Verbrugge, R., Verheij, B.: Higher-order social cognition in rock-paper-scissors: a simulation study. In: Proceedings of the 11th International Conference on Autonomous Agents and Multiagent Systems, pp. 1195–1196 (2012)
8. Finin, T., Fritzson, R., McKay, D., McEntire, R.: KQML as an agent communication language. In: Proceedings of the 3rd International Conference on Information and knowledge management, pp. 456–463. ACM (1994)
9. TCC FIPA: FIPA communicative act library specification. Foundation for Intelligent Physical Agents (2008). http://www.fipa.org/specs/fipa00037/SC00037J.html. 15 Feb 2018
10. Goldman, A.I.: Theory of mind. In: The Oxford Handbook of Philosophy of Cognitive Science, vol. 1. Oxford Handbooks Online, 2012 edn. (2012)
11. Hadidi, N., Dimopoulos, Y., Moraitis, P., et al.: Tactics and concessions for argumentation-based negotiation. In: COMMA, pp. 285–296 (2012)
12. Hadjinikolis, C., Siantos, Y., Modgil, S., Black, E., McBurney, P.: Opponent modelling in persuasion dialogues. In: International Joint Conference on Artificial Intelligence IJCAI, pp. 164–170 (2013)
13. Kumar, S., Cohen, P.R.: Staple: an agent programming language based on the joint intention theory. In: Proceedings of the 3rd International Joint Conference on Autonomous Agents and Multiagent Systems, pp. 1390–1391 (2004)
14. Kumar, S., Cohen, P.R., Huber, M.J.: Direct execution of team specifications in STAPLE. In: Proceedings of the 1st International Joint Conference on Autonomous Agents and Multiagent Systems, pp. 567–568. ACM (2002)
15. Kumar, S., Cohen, P.R., Levesque, H.J.: The adaptive agent architecture: achieving fault-tolerance using persistent broker teams. In: Proceedings of the 4th International Conference on MultiAgent Systems, pp. 159–166 (2000)
16. Labrou, Y., Finin, T.: A semantics approach for KQML - a general purpose communication language for software agents. In: Proceedings of the 3rd International Conference on Information and Knowledge Management, pp. 447–455. ACM (1994)
17. Mayfield, J., Labrou, Y., Finin, T.: Evaluation of KQML as an agent communication language. In: Wooldridge, M., Müller, J.P., Tambe, M. (eds.) ATAL 1995. LNCS, vol. 1037, pp. 347–360. Springer, Heidelberg (1996). https://doi.org/10.1007/3540608052_77

18. McBurney, P., Parsons, S.: Dialogue games for agent argumentation. In: Simari, G., Rahwan, I. (eds.) Argumentation in Artificial Intelligence, pp. 261–280. Springer, Boston (2009). https://doi.org/10.1007/978-0-387-98197-0_13

19. Melo, V.S., Panisson, A.R., Bordini, R.H.: Argumentation-based reasoning using preferences over sources of information. In: Fifteenth International Conference on Autonomous Agents and Multiagent Systems (AAMAS) (2016)

20. Oren, N., Norman, T.J.: Arguing using opponent models. In: McBurney, P., Rahwan, I., Parsons, S., Maudet, N. (eds.) ArgMAS 2009. LNCS (LNAI), vol. 6057, pp. 160–174. Springer, Heidelberg (2010). https://doi.org/10.1007/978-3-642-12805-9_10

21. Panisson, A.R., Melo, V.S., Bordini, R.H.: Using preferences over sources of information in argumentation-based reasoning. In: 5th Brazilian Conference on Intelligent Systems, pp. 31–36 (2016)

22. Panisson, A.R., Meneguzzi, F., Fagundes, M., Vieira, R., Bordini, R.H.: Formal semantics of speech acts for argumentative dialogues. In: 13th International Conference on Autonomous Agents and Multiagent Systems, pp. 1437–1438 (2014)

23. Panisson, A.R., Meneguzzi, F., Vieira, R., Bordini, R.H.: Towards practical argumentation in multi-agent systems. In: Brazilian Conference on Intelligent Systems, pp. 98–103 (2015)

24. Panisson, A.R., Sarkadi, S., McBurney, P., Parsons, S., Bordini, R.H.: Lies, bullshit, and deception in agent-oriented programming languages. In: Proceedings of the 20th International Trust Workshop, pp. 50–61 (2018)

25. Parsons, S., Sklar, E., McBurney, P.: Using argumentation to reason with and about trust. In: McBurney, P., Parsons, S., Rahwan, I. (eds.) ArgMAS 2011. LNCS (LNAI), vol. 7543, pp. 194–212. Springer, Heidelberg (2012). https://doi.org/10.1007/978-3-642-33152-7_12

26. Parsons, S., Tang, Y., Sklar, E., McBurney, P., Cai, K.: Argumentation-based reasoning in agents with varying degrees of trust. In: The 10th International Conference on Autonomous Agents and Multiagent Systems, pp. 879–886 (2011)

27. Plotkin, G.D.: A structural approach to operational semantics (1981)

28. Rao, A.S.: AgentSpeak(L): BDI agents speak out in a logical computable language. In: Van de Velde, W., Perram, J.W. (eds.) MAAMAW 1996. LNCS, vol. 1038, pp. 42–55. Springer, Heidelberg (1996). https://doi.org/10.1007/BFb0031845

29. Rienstra, T., Thimm, M., Oren, N.: Opponent models with uncertainty for strategic argumentation. In: International Joint Conference on Artificial Intelligence IJCAI, pp. 332–338 (2013)

30. Searle, J.R.: Speech Acts: An Essay in the Philosophy of Language. Cambridge University Press, Cambridge (1969)

31. Sarkadi, S., Panisson, A.R., McBurney, P., Parsons, S., Bordini, R.H.: Towards an approach for modelling uncertain theory of mind in multi-agent systems. In: 6th International Conference on Agreement Technologies (2018)

32. Thimm, M.: Strategic argumentation in multi-agent systems. KI-Künstliche Intelligenz 28(3), 159–168 (2014)

33. Vieira, R., Moreira, A., Wooldridge, M., Bordini, R.H.: On the formal semantics of speech-act based communication in an agent-oriented programming language. J. Artif. Int. Res. 29(1), 221–267 (2007)

34. Wooldridge, M.: An Introduction to Multiagent Systems. Wiley, New York (2009)

Accountability for Practical Reasoning Agents

Stephen Cranefield[1]([⊠]) (iD), Nir Oren[2]([⊠]) (iD),
and Wamberto W. Vasconcelos[2]([⊠]) (iD)

[1] University of Otago, Dunedin, New Zealand
`stephen.cranefield@otago.ac.nz`
[2] University of Aberdeen, Aberdeen, UK
`n.oren@abdn.ac.uk, w.w.vasconcelos@abdn.ac.uk`

Abstract. Artificial intelligence has been increasing the autonomy of man-made artefacts such as software agents, self-driving vehicles and military drones. This increase in autonomy together with the ubiquity and impact of such artefacts in our daily lives have raised many concerns in society. Initiatives such as transparent and ethical AI aim to allay fears of a "free for all" future where amoral technology (or technology amorally designed) will replace humans with terrible consequences. We discuss the notion of accountable autonomy, and explore this concept within the context of practical reasoning agents. We survey literature from distinct fields such as management, healthcare, policy-making, and others, and differentiate and relate concepts connected to accountability. We present a list of justified requirements for accountable software agents and discuss research questions stemming from these requirements. We also propose a preliminary formalisation of one core aspect of accountability: responsibility.

1 Introduction

Accountability has become an increasingly common term in public discourse, with frequent demands for organisations and officials such as politicians, business leaders, government agencies and public service organisations to be held accountable for their actions (or lack of action). Dubnick [1] describes the term "accountability" as a *cultural keyword*—one that was "culturally innocuous" until the 1960s–70s, but has since undergone a massive growth in usage and become an "expansive, ambiguous, and often enigmatic term with considerable cultural gravitas".

With the increasing capabilities and uptake of machine learning and other AI techniques to aid human decision-making, the public desire for accountability has begun to encompass the development and deployment of AI software [2,3], and is likely to provide increasing urgency for researchers to address the emerging field of the ethical use of AI [4–6] (see also DeepMind's "Ethics and Society" initiative[1]). Due to the conspicuous success of deep learning classifiers and

---

[1] https://deepmind.com/applied/deepmind-ethics-society/.

© Springer Nature Switzerland AG 2019
M. Lujak (Ed.): AT 2018, LNAI 11327, pp. 33–48, 2019.
https://doi.org/10.1007/978-3-030-17294-7_3

reinforcement learning systems (e.g., Alphabet's AlphaGo[2]), one particular research focus is on understanding and addressing the inherent biases due to the dependency of such systems on large sets of training data [7]. This is an example of accountability applied to the *people and organisations* involved in developing and deploying AI: academic (and increasingly public) debate is driving the development and application of norms of best practice [7].

However, in the context of AI systems that can *act autonomously*, the question arises of whether, and how, such systems could themselves be considered as "accountable". This is particularly important for systems that are adaptive, i.e., those that have the flexibility to modify their behaviour-generating processes due to changes in their current knowledge of the world and their interactions with other "agents", which might be humans or other autonomous software systems. This paper addresses the accountability of adaptive autonomous systems, with a particular focus on agents that reason using goals and plans, such as belief-desire-intention (BDI) agents [8–10], which have a long history of investigation by researchers in the field of multi-agent systems.

The contributions of this article are: (i) a survey of the relevant literature on accountability, drawing from diverse areas such as sociology, healthcare, management, policy-making and artificial intelligence (especially autonomous and multi-agent systems); (ii) a differentiation and correlation among concepts closely connected to accountability such as responsibility, answerability, and others; we also discuss the functional purpose of accountability; (iii) a justified list of requirements for accountable autonomous agents and research questions stemming from these; and (iv) a preliminary formalisation of one core aspect of accountability: answerability.

The rest of this paper is organised as follows. Section 2 surveys contributions from disparate areas, to answer the question "what is accountability?". Section 3 proposes, based on the literature surveyed, requirements to support accountability in autonomous practical reasoning agents; for each requirement we list associated research questions. In Sect. 4 we present a preliminary formal model of one aspect of accountability: answerability. We conclude the paper in Sect. 5, discussing our approach, contributions and further research.

2   What Is Accountability?

There has been a small amount of prior work related to accountability of autonomous systems, but it is not clear that this work has formed a consensus on what accountability entails, or how well that work aligns with the view of accountability in other academic fields. Therefore, in this section we survey the literature on accountability from disparate fields such as policy-making, sociology, management and computing science (especially artificial intelligence and multi-agent systems). Our aim is to identify the key requirements that an autonomous agent would need to satisfy in order to be considered accountable.

---

[2] https://deepmind.com/research/alphago/.

Chopra and Singh [11] describe accountability as a normative concept in the context of socio-technical systems: "accountability requirements describe how principals ought to act in each other's eyes, providing a basis for their mutual expectations". They give two examples of accountability requirements: a meeting participant who is accountable for turning up to a meeting after accepting an invitation, and a food company that is accountable to a regulator for maintaining certain tracking information and providing it to a regulator on demand. However, it is not clear from this discussion to what degree (if any) the authors believe the computational representations and processes needed to support accountability might differ from existing techniques developed by multi-agent systems researchers for reasoning about norms and commitments [12,13].

Baldoni et al. [14] propose the study of *computational accountability*. They consider accountability to be an ethical value, and define accountability as "the acknowledgment and assumption of responsibility for decisions and actions that an individual, or an organization, has towards another party". They note that, implicitly, "individuals are expected to account for their actions and decisions when put under examination". The paper focuses on multi-agent systems that track the state of conditional social commitments using business artifacts, in order to "coordinate their activities, e.g. through responsibility assignment, as well as to identify liabilities". It is argued that the "analysis of accountability can be accomplished by looking at commitment relationships".

In later work, Baldoni et al. [15,16] take the viewpoint of *accountability as a mechanism*, summarised by Bovens et al. [17] as "an institutional relation or arrangement in which an agent can be held to account by another agent or institution". They consider how such an institutional mechanism can be provided by design in a multi-agent system (MAS), and seek to provide "structures that allow assessing who is accountable without actually infringing on the individual and private nature of agents" and to "determine action impact or significance by identifying the amount of disruption it causes in terms of other agents and/or work affected" [15]. To this end, they present five "necessary-but-not-sufficient principles that an MAS system must exhibit in order to support accountability determination" [15]. These principles state that (i) agents should interact within the scope of an organisation, (ii) must join the organisation by taking on a role, (iii) can be accountable only for goals they have explicitly accepted, and (iv) may specify the resources they need to satisfy a goal (which may be provided, or not, at the organisation's discretion). The fourth principle is endowed with particular significance for accountability determination: "Should an uniformed agent stipulate insufficient provisions for an impossible goal that is then accepted by an organization, that agent will be held accountable because by voicing its provisions, it declared an impossible goal possible" [16]. Baldoni et al. operationalise these principles as an "accountability protocol" to be followed when an agent joins an organisation. This protocol ensures the creation of specific types of commitment between agents and between agents and the organisation. This work is situated within a particular paradigm of organisational multi-agent systems in which organisations are supported by specialised coordination artifacts, whereas we seek a more general model of computational accountability.

Dignum [18] addresses the question of how AI systems can be designed responsibly to ensure they are "sensitive to moral principles and human value [sic]". She discusses three principles of responsible AI: accountability, responsibility and transparency (ART). Accountability is described as "the need to explain and justify one's decisions and actions to its partners, users and others with whom the system interacts". In addition, there is a need for moral values and social norms to be represented and included in the system's deliberations and explanations of its decisions.

Other multi-agent systems researchers have investigated related concepts such as responsibility, which we discuss in Sect. 2.1, after a more general look at the literature on accountability.

Dubnick [1] notes that it is difficult to find a definition of accountability that is not circular or specific to a qualifying adjective (e.g. "political accountability"). In the latter case, Dubnick observes that "whatever substantive meaning might be in the word accountability is overwhelmed and subordinated to the demands of the specific task environment". Fox [19] also notes the lack of clarity around the meaning of accountability and related concepts, stating that "the terms *transparency* and *accountability* are both quite malleable and therefore – conveniently – can mean all things to all people".

Bovens et al. [17] discuss the views of accountability in the social psychological, accounting, public administration, political science, international relations and constitutional law literature. They observe that there is a "minimal consensus" in the academic literature. Schillemans [20] expresses this consensus as follows:

> (1) Accountability is about providing answers, about answerability, towards others with a legitimate claim in some agents' work. (2) Accountability is furthermore a relational concept: it focuses our attention on agents who perform tasks for others.... (3) Accountability is retrospective... and focuses on the behavior of some agent in general, ranging from performance and results to financial management, regularity or normative and professional standards. (4) ... accountability consists of three analytically distinct phases. In the first phase, the agent/accountor/actor renders an account on his conduct and performance to a significant other. This may be coined the information phase. In the second phase, the principal/accountee/forum assesses the... transmitted information and both parties often engage in a debate on this account. The principal/accountee/forum may ask for additional information and pass judgment on the behaviour of the agent/accountor/actor. The agent/accountor/actor will then answer to questions and if necessary justify and defend his course of action. This is the debating phase. Finally, the principal/accountee/forum comes to a concluding judgment and decides whether and how to make use of available sanctions. This is the sanctions or judgment phase.

From this, we note that accountability revolves around some form of *accountability relationship* between an accountee and accountor. As discussed in Sect. 3.1, many of the properties of this relationship have not yet been formalised.

Emanuel and Emanuel [21] give a definition of accountability in the domain of healthcare: "Accountability . . . entails procedures and processes by which one party provides a justification and is held responsible for its actions by another party that has an interest in the actions". They consider the following components of accountability: the locus of accountability, i.e. *who* can be held accountable, the *domain* of accountability, i.e. for what activities, practices or issues "a party can legitimately be held responsible and called on to justify or change its action", and the *procedures* of accountability, divided into evaluation of compliance and dissemination of evaluations to seek "responses or justifications" from accountable parties.

2.1 Related Concepts

Dubnick [1, Fig. 2.4] categorises various concepts related to accountability that are motivated by "moral pull" (i.e., due to external forces): liability, answerability, responsibility, responsiveness (in the legal, organisational, professional and political settings, respectively), and those motivated by "moral push" (i.e., due to internal managerial efforts): obligation, obediance, fidelity, amenability (in the same four settings, respectively).

The relationships between accountability, responsibility and answerability seem especially subject to varying viewpoints. Dubnick [1] notes that one can be "responsible for some event, for example the marriage of two people who met because (one) did not take the empty seat between them on the bus, without being held to account for it". Eshleman [22] discusses various philosophical views on *moral* responsibility. The *accountability* view holds that "an agent is responsible, if and only if it is appropriate for us to hold her responsible, or accountable, via the reactive attitudes . . . (e.g. resentment)". Another influential view, referred to by Eshleman as the *answerability* view, is that "someone is responsible for an action or attitude just in case it is connected to her capacity for evaluative judgment in a way that opens her up, in principle, to demands for justification from others".

In the practice of business management, a Responsible, Accountable, Consulted, and Informed (RACI) matrix is a recognised [23] tool to map where responsibility and accountability are assigned for activities. In this context, the responsible parties are those who work on the activity (responsibility may be shared), whereas the accountable party is the (unique) person with "yes or no authority" over the activity and "about whom it is said 'The buck stops here'" [24].

Researchers in multi-agent systems and deontic logic have addressed the concept of responsibility as the problem of assigning blame for failures of group plans or norms [25–36]. This problem has been well studied in the literature, and as determining responsibility is a process performed by a principal, it is largely orthogonal to our focus in this paper: the capabilities needed for an accountable agent to play its role in an accountability relationship with a principal. Therefore, we do not attempt to summarise the literature on responsibility as blame assignment.

In the context of the responsible development of AI systems, Dignum [18] defines *transparency* as "the need to describe, inspect and reproduce the mechanisms through which AI systems make decisions and learn to adapt to their environment, and to the governance of the data used or created". Fox [19] discusses the relationship between transparency and accountability in human institutions, which is conventionally expressed as "transparency generates accountability". After reviewing the empirical literature he concludes that transparency is necessary for accountability, but far from sufficient. In particular, his analysis shows that "opaque transparency" (limited to providing access to information) does not necessarily result in accountability, whereas an overlap between transparency and accountability occurs when there is answerability, i.e. the capacity or right to demand answers. However, answerability without consequences (e.g. sanctions) is a "soft" form of accountability. To guarantee "hard accountability" (answerability plus consequence, such as sanctions), the intervention of other "public sector actors" is needed.

Winikoff [37] considers the question of the *trustability* of autonomous systems, i.e., how humans can come to trust them, and proposes three prerequisites for such trust: there should be a social framework for recourse; if the system makes a decision with negative consequences for the user, the system should be able to explain its behaviour; and the system should be subject to verification and validation to give assurance that key behavioural properties hold.

2.2   The Functional Purpose of Accountability

When setting out to design accountable software agents it is important to consider the functional purpose of accountability. Is accountability simply something that satisfies a human desire to feel empowered (even if there is no other effect), or are there some system-level benefits? In the former case, there may be no point in creating accountable agents unless they are interacting with people or other agents. In the latter case, it is necessary to identify the benefits that we wish our agents (or their society) to enjoy.

The purpose of accountability has been analysed in the human context. Bovens provides this commentary [38]:

> "So why is accountability important? ... In the academic literature and in policy publications about public accountability, three answers recur, albeit implicitly, time and again. Accountability is important to provide a democratic means to monitor and control government conduct, for preventing the development of concentrations of power, and to enhance the learning capacity and effectiveness of public administration."

The first and last of these answers seem most relevant to software agents (assuming that our agents are not power-seeking). The first reason (control) is also noted by Mulgan [39]:

> "The core sense of accountability is clearly grounded in the general purpose of making agents or sub-ordinates act in accordance with the wishes of their superiors. Subordinates are called to account and, if necessary, penalized as means of bringing them under control."

We note that this also highlights a *motivational* aspect of accountability: a rational agent (as software agents are generally designed to be) will be likely to prioritise goals for which it is accountable, and devote more resources to them. This is due to the expected costs of requests for answers and possible sanctions in the event of sub-standard performance or failure.

Bovens elaborates on the third reason above (enhancing learning) as follows:

> "The purpose of public accountability is to induce the executive branch to learn. The possibility of sanctions from clients and other stakeholders in their environment in the event of errors and shortcomings motivates them to search for more intelligent ways of organising their business. Moreover, the public nature of the accountability process teaches others in similar positions what is expected of them, what works and what does not."

The last sentence implies a norm-alignment and spreading function of accountability, as Bovens notes elsewhere in his article: "Norms are (re)produced, internalised and, where necessary, adjusted through accountability".

We conclude that for (software) multi-agent systems, accountability has a role to play in motivating good performance, and in monitoring and control (when one agent is a subordinate of another). It can also allow for incremental system improvement through learning or instruction, e.g. one agent may send new plans to another agent as an outcome of an accountability dialogue, and can enable the alignment and spreading of norms. When human users or partners are involved, we also see accountability contributing to the alignment of values.

3   Requirements for Accountable Autonomous Agents

Based on the literature discussed above, we propose that in order to support accountability, an autonomous practical reasoning agent should have the following four properties:

Expectation-Aware. The agent should be able to understand when it becomes subject to the expectations of others, for example through norms and commitments, such as the obligation to provide answers to accountability queries. It should also expect to be held to account, and possibly incur a sanction, after poor performance and failure—this provides the motivation to perform well. Its practical reasoning should be informed by these expectations. This property is likely to be crucial in ensuring that the following two properties are exercised correctly.

Answerable. The agent should be able to answer retrospective queries about its decision-making, within some pre-established scope. These queries may not be made immediately, so it must maintain sufficient information about its past reasoning to enable these queries to be answered. Note that answerability is similar to the concept of explainability, but includes the relational aspects of accountability: an accountable agent is answerable to a specific party that may send queries within some (possibly limited) scope, and these must be answered.

Argumentative. Full accountability cannot be achieved by one-off queries alone. To enable accountability processes to lead to system improvement (including norm and value alignment), an accountable agent should be capable of undertaking extended accountability dialogues in which beliefs, plans, norms and values are challenged, justified and further queried.

Meta-Cognitive. The agent must be able to adapt its reasoning mechanisms as a result of accountability dialogues. For example, an agent may need to update its plans, its plan selection mechanism, its failure-handing mechanism, its norms, or its values as a result of advice from its principal. The ability of an agent to alter its own decision-making components is known as meta-cognition [40], although we do not require the agent to monitor its own cognition, but rather to make changes when required by accountability mechanisms.

Additionally, when the scope of accountability includes actions that affect people, the following property is also required:

Value-Aware. The agent should maintain information about the relative importance of human values to its organisation or human partner(s) or client(s), and take these into account during its reasoning [41]. This in line with Dignum's ART model of responsible AI [18].

3.1   Research Questions

Various research questions stem from the requirements above. When extending autonomous agents to meet the requirements, we have:

Expectation-Aware. Research on norm-aware planning in BDI agents, e.g., [42], indicate that it is desirable and possible to extend a standard practical reasoning mechanism to address normative concerns. Our research questions are
  - What practical reasoning approach is most appropriate to be extended with expectations stemming from accountability relationships?
  - What is the minimal information required to enable expectation-aware behaviour in autonomous agents?
  - What game-theoretic aspects are there when agreeing (or not) to be accountable for something?

Answerable. There is a wealth of research on summarising and presenting data and information to different stakeholders, e.g., [43,44]. We anticipate queries to refer to rich and comprehensive records of decision-making processes and their rationale. Some questions arising are

- What knowledge/information should be represented to support accountability?
- What extensions/adaptations are required in the decision-making process(es) to ensure the knowledge and information of the previous question is adequately represented?
- What kinds of queries should be supported in accountability relations?

Argumentative. Research on formal argumentation has matured and has been applied to many contexts/domains [45]. Some issues arising are:

- Which formal argumentation techniques can be (re-)used, adapted or extended in the context of accountability queries and how this can be done?
- How can accountable behaviour (stemming from practical reasoning) be combined/extended with argumentation capabilities?
- How can argumentation interactions support and affect accountable behaviour (stemming from practical reasoning)?

Meta-Cognitive. Multi-agent plan selection and revision have been explored through different approaches (e.g., [41,46,47]) indicating that practical reasoning must tackle meta-cognitive issues – agents not only build and follow plans, but they must also reconsider/revisit decisions and reason about the actual decision processes. Some questions arising are:

- Is there a need for many levels of meta-cognition, whereby agents become aware about being aware about being aware and so on, or would a single meta-cognition level suffice?
- Would meta-interpretation [48,49] be an adequate and flexible approach to both meta-cognition and answerability?
- Should practical reasoning always embed meta-cognitive concerns or should these only be addressed when agents are accountable for some behaviour or result?

Value-Aware. Accountable agents seek to act, or answer queries, in a manner which promotes the values of the organisation(s), human partner(s) or client(s) to which they are accountable. In this context, research questions include

- How can the actions for which one is held accountable be shown to align to the values that should be promoted? Existing work on argument based practical reasoning (e.g., [50]) demonstrates the links between action and values, but not between accountability and values.
- How can the lack of promotion of a value (e.g., due to the sub-standard execution of a task) trigger the accountability process?

4 Towards a Formalisation of Accountability

In this section we propose an initial high-level formalism of accountability, focusing on answerability. We assume the accountable agent is equipped with a well studied form of expectation-awareness: the ability to represent and perform practical reasoning informed by norms such as obligations [51]. We consider that answerability is naturally expressed as an organisational norm, or as a commitment (if implicitly created via a *commitment protocol* [52]). We focus here on the normative view and model answerability as a conditional obligation norm. It is not the intention of this paper to define or commit to any specific formalisation for obligations, so for brevity we use an existing notation from the literature: the logic of Dignum et al. [53] for specifying temporal deontic constraints[3].

$$answerable(ag, at, QL, S, \delta t, rt) \equiv$$
$$\forall q \, PREV(ask(at, ag, q)) \wedge in\_scope(q, QL, S) \longrightarrow$$
$$O(valid\_reply(ag, at, q, S, \delta t) < now + rt)$$

where:

- ag and at refer to the *account-giver* (or accountable party) and the *account-taker* (or principal), following the terminology of Chopra and Singh [11].
- QL is an agreed (or imposed) query language in which accountability queries will be expressed.
- S is an agreed (or imposed) scope of queries—not all queries that can be expressed in QL may be relevant to the accountability relationship. Restrictions might include the types of goal considered, and the roles under which the queried activities are performed. We make no commitment regarding how S is expressed.
- δt is the length of the retrospective time period that accountability queries can ask about (where $\delta_t = \infty$ means there is no limit). This limits the time interval for which ag must keep records of its decision-making processes.
- rt is the maximum time allowed for an answer to an accountability query to be sent.
- $PREV(a)$ means that the action leading to the current state was a.
- $ask(at, ag, q)$ is the action of at asking ag the query q.
- $in\_scope(q, QL, S)$ denotes the condition that the query q is expressed in the query language QL and is within the scope S.
- $O(a < t)$ denotes the obligation for action a to be done before time t.
- $valid\_reply(ag, at, q, S, \delta t)$ is the action of ag sending at a valid answer for query q within scope S, based on a trace of its reasoning for the last δt time units. We do not attempt, within this obligation, to specify the notion of a valid reply. Instead, we consider this an abstract action, and assume that ag and at have a common understanding of what *counts as* [54] a valid reply. Below we propose one option.
- now is a special variable used in the logic of Dignum et al. [53] to refer to the time at which the obligation's conditions become true.

---

[3] This formalism is based on dynamic logic, but it is out of scope of this paper to describe the semantics. Also, note that our purpose here is to *specify* the nature of the obligation implied by answerability. For implementing accountability processes, it is likely that agents can use less expresssive and possibly more specialised, representations of their obligations.

We now consider what could count as a valid answer to the query. An answerable agent should be obliged to provide information about its practical reasoning that led to the queried behaviour, and that is relevant to the query. Before formalising this, we define some notation.

- $\tau_{ag}^{[t-\delta t,t]}$ denotes a full trace of the agent ag's reasoning during the interval $[t - \delta t, t]$. As well as recording successful plan executions, this trace must include information about options considered and not selected, and action and plan failures.
- Given a full trace τ, we write $\tau \lceil q,S$ to denote the restriction of the trace to contain only information relevant to the query q and scope S, and omit S if there is no scope restriction. We leave as an open question whether such a notion of relevance can be defined—if not, $\tau \lceil q,S = \tau$.

We assume that queries are expressed declaratively, with answers returned as variable bindings (or $\perp$ to indicate failure), and that the trace is viewed as a set of facts, and can therefore be decomposed into disjoint sets of facts. We then propose the following conditions for a query reply to be considered valid (where σ ranges over variable substitutions and $\uplus$ denotes disjoint union):

$$\nexists \sigma : (\tau_{ag}^{[t-\delta t,t]} \lceil q,S \models \sigma(q)) \longrightarrow$$
$$reply(ag, at, q, \perp) \; counts\_as \; valid\_reply(ag, at, q, S, \delta t)$$

$$\tau_{ag}^{[t-\delta t,t]} \lceil q,S \models \sigma(q) \; \wedge$$
$$\tau_{ag}^{[t-\delta t,t]} \lceil q,S = reasons \uplus rest \wedge rest \not\models \sigma(q) \longrightarrow$$
$$reply(ag, at, q, \langle \sigma, reasons \rangle) \; counts \; as \; valid\_reply(ag, at, q, S, \delta t)$$

The first clause states that a reply containing $\perp$ is valid if the query cannot be answered using the time- and scope-restricted trace. The first line of the second clause expresses the condition that the answer is correct, i.e. $\sigma(q)$ is entailed by the scope- and time-restricted trace. The second line first extracts a set of reasons from the trace, to help justify the query result, and then requires that at least some of the reasons provided in the answer are necessary for the truth of the answer—removing them from the trace would not allow the query to be answered. When these conditions hold, a reply containing the substitution, i.e. a set of variable bindings, and the reasons is considered valid. This notion of a valid answer does not fully specify the reasons that should be given to justify the answer. We believe these will be domain- and context-dependent, and in general, we envisage the need for a dialogue between the two agents to build up mutual information through a series of queries.

The use of $\tau_{ag}^{[t-\delta t,t]}$ above implies that ag should give an answer that is correct with respect to the *full trace* over the required retrospective time window. However, that does not necessarily mean that ag must actually record the full trace as implied by its semantics. Given a query scope S, it may be possible to answer queries within that scope using a subset of the information in $\tau_{ag}^{[t-\delta t,t]}$.

We explain this intuition by using the notion of an *abstraction* of a transition system. We can view the full trace as a transition system on time-stamped agent internal states (but note that the transitions must include the evaluation of failed reasoning rule conditions, as well as successes). Answering queries with a subset of information means reasoning with an abstraction of the transition system [55], which is defined over information states that are (potentially lossy) *projections* of the full agent states.

For a projection function f and a trace τ, we denote the abstracted transition system that f induces by τ^f. The task for the account-giver (or its designer) is then, given a scope S, to find a projection function f_S such that the following property holds:

$$\forall q : in\_scope(q, S), \forall \tau \in Traces, \forall \sigma, (\tau \upharpoonright q, S) \models \sigma(q)) \iff (\tau^{f_S} \upharpoonright q \models \sigma(q))$$

This states that answering queries within scope S by projecting traces using f_S produces the same answers as would be obtained using scope-restricted traces.

This model of answerability opens a number of research directions, including the following:

– There is a need to underpin the notation above with a formal model of agent reasoning. In the context of debugging BDI agent programs, Winikoff [49] provides such a model in the context of debugging agents by asking "why?" and "why not?" questions, which are answered using traces of agent reasoning. His formalism provides much of what is needed here. However, some aspects of this approach may not suit the problem of answerability. For example, queries may be asked some time after the computation in question was run, especially in the case of suboptimal outcomes or failures, and the account-taker may only have partial observability of the agent trace when asking its queries. Also, Winikoff's semantics assume that new beliefs can be semantically associated with the actions they were consequences of. In practice, the world is more complicated: actions can have various degrees of success and failure, and their effects can vary accordingly. Also, the effects may not always be immediately observable. To cater for these complexities, a richer domain model may be needed, and explanations may need to be contingent on the most likely causes of observations.
– A range of useful notions of query language and scope should be investigated. Winikoff investigated questions seeking reasons for why, at a given point of execution, plan steps were or were not performed, or specific conditions were or were not believed. These could be extended to consider extended models of agent reasoning, e.g., those incorporating norms [51] and values [41]. Another potentially useful query type when the account-taker lacks the full trace is "could you have performed X?" for a plan or action X. For argumentative agents, the notion of a query language should be extended to include assertions such as "P would have been a better plan to choose".
– The problem of choosing a projection function f_S given a scope S is important to ensure that agents only need to record the minimal required information. Also, there is the inverse question of what scope of queries can be answered by an agent that keeps a specific type of audit trail.

5 Conclusions, Discussion and Future Work

This paper surveyed the meaning and purpose of accountability in many areas, connecting and differentiating it from closely related concepts such as responsibility and transparency, among others. We identify the functional purpose of accountability: it enables monitoring and control of self-interested agents of a multi-agent system, and facilitates incremental improvements in the system. The improvement comes about as agents, aware of what they are accountable for, factor this in their choices of autonomous behaviour; the interactions among agents as they query and answer each other (this being guided by their accountability relations) will enable sharing of "best practices" (plans which withstand scrutiny and criticism), whilst aligning and spreading global norms. We have put forward requirements for accountable practical reasoning agents, and for each of these requirements we listed related research questions. We sketched a formalisation for one aspect of accountability: answerability, as part of an investigation into the normative constructs, the information model and reasoning mechanisms necessary for accountable practical reasoning.

Concerns about advances in AI and their impact in society have caught the attention of the media, governments and people in general. AI, coupled with autonomous behaviour, has immense potential, and initiatives have championed ethical and responsible principles for systems and their design. We hope we have made a step towards accountable autonomy, whereby the design and execution of practical reasoning agents is influenced by accountability. Ultimately, this paper aims to increase awareness among the multi-agent systems and software agents community of accountability and related ethical matters in our research. We would also like to consider this paper as a call-to-arms: we can, as a community, and building on the wealth of our research, lead the AI community in this quest for ethical and responsible AI.

In addition to the various research questions raised in previous sections, we are currently extending BDI practical reasoning technologies to explore accountability issues. We are also developing our formalisation of accountability, especially its connections with normative aspects as well as norm-aware BDI reasoning.

References

1. Dubnick, M.J.: Accountability as a cultural keyword. In: Bovens et al. [56]
2. Billingham, P., Colin, A.: The democratisation of accountability in the digital age: promise and pitfalls. In: Winner of Robert Davies Essay Competition 2016, Skoll Centre for Social Entrepreneurship, Saïd Business School, The University of Oxford, U.K. (2016). https://www.sbs.ox.ac.uk/sites/default/files/Skoll_Centre/Docs/Accountability_BillinghamColin-Jones.pdf
3. Wachter, S.: Towards accountable A.I. in Europe? The Alan Turing Institute, U.K. https://www.turing.ac.uk/blog/towards-accountable-ai-europe. Accessed 25 July 2018

4. Bostrom, N., Yudkowsky, E.: The ethics of artificial intelligence. In: Frankish, K., Ramsey, W.M. (eds.) The Cambridge Handbook of Artificial Intelligence, pp. 316–334. Cambridge University Press (2014)
5. Dignum, V.: Ethics in artificial intelligence: introduction to the special issue. Ethics Inf. Technol. **20**(1), 1–3 (2018)
6. Simonite, T.: Tech firms move to put ethical guard rails around AI. Wired, May 2018. https://www.wired.com/story/tech-firms-move-to-put-ethical-guard-rails-around-ai/. Accessed 29 July 2018
7. Zou, J., Schiebinger, L.: AI can be sexist and racist – it's time to make it fair. Nature **559**, 324–326 (2018)
8. Georgeff, M., Pell, B., Pollack, M., Tambe, M., Wooldridge, M.: The belief-desire-intention model of agency. In: Müller, J.P., Rao, A.S., Singh, M.P. (eds.) ATAL 1998. LNCS, vol. 1555, pp. 1–10. Springer, Heidelberg (1999). https://doi.org/10.1007/3-540-49057-4_1
9. Meneguzzi, F.R., Zorzo, A.F., da Costa Móra, M.: Propositional planning in BDI agents. In: Proceedings of the ACM Symposium on Applied Computing, pp. 58–63. ACM, New York (2004)
10. Rao, A.S., Georgeff, M.P.: BDI agents: from theory to practice. In: Proceedings of the 1st International Conference on Multi-Agent Systems (ICMAS 1995), pp. 312–319. AAAI (1995). https://www.aaai.org/Papers/ICMAS/1995/ICMAS95-042.pdf
11. Chopra, A.K., Singh, M.P.: The thing itself speaks: accountability as a foundation for requirements in sociotechnical systems. In: 2014 IEEE 7th International Workshop on Requirements Engineering and Law, p. 22. IEEE (2014)
12. Dastani, M., van der Torre, L., Yorke-Smith, N.: Commitments and interaction norms in organisations. Auton. Agent. Multi-Agent Syst. **31**(2), 207–249 (2017)
13. Fornara, N., Colombetti, M.: Representation and monitoring of commitments and norms using OWL. AI Commun. **23**(4), 341–356 (2010)
14. Baldoni, M., Baroglio, C., May, K.M., Micalizio, R., Tedeschi, S.: Computational accountability. In: Proceedings of the AI*IA Workshop on Deep Understanding and Reasoning: A Challenge for Next-generation Intelligent Agents, volume 1802 of CEUR Workshop Proceedings, pp. 56–62. CEUR-WS.org (2017)
15. Baldoni, M., Baroglio, C., May, K.M., Micalizio, R., Tedeschi, S.: ADOPT JaCaMo: accountability-driven organization programming technique for JaCaMo. In: An, B., Bazzan, A., Leite, J., Villata, S., van der Torre, L. (eds.) PRIMA 2017. LNCS (LNAI), vol. 10621, pp. 295–312. Springer, Cham (2017). https://doi.org/10.1007/978-3-319-69131-2_18
16. Baldoni, M., Baroglio, C., Micalizio, R.: The AThOS project: first steps towards computational accountability. In: Proceedings of the 1st Workshop on Computational Accountability and Responsibility in Multiagent Systems, volume 2051 of CEUR Workshop Proceedings, pp. 3–19. CEUR-WS.org (2018)
17. Bovens, M., Schillemans, T., Goodin, R.E.: Public accountability. In: Bovens et al. [56]
18. Dignum, V.: Responsible artificial intelligence: designing AI for human values. ITU J. ICT Discov. **1**(1), 1–8 (2018)
19. Fox, J.: The uncertain relationship between transparency and accountability. Dev. Pract. **17**(4–5), 663–671 (2007)
20. Schillemans, T.: The public accountability review: a meta-analysis of public accountability research in six academic disciplines. Working paper, Utrecht University School of Governance (2013). https://dspace.library.uu.nl/handle/1874/275784

21. Emanuel, E.J., Emanuel, L.L.: What is accountability in health care? Ann. Intern. Med. **124**(2), 229–239 (1996)
22. Eshleman, A.: Moral responsibility. In: Zalta, E.N. (ed.) The Stanford Encyclopedia of Philosophy. Metaphysics Research Lab, Stanford University, winter 2016 edn. (2016)
23. PMI: Guide to the Project Management Body of Knowledge (PMBOK®Guide), 5th edn. Project Management Institute (2013)
24. Jacka, J.M., Keller, P.J.: Business Process Mapping: Improving Customer Satisfaction, 2nd edn. Wiley, Hoboken (2009)
25. Grossi, D., Dignum, F., Royakkers, L.M.M., Meyer, J.-J.C.: Collective obligations and agents: who gets the blame? In: Lomuscio, A., Nute, D. (eds.) DEON 2004. LNCS (LNAI), vol. 3065, pp. 129–145. Springer, Heidelberg (2004). https://doi.org/10.1007/978-3-540-25927-5_9
26. Micalizio, R., Torasso, P., Torta, G.: On-line monitoring and diagnosis of multi-agent systems: a model based approach. In: Proceedings of the 16th European Conference on Artificial Intelligence, pp. 848–852. IOS Press (2004)
27. Witteveen, C., Roos, N., van der Krogt, R., de Weerdt, M.: Diagnosis of single and multi-agent plans. In: Proceedings of the Fourth International Joint Conference on Autonomous Agents and Multiagent Systems, pp. 805–812. ACM (2005)
28. Grossi, D., Royakkers, L., Dignum, F.: Organizational structure and responsibility. Artif. Intell. Law **15**(3), 223–249 (2007)
29. de Jonge, F., Roos, N., Witteveen, C.: Primary and secondary diagnosis of multi-agent plan execution. Auton. Agent. Multi-Agent Syst. **18**(2), 267–294 (2009)
30. Mastop, R.: Characterising responsibility in organisational structures: the problem of many hands. In: Governatori, G., Sartor, G. (eds.) DEON 2010. LNCS (LNAI), vol. 6181, pp. 274–287. Springer, Heidelberg (2010). https://doi.org/10.1007/978-3-642-14183-6_20
31. De Lima, T., Royakkers, L.M.M., Dignum, F.: Modeling the problem of many hands in organisations. In: Proceedings of the 19th European Conference on Artificial Intelligence, volume 215 of Frontiers in Artificial Intelligence and Applications, pp. 79–84. IOS Press (2010)
32. Bulling, N., Dastani, M.: Coalitional responsibility in strategic settings. In: Leite, J., Son, T.C., Torroni, P., van der Torre, L., Woltran, S. (eds.) CLIMA 2013. LNCS (LNAI), vol. 8143, pp. 172–189. Springer, Heidelberg (2013). https://doi.org/10.1007/978-3-642-40624-9_11
33. Micalizio, R., Torasso, P.: Cooperative monitoring to diagnose multiagent plans. J. Artif. Intell. Res. **51**, 1–70 (2014)
34. Lorini, E., Longin, D., Mayor, E.: A logical analysis of responsibility attribution: emotions, individuals and collectives. J. Log. Comput. **24**(6), 1313–1339 (2014)
35. Aldewereld, H., Dignum, V., Vasconcelos, W.W.: Group norms for multi-agent organisations. ACM Trans. Auton. Adapt. Syst. **11**(2), 15:1–15:31 (2016)
36. Alechina, N., Halpern, J.Y., Logan,B.: Causality, responsibility and blame in team plans. In: Proceedings of the 16th International Conference on Autonomous Agents and Multiagent Systems, pp. 1091–1099. IFAAMAS (2017)
37. Winikoff, M.: Towards trusting autonomous systems. In: El Fallah-Seghrouchni, A., Ricci, A., Son, T.C. (eds.) EMAS 2017. LNCS (LNAI), vol. 10738, pp. 3–20. Springer, Cham (2018). https://doi.org/10.1007/978-3-319-91899-0_1
38. Bovens, M.: Analysing and assessing accountability: a conceptual framework. Eur. Law J. **13**(4), 447–468 (2007)
39. Richard, M.: 'accountability': An ever-expanding concept? Public Adm. **78**(3), 555–573 (2000)

40. Anderson, M.L., Perlis, D.R.: Logic, self-awareness and self-improvement: the metacognitive loop and the problem of brittleness. J. Log. Comput. **15**(1), 21–40 (2005)

41. Cranefield, S., Winikoff, M., Dignum, V., Dignum, F.: No pizza for you: Value-based plan selection in BDI agents. In: Proceedings of the Twenty-Sixth International Joint Conference on Artificial Intelligence, pp. 178–184. ijcai.org (2017)

42. Meneguzzi, F., Rodrigues, O., Oren, N., Vasconcelos, W.W., Luck, M.: BDI reasoning with normative considerations. Eng. Appl. Artif. Intell. **43**, 127–146 (2015)

43. Gatt, A., et al.: From data to text in the neonatal intensive care unit: using NLG technology for decision support and information management. AI Commun. **22**(3), 153–186 (2009)

44. Mulwa, C., Lawless, S., Sharp, M., Wade, V.: The evaluation of adaptive and personalised information retrieval systems: a review. Int. J. Knowl. Web Intell. **2**(2/3), 138–156 (2011)

45. Bex, F., Grasso, F., Green, N., Paglieri, F., Reed, C.: Argument Technologies: Theory, Analysis, and Applications. Studies in Logic and Argumentation. College Publications (2017)

46. Alechina, N., Dastani, M., Logan, B., Meyer, J.-J.C.: Reasoning about plan revision in BDI agent programs. Theoret. Comput. Sci. **412**(44), 6115–6134 (2011)

47. Ma, J., Liu, W., Hong, J., Godo, L., Sierra, C.: Plan selection for probabilistic BDI agents. In: 2014 IEEE 26th International Conference on Tools with Artificial Intelligence, pp. 83–90, November 2014

48. Winikoff, M.: An AgentSpeak meta-interpreter and its applications. In: Bordini, R.H., Dastani, M.M., Dix, J., El Fallah Seghrouchni, A. (eds.) ProMAS 2005. LNCS (LNAI), vol. 3862, pp. 123–138. Springer, Heidelberg (2006). https://doi.org/10.1007/11678823_8

49. Winikoff, M.: Debugging agent programs with "why?" questions. In: Proceedings of the 16th International Conference on Autonomous Agents and Multiagent Systems, pp. 251–259. IFAAMAS (2017)

50. Atkinson, K., Bench-Capon, T.J.M.: Practical reasoning as presumptive argumentation using action based alternating transition systems. Artifi. Intell. **171**(10–15), 855–874 (2007)

51. Andrighetto, G., Governatori, G., Noriega, P., van der Torre, L.W.N. (eds.) Normative Multi-Agent Systems, volume 4 of Dagstuhl Follow-Ups. Schloss Dagstuhl - Leibniz-Zentrum für Informatik (2013)

52. Mallya, A.U., Singh, M.P.: An algebra for commitment protocols. Auton. Agent. Multi-Agent Syst. **14**(2), 143–163 (2007)

53. Dignum, F., Weigand, H., Verharen, E.: Meeting the deadline: on the formal specification of temporal deontic constraints. In: Raś, Z.W., Michalewicz, M. (eds.) ISMIS 1996. LNCS, vol. 1079, pp. 243–252. Springer, Heidelberg (1996). https://doi.org/10.1007/3-540-61286-6_149

54. Searle, J.R.: The Construction of Social Reality. Free Press, New York (1995)

55. Finkel, A., Iyer, S.P., Sutre, G.: Well-abstracted transition systems: application to FIFO automata. Inf. Comput. **181**(1), 1–31 (2003)

56. Bovens, M., Goodin, R.E., Schillemans, T. (eds.): The Oxford Handbook of Public Accountability. Oxford University Press, Oxford (2014)

Using Semantic Web Technologies and Production Rules for Reasoning on Obligations and Permissions

Nicoletta Fornara[1]([✉])[iD], Alessia Chiappa[2], and Marco Colombetti[2][iD]

[1] Università della Svizzera italiana, via G. Buffi 13, 6900 Lugano, Switzerland
nicoletta.fornara@usi.ch
[2] Politecnico di Milano, Piazza Leonardo Da Vinci 32, Milano, Italy
alessia.chiappa@gmail.com, marco.colombetti@polimi.it

Abstract. Nowadays the studies on the formalization, enforcement, and monitoring of policies and norms is crucial in different fields of research and in numerous applications. ODRL 2.2 (Open Digital Right Language) is a W3C standard policy expression language formalized using semantic web technologies. It is used to represent permitted and prohibited actions over a certain asset, and obligations required to be met by parties involved in the exchange of a digital asset. In this paper, we propose to extend the model of permission and obligation proposed by ODRL 2.2 in two directions. Firstly, by inserting in the model the notion of activation event or action and by expressing event and action as complex constructs having types and application-independent properties. Secondly, by considering the temporal aspects of obligations and permissions (expiration dates and deadlines) as part of their application independent model. The operational semantics of the proposed model of obligations and permissions is specified using Discrete State Machines and is computed using a production rule system. The proposed approach has been tested by developing a framework in Java able to get as input a set of policies formalized using Semantic Web languages, and to compute their evolution in time based on the events and actions that happen in the interaction among the parties involved in the policies.

1 Introduction

Nowadays the study of policies and norms is crucial in different fields of research and applications. Policies may be used for regulating access to data and digital assets in policy-based access control frameworks. They may be used to unambiguously specify licenses for software, images, video and data or to formalize contracts, agreements, and offers between different parties in e-commerce applications. Privacy policy may also be used to express regulations on the management of personal and sensitive data.

Funded by the SNSF (Swiss National Science Foundation) grant no. 200021_175759/1.

M. Lujak (Ed.): AT 2018, LNAI 11327, pp. 49–63, 2019.
https://doi.org/10.1007/978-3-030-17294-7_4

In principle policies and norms can be specified using human-readable formats; however, it is crucial to specify them with formal and machine-readable languages in order to enable machine-to-machine interactions combined with a number of useful services, like: (i) advanced search of resources based on the actions that it is possible to perform on them; (ii) aggregation of different resources released under different policies by computing policies compatibility or conflicts; (iii) checking the satisfaction or violation of the normative or legal relations that an intensive exchange of digital assets creates in the chain of interactions among data producers, data publishers, and data consumers.

In order to perform services of this type it is crucial not only to propose a language for expressing policies, but also to unambiguously specify the meaning of such policies. This with the goal of being able to automatically monitor the fulfilment or violation of obligations and the correct use of permissions, and to simulate what would happen if one of the parties, related by a set of policies, performs certain actions.

ODRL 2.2 (Open Digital Right Language)[1] is a W3C standard policy expression language, which is used to represent permitted and prohibited actions over a certain asset, and obligations required to be met by the parties involved in the exchange of a digital asset. Originally, in 2001, ODRL was an XML language for expressing digital rights, that is, digital content usage terms and conditions. In 2012 (version 2.0) and in 2015 (version 2.1) [12], ODRL evolved into a more general policy language: it is no longer focused only on the formalization of rights expressions, but also on the specification of privacy statements, like duties, permissions, and prohibitions. ORDL started to be formalized in RDF with an abstract model specified by an RDF Schema Ontology. In March 2016, a W3C Working Group was created with the goal of bringing the specifications through the W3C Process to "Recommendation" status. ODRL 2.2 became a W3C Recommendation on 15th February 2018. In all the specifications of ODRL, its semantics is described informally in English, and no formal specification is provided. In [13] an OWL representation of ODRL 1.1 is presented, but the use of OWL is limited to the representation of classes and properties, and no representation is given of the dynamic semantics of policies, that is, of how they evolve in time. In [19] the semantics of ODRL 2.1 policies used for access control is investigated. When a request to perform an action on an asset is issued, the system evaluates which rules (prohibition, permission, or duty rules) are triggered (taking into account explicit and implicit dependencies among regulated actions), then it checks whether these rules hold based on certain constraints (i.e., activation conditions); however there is no hint on how the satisfaction of constraints can be computed.

In this paper, we propose to extend the model of permission and obligation proposed by ODRL 2.2 in two directions. Firstly, by inserting in the model the notion of activation event/action and by expressing event and action as complex constructs having types and application-independent properties. Secondly, by considering the temporal aspects of obligations and permissions (their expiration

---

dates and the deadlines) as part of their application-independent model. The operational semantics of the proposed model of obligations and permissions is then specified using Discrete State Machines, which are used to unambiguously specify the temporal evolution of the *deontic state* of obligations and permissions while time passes and relevant events (e.g. the elapsing of a deadline) or actions (e.g. downloading a music file) happen. Such an operational semantics can be efficiently computed by a *monitor* component by using a production rule system. The proposed approach has been tested by developing a framework in Java able to get as input a set of policies formalized using Semantic Web languages, and to compute their evolution in time based on the events and actions that take place. Such a framework uses the forward chaining rule-based RETE engine of the Apache Jena framework[2] (which is compatible with semantic web languages) for realizing the production system.

The paper is organized as follows. In Sect. 2, a semantic meta-model for expressing temporal and conditional permissions and obligations is introduced. In Sect. 3, the life cycles of those two deontic relations is formally specified. In Sect. 4, a production rule system is used for computing the deontic state of obligations and permissions. In Sect. 5, a prototype for simulating the evolution in time of deontic relations is described. Finally, in Sect. 6 other approaches for expressing policies and norms are presented and discussed.

2 A Semantic Web Meta-model of Conditional Obligations and Permissions

Following ODRL 2.2 Information Model, a policy must have at least one permission, prohibition or obligation. In ODRL model, the regulated *actions* are expressed by means of their textual name (e.g. print), and their semantics can be narrowed by using *constraints* (i.e. expressions which compare two operands), for example "print less than or equal to 1200 dpi resolution". A permission may be conditioned by a duty and its intuitive meaning is that the duty represents a pre-condition that must be fulfilled to obtain a valid permission. From our perspective, it sounds quite unnatural to say that for acquiring a valid permission, for example to listen to an audio file, I have the duty to do something, for example to pay x euro. This because a duty is an action than an agent is obligated to do, not an action that an agent can freely decide to perform. In ODRL model, an obligation is a duty and it is fulfilled if all constraints are satisfied and if the regulated action, with all constraints satisfied, has been exercised.

The ODRL model does not highlight two crucial application-independent characteristics of the modelled deontic concepts. The first one is the important role played by the event/action that can *activate* an obligation or make a permission *valid*. In ODRL, an activation condition is represented as a generic constraint, even if it is a crucial part of the deontic model. For example, only when an agent enters a limited traffic area he becomes obligated to pay an amount

---

[2] https://jena.apache.org/documentation/inference/index.html.

of money within a given interval of time; similarly, only after paying a fee an agent gets a valid permission to play a music file in a party. It is also important to model those actions and events using complex constructs having a type and application-independent properties.

The second relevant application-independent characteristic of the modelled deontic concepts is their relation with time. Usually an obligatory action has to be performed before a specific *deadline*, and a permission can be used within a certain interval of time (e.g., the obligation to pay 5 euro before the end of the month, or the permission to play a music file within one week). A conditional obligation/permission may also become *expired* if it is not activated or made valid before a given expiration date. For example, as long as an agent is a bidder in an auction, such an agent has the obligation to pay his bids if it becomes the winner of the auction. When the auction is closed, the obligation expires and cannot become active anymore.

In this paper, we propose to extend ODRL 2.2 information model with two new types of deontic relations: *conditional obligations* and *conditional permissions*, i.e. obligations and permissions that become activated/valid when a condition is satisfied and having in their meta-model expiration dates and deadlines. What we model is a notion of *strong* permission, i.e. the explicit permission to do an otherwise prohibited action, which is different from the *weak* permission, i.e. the absence of the prohibition to do an action [22].

Given that ODRL is a W3C standard, the ODRL 2.2 ontology[3] is formalized using RDF Schema[4], a semantic web standard language for expressing data-model vocabulary for RDF data. RDF Schema can be used for defining classes, domain and range of properties and hierarchies of classes and of properties. The provided ODRL specification is compatible with another standard semantic web language for expressing ontologies, the OWL 2 Web Ontology Language, which is a practical serialization of the SROIQ(D) Description Logic. Therefore, given that we want to propose an extension of ODRL, we will formalize our meta-model of temporal-conditional obligations and permissions using an OWL ontology: the *Normative Language Ontology* (NL Ontology). This choice involves also the advantage of being able to perform automatic reasoning on the OWL formalization of the proposed deontic concepts.

In the definition of the *Normative Language Ontology* we exploit the possibility, given by the adoption of Semantic Web Languages, to connect our ontology with other, quite well known, ontologies. We re-use the core model of temporal entities specified in the *OWL Time Ontology*[5] for being able to specify deadline and expiration dates, and the time when real events or actions happen. We re-use the *Schema.org* ontology[6] a well-known ontology that has been developed to support web search engines. We re-use it for the specification of actions as complex objects, contrary to their treatment in ODRL, where they are represented

---

[3] https://www.w3.org/ns/odrl/2/.

[4] https://www.w3.org/TR/rdf-schema/.

[5] W3C Recommendation 19 October 2017 https://www.w3.org/TR/owl-time/.

[6] http://schema.org/docs/developers.html.

by atomic symbols. We extend the ODRL 2.2 ontology in various ways, as will be detailed in the sequel. Finally, we re-use the *Event Ontology* presented in [5] for expressing events as a super-class of actions and for connecting events to time instants and intervals. The import relationship among the various ontologies is depicted in Fig. 1

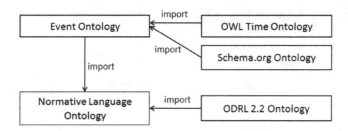

Fig. 1. The import relationship among the various ontologies

The *Normative Language Ontology* is depicted in Fig. 2. It defines two new types of deontic relations, as subclass of the ODRL Rule class: the nl:Obligation and the nl:Permission classes.

Obligations and permissions have the following common characteristics. They are *deontic relations* between two *parties*. They are characterized by two fundamental components: the *activation condition* and the *content*. The activation condition describes an event or an action, the content describes an action. When the activation event/action of an obligation actually happens, the obligation to perform the action described in the content component becomes active. Differently, when the activation event/action of a permission actually happens, the permission to perform the action described in the content component becomes valid. A *counter* is used for managing obligations and permissions to perform an action more than once. Obligations and permission have an *expiration* date and a *deadline*. Expiration and deadline usually refer to different instants of time. The expiration is the instant of time when the deontic relation ceases to exist. The deadline is the instant of time before which it is obligatory to satisfy the content of an active obligation or it permitted to exercise a valid permission. Deadlines and expiration dates may be computed at run-time by using the specified interval of time, in those cases their value depends on when the obligation/permission is created or activated/made valid. Finally, obligation and permission have a *deontic state*, it is used to compute their life cycle as discussed in next section.

An example of a conditional permission may be: when person:bob:01 pays 5 euros to organization:SOYN, he obtains a valid permission to listen to, at most ten times, a music record by the Beatles within 48 h from the

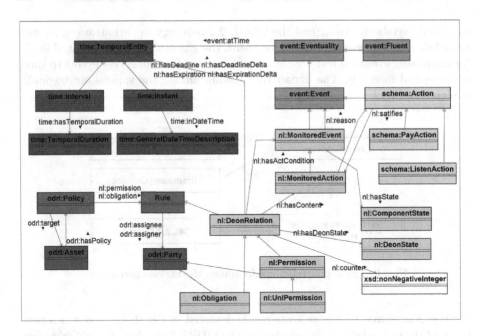

Fig. 2. The OWL Normative Language Ontology and its connections with other ontologies

payment; this permission expires at the end of 2018. Its formalization using the proposed ontology serialized using the Turtle language[7] is as follows:

```
ex:policy:01 a odrl:Policy;
   nl:permission    ex:perm:policy:01:1.
ex:perm:policy:01:1  a   nl:Permission;
   odrl:assigner    ex:org:SOYN;
   odrl:assignee    ex:person:bob:01;
   nl:hasActCond    ex:actCond:1;
   nl:hasContent    ex:content:1;
   nl:hasDeadlineDelta [time:hasTemporalDuration "PT48H0M0S"^^xsd:duration];
   nl:hasExpiration    [time:inDateTime "2018-12-31T09:00:00Z"^^xsd:dateTime];
   nl:counter       10^^xsd:integer.
ex:actCond:01:1  a   schema:PayAction;
   schema:agent     ex:person:bob:01;
   schema:recipient ex:org:SOYN;
   schema:price     5.00;
   schema:priceCurrency "euro".
ex:content:01:1  a   schema:ListenAction;
   schema:agent     ex:person:bob:01;
   schema:object  [ a schema:MusicRecording;
                    schema:byArtist ex:Beatles].
```

---

[7] https://www.w3.org/TR/2014/REC-turtle-20140225/. In Turtle every row is an RDF triple statement (subject, predicate, object) terminated by '.'; a ';' symbol is used to repeat the subject of triples that vary only in the predicate and object parts.

This is an example of a *policy instance*, with all its properties filled with a specific value. In a real system, it is desirable that digital assets are associated with a *policy schema* that can be re-used in different circumstances, for example the schema of a contract or of an agreement. Policy schemas contain variables and are transformed into policy instances through a procedure of substitution of variables with actual values, specified during an interaction with a specific user.

3 Life Cycles of Obligation and Permission

Obligations and *permissions* are two fundamental deontic relations widely used for regulating the *actions* that various individuals should or may perform. *Actions*, and more generally *events* (i.e. something that happens in a system, but is not necessarily done by an actor) change the state of the interaction among various parties, and their effects are strictly related to the instant of time when they happen. In order to specify what it means for an agent to have an obligation or a permission, it is fundamental to model their *deontic state* and to formally specify its evolution in time based on actual events (e.g. the elapsing of a deadline) and actions (e.g. downloading a music file).

In this section, we propose to formally describe such a temporal evolution using two *life cycles*, one for the notion of obligation and one for the notion of permission. They are the result of a deep analysis of the literature and of the textual description of permissions and duties given in the ODRL Information Model 2.2. Those life cycles are unambiguously specified using Discrete State Machines. More precisely, we use two simple types of *Discrete State Machines* (DSMs): pure *Finite State Machines* for modelling the conditional permission to perform an action for an unlimited number of times, and *Finite State Machines* augmented with a *decreasing counter* (with 0 lower bound), for modelling conditional obligations and permissions to perform an action for a limited number of times.

It is important to notice that the evolution of the *deontic state* of obligations and permissions in turn depends on the satisfaction of their *activation condition* and *content*. It is necessary to define a *procedure* for checking if actual events or actions satisfy the description of events and actions that appear in obligations and permissions. One possible approach for the realization of such a procedure will be described and discussed in next section.

In order to represent in our model the satisfaction of the content or of the activation condition of a deontic object, we introduce in the *NL Ontology* the following two properties. The hasState property is used to connect the content and the activation condition of a deontic object with their *state*. Such a state is initially *unsatisfied* and becomes *satisfied* when the described event/action occurs. The reason property is used to connect the content and the activation condition of a deontic object with the real event or action that produced its satisfaction. This property is necessary for comparing expiration dates and deadlines of the deontic objects with the instant of time when events or actions actually happen.

The life cycle of conditional obligations is depicted in Fig. 3. When a conditional obligation is created, it is in the *conditional* state and its condition and content are *unsatisfied*. When the activation condition becomes *satisfied* and the current time is less than or equal to the expiration date of the deontic relation, the transition from the conditional state to the *activated* state is fired. Differently if the expiration date is elapsed the transition leads from the conditional to the *expired* state. Then, whenever the content becomes satisfied before the deadline and its counter is greater than zero the conditional obligation remains *activated*, the counter is decremented, and the content is set back to *unsatisfied*. If the content becomes again satisfied before the deadline and the counter is equal to zero the state becomes *fulfilled*. Differently if the state is still activated and the deadline becomes elapsed, the state becomes *violated*.

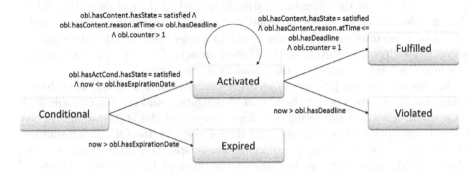

Fig. 3. Life cycle of conditional obligation

The life cycle of a conditional permission is depicted in Fig. 4. A *conditional* permission becomes *valid* when its condition is satisfied. Then every time it is exercised, a counter is decremented and when the counter is equal to zero the state becomes *exercised*. If the expiration date of a conditional permission is expired its state becomes *expiredConditional*, differently if the deadline of a valid permission is expired the permission becomes *expiredValid*. The conditional permission to perform an action for an unlimited number of times is represented with a Finite State Machine and the main difference is the absence of the counter and of the exercised state, in fact only when the deadline is elapsed the permission becomes expiredValid.

It is interesting to observe that the conditions that trigger the transitions of the two life cycles are identical. The fundamental difference between the two deontic relations, which is enlightened by the different name of the deontic states, is that for obligations the *fulfilled* state is a final and desired state, contrary to the *violated* final state which may bring about a sanction, differently, for permissions the *exercised* final state has no positive or negative connotation.

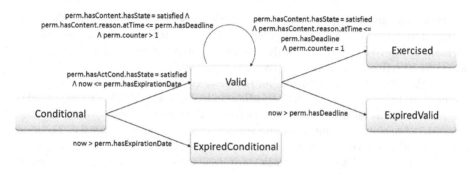

Fig. 4. Life cycle of conditional permission

4   Operational Semantics of Obligation and Permission

In order to realize services able to automatically monitor or simulate the dynamic evolution of the proposed deontic relations, it is necessary to define a *procedure* for automatically computing their *deontic state*. Such a deontic state, in turn, depends on the satisfaction of the *state* of the *activation condition* and *content* of the relevant deontic objects.

This procedure requires an application-dependent component, able to "sense" the actual events or actions and represent them as individuals of the *State Ontology* by using the vocabulary defined by the *Event* and *Schema.org* ontologies. This procedure also requires two application-independent components: one for computing the satisfaction of the *state* and one for computing the *deontic state*.

In this section we propose to realize those components using a *production system* [1], i.e. a forward-chaining reasoning system that uses *production rules*. The *ongoing memory* of assertions (stored in the working memory of the proposed production system) is composed of: the *State Ontology*, a representation, in the form of RDF triples, of the state of the interaction in terms of actual actions, events, and current time; the *Normative Ontology*, a representation of the set of policies containing obligations and permissions. While time flows, the *ongoing memory* is continuously updated with new assertions representing actual events or actions and the elapsing of time, and it is updated due to the execution of production rules.

A production rule has two parts: a set of *conditions*, to be tested on the ongoing memory, and a set of *actions*, whose execution has an effect on the ongoing memory. The generic form of a production rule is:

IF conditions THEN actions

Production rules may be used to generate an event-based computation, which can carry out an inference process or implement a discrete dynamic system. We will exploit the latter use of production rules for proposing an operation model of the life cycles of obligations and permissions introduced in the previous section.

A crucial advantage of production rules is the possibility to represent the logic of the dynamic evolution of the proposed deontic relations using a declarative paradigm, where rules can be easily modified, instead of embedding such a logic in the code written in an imperative programming language.

In this section we will formalize our production rules using the Abstract Syntax of the W3C Recommendation RIF Production Rule Dialect[8] (RIF PRD). Initially, we present the application independent productions rules for computing the satisfaction of *activation conditions* and *content*. Subsequently, we present the productions rules for computing the *deontic state* of obligations and permissions.

The first type of production rules are used for matching the description of events and actions with actual events or actions as soon as they are represented in the system. In the meta-model of obligations and permissions proposed in this paper, a description of an event or an action is characterized by the specification of its class and of a list of values for significant properties. The matching can be realized by a production rule used for checking the exact match between the described values and the real values. Given that the list of properties used for describing an event or an action can vary, we need to specify a production rule for every monitored type of event or action (characterized by the list of properties used for its description). In the future we plan to study a more flexible mechanism for matching an actual event/action with an event/action description.

Due to space limitation we report only one production rule of this type. It can be used for matching a real payment with the activation condition of the permission presented in Sect. 2 and with all the activation conditions where the same parameters are used[9].

```
(* PayAction *)
Forall  ?realAction ?component ?agent ?recipient ?price ?currency(
  If And( rdf:type(?obl nl:Obligation)
    nl:hasDeonState(?obl nl:conditional)
    nl:hasActCond(?obl ?activation)
    nl:hasState(?activation nl:unSatisfied)
    rdf:type(?activation schema:PayAction)
    schema:agent(?activation ?agent)
    schema:recipient(?activation ?recipient)
    schema:price(?activation ?price)
    schema:priceCurrency(?activation ?currency)
    rdf:type(?realAction schema:PayAction)
    schema:agent(?realAction ?agent)
    schema:recipient(?realAction ?recipient)
    schema:price(?realAction ?price)
    schema:priceCurrency(?realAction ?currency) )
  Then (Assert(nl:reason(?activation ?realAction))
        Retract(nl:hasState(?activation nl:unSatisfied))
        Assert( nl:hasState(?activation nl:satisfied)) )  )
```

---

[8] https://www.w3.org/TR/rif-prd/, http://www.w3.org/TR/rif-primer/.

[9] We assume that it is impossible to insert in the State Ontology an event that will happen in the future.

The production rules of the second type are used for computing the *deontic state* of obligations and permissions. It is necessary to define one production rule for every transition of the life cycles presented in Sect. 3. The *conditions* of these production rules are used for testing the type of the deontic relation (permission or obligation), the current deontic state, and the conditions that appear on the transition of the life cycle. The *action* component of the rules is used to retract the current deontic state, assert the new one and, if necessary, decrement the counter.

Due to space limitation, we present only the production rule used for computing the transition from *conditional* to *valid* of a permission.

```
(* validatePermission *)
Forall ?perm ?activation ?expiration ?expirationDateTime ?now (
  If And( rdf:type(?perm nl:Permission)
    nl:hasDeonState(?perm nl:conditional)
    nl:hasActCond(?perm ?activation)
      nl:hasState(?activation nl:satisfied)
    nl:hasExpiration(?perm ?expiration)
      time:inDateTime(?expiration ?expirationDateTime)
      time:inDateTime(ex:currentTime ?now)
    External(pred:numeric-less-than(?now ?expirationDateTime) ) )
  Then (Retract(nl:hasDeonState(?perm nl:conditional))
      Assert(nl:hasDeonState(?perm nl:valid)) )   )
```

5   Implementation of a Prototype

For testing our proposal, we have developed a Java prototype, specifically a system able to *simulate* the evolution of policies containing obligations and permissions. We use Apache Jena[10], a free and open source Java framework for building semantic web applications. For the implementation of the *production system*, described in Sect. 4, we use the Jena general-purpose rule-based reasoner and a translation of the RIF PRD rules into Jena Rules[11]. This reasoner supports rule-based inference over RDF graphs, and provides forward chaining realized by means of an internal RETE-based forward chaining interpreter [4]. The main advantage of using the JENA interpreter with respect to other Java compatible production rules interpreters, like for instance the Jess engine inspired by the open-source CLIPS project, is its direct compatibility with RDF data [16].

An interesting feature of the Jena forward chaining interpreter is that it works incrementally, meaning that if the inference model is modified by adding or removing statements, the reasoning process automatically resumes, potentially producing the activation of new rules. The efficiency of the reasoning with respect to these incremental changes is guaranteed by the use of the RETE algorithm, through which matching tests are performed only for those rules whose conditions include an updated fact in the previous iteration.

In our prototype, the RIF PRD external built-in operations of *Retract()* and *Assert()* are realized by means of the default Jena built-in *remove(n)* and the ad-hoc realized *add(triple)* built-in. The *remove(n)* Jena built-in has the side effect of

---

[10] https://jena.apache.org/.

[11] https://jena.apache.org/documentation/inference/#rules.

recursively retracting, from the inference model, the consequences of the already fired rules, if their conditions matched with the removed statement. In fact, coherently with its main goal of implementing logical reasoning in RDF and OWL, the Jena interpreter is designed to have a monotonic behaviour. Given that our productions rules are meant to implement Finite State Machines (and not monotonic logical reasoning), we implemented the ad-hoc *add(triple)* built-in, having the effect of inserting a new triple that will not be retracted as a side effect of removing another statement.

A useful service is the *monitoring* of deontic relations for those applications where it is crucial to check the fulfilment or violation of norms and the use of valid permissions. Another relevant service is the *simulation* of the evolution of deontic relations based on a set of hypothetical actions. In order to realize these services it is important to take into account that a few *relevant instants* are truly significant in the life cycle of a permission or obligation. Significant instants are the instants when real actions and events happen and the elapsing of deadline and expiration dates. Therefore in order to realize an efficient simulator[12] it is important that the comparison between the simulated current time and the *significant instants* (stored in an ordered list) occurs only if strictly necessary, i.e. when one of these relevant instants are reached. This is obtained by forcing the current time to evolve to the nearest relevant instant of time. Each update of the current time in the inference model leads to a new cycle of the interpreter, during which the states of obligations and permissions eventually evolve.

6   Related Work

Studies on Normative Multiagent Systems (NorMAS) concern mainly the proposals of formalisms for expressing norms or policies containing obligations, permissions, and prohibitions. Those studies also investigate the realization of fundamental functionalities for norm promulgation, monitoring, and enforcement, as well as norm adoption and reasoning. In the NorMAS literature there are various proposals for the formalization of norms and policies using different languages [3,5] and different frameworks [2,18] for their management.

As we already discussed, the W3C standard for expressing policies is ODRL 2.2. Another interesting proposal, which is in the process of becoming an OASIS standard in the legal domain, is the LegalRuleML language[13].

Many approaches to the formalization of norms are based on different logics, which are declarative in nature. The most well-known are the studies on Deontic Logic [21], a family of logical systems where the essential features of obligations, prohibitions and related concepts are captured. An interesting approach to the specification of the semantics of obligations, permissions, and prohibitions is given in [11], where the L4LOD vocabulary for expressing licenses for Linked Open Data is presented. The semantics of the deontic component of licenses is formalized using an extension of Defeasible Logic [10]. This extension is a non-monotonic logic able to deal with permissions as defeaters of prohibitions (understood as negative obligations). The actions that are regulated are those typical of linked open data licences (e.g., ShareAlike, Attribution, etc.). Such actions are represented as atomic symbols, and no treatment of time or relevant action attributes is proposed. Another interesting approach, where time is

---

[12] Taking into account that the *monitoring* service can be realized using the simulator where time and events are real.

[13] https://www.oasis-open.org/committees/legalruleml/.

taken into account, is based on Linear Temporal Logic (LTL) [17]. This paper proposes a life cycle for obligations where deadlines and expiration dates are not modelled, and the content of the obligation is a maintenance condition, like for example "do not cross on a red light". Similarly to our proposal the transition rules are computed using a production system. In [9], a normative language for the specification of norms is presented. In such a normative language norms have the form of *preconditions → postconditions*, and the execution of every norm is implemented by means of an ad-hoc forward rule written for the Jess interpreter[14]. Differently in this paper, we propose a production rule system for computing the application-independent life cycle of policies containing deontic relations.

In this paper, we propose to formalize policies using Semantic Web Technologies; therefore here we will mainly discuss other approaches where those technologies were adopted. In particular, an interesting literature review of various approaches to policies specification using Semantic Web Technologies is given in [14]. [5,7] presents a proposal to specify and reason on obligations using OWL 2, SWRL rules, and OWL-API. These papers present an OWL ontology of obligations whose content is a class of possible actions that have to be performed within a given deadline. The monitoring of such obligations (checking if they are fulfilled of violated on the basis of the actions performed by the agents) is realized by means of a specific framework used for managing the elapsing of time and for performing closed-world reasoning on certain classes. Unfortunately, the scalability of this approach is not good enough to make it usable in real applications.

An interesting approach that uses Semantic Web Technologies for policy formalization and management is the OWL-POLAR framework [18]. This framework investigates the possibility of using OWL ontologies for representing the state of the interaction among agents and SPARQL queries for reasoning on policies activation, for anticipating possible conflicts among policies, and for conflicts avoidance and resolution. In the OWL-POLAR model, the activation condition and the content of the policies are represented using conjunctive semantic formulas. Reasoning on a set of policies for deducing their state is realized by translating the activation condition and the content of a policy into the SPARQL query language and then evaluating the resulting queries on the OWL ontology used for representing the state of the world. In OWL-POLAR, there is no treatment of time.

Another relevant proposal is the KAoS policy management framework [2,20]. In KAoS Semantic Web technologies are used for policy specification and management, in particular policy monitoring and enforcing is realized by a component that compiles OWL policies into an efficient format. In [15] social commitments [6] are used for modelling privacy requirements for social networks formalized using OWL. Similarly to our approach, the antecedent of commitments is a description of conditions that have to be matched with the content of the ontology. However, the consequent of commitments is limited to permissions or prohibitions to see a set of posts, and time is not modelled at all.

In [8] a proposal of expressing conditional obligations to perform one action, as an extension of ODRL 2.1 having a life cycle computed using Jena Rules is presented. In this paper we improved that work by proposing an extension of the new version of ODRL (ODRL 2.2), by formalizing the life cycle of both condition permissions and obligations which regulate the performance of an action for a limited number of

---

[14] http://www.jessrules.com/.

times, and by expressing the operational semantics of those deontic concepts using a production system.

In our future work, we plan to investigate the dynamic connections between obligations, permissions and prohibitions. We plan also to study how to efficiently integrate OWL reasoning into the proposed production system, and to further investigate the possibility to use the event of violation or fulfilment of an obligation for applying rewards or sanctions.

References

1. Brachman, R., Levesque, H.: Knowledge Representation and Reasoning. Morgan Kaufmann Publishers Inc., San Francisco (2004)
2. Bradshaw, J.M., et al.: The KAoS policy services framework. In: Eighth Cyber Security and Information Intelligence Research Workshop, CSIIRW 2013. Oak Ridge National Labs, Oak Ridge (2013)
3. da Silva Figueiredo, K., Torres da Silva, V., de Oliveira Braga, C.: Modeling norms in multi-agent systems with NormML. In: De Vos, M., Fornara, N., Pitt, J.V., Vouros, G. (eds.) COIN -2010. LNCS, vol. 6541, pp. 39–57. Springer, Heidelberg (2011). https://doi.org/10.1007/978-3-642-21268-0_3
4. Forgy, C.L.: On the efficient implementation of production systems. Ph.D. thesis, Pittsburgh, PA, USA (1979). AAI7919143
5. Fornara, N.: Specifying and monitoring obligations in open multiagent systems using semantic web technology. In: Elçi, A., Koné, M.T., Orgun, M.A. (eds.) Semantic Agent Systems: Foundations and Applications. Studies in Computational Intelligence, chap. 2, vol. 344, pp. 25–46. Springer, Heidelberg (2011)
6. Fornara, N., Colombetti, M.: Operational specification of a commitment-based agent communication language. In: Proceedings of the First International Joint Conference on Autonomous Agents and Multiagent Systems: Part 2, AAMAS 2002, pp. 536–542. ACM, New York (2002)
7. Fornara, N., Colombetti, M.: Representation and monitoring of commitments and norms using OWL. AI Commun. **23**(4), 341–356 (2010)
8. Fornara, N., Colombetti, M.: Operational semantics of an extension of ODRL able to express obligations. In: Belardinelli, F., Argente, E. (eds.) EUMAS/AT -2017. LNCS, vol. 10767, pp. 172–186. Springer, Cham (2018). https://doi.org/10.1007/978-3-030-01713-2_13
9. Garcia-Camino, A., Noriega, P., Rodriguez-Aguilar, J.A.: Implementing norms in electronic institutions. In: Proceedings of the Fourth International Joint Conference on Autonomous Agents and Multiagent Systems, AAMAS 2005, pp. 667–673. ACM, New York (2005)
10. Governatori, G., Rotolo, A.: BIO logical agents: norms, beliefs, intentions in defeasible logic. Auton. Agents Multi-Agent Syst. **17**(1), 36–69 (2008)
11. Governatori, G., Rotolo, A., Villata, S., Gandon, F.: One license to compose them all. In: Alani, H., et al. (eds.) ISWC 2013. LNCS, vol. 8218, pp. 151–166. Springer, Heidelberg (2013). https://doi.org/10.1007/978-3-642-41335-3_10
12. Iannella, R., Guth, S., Paehler, D., Kasten, A.: ODRL Version 2.1 Core Model (2015). https://www.w3.org/community/odrl/model/2.1/. Accessed 15 Sept 2017
13. Kasten, A., Grimm, R.: Making the semantics of ODRL and URM explicit using web ontologies. In: Virtual Goods, pp. 77–91 (2010)

14. Kirrane, S., Villata, S., d'Aquin, M.: Privacy, security and policies: a review of problems and solutions with semantic web technologies. Semant. Web **9**(2), 153–161 (2018)
15. Kokciyan, N., Yolum, P.: PriGuard: a semantic approach to detect privacy violations in online social networks. IEEE Trans. Knowl. Data Eng. **28**(10), 2724–2737 (2016)
16. Moskal, J., Matheus, C.J.: Detection of suspicious activity using different rule engines—comparison of BaseVISor, Jena and Jess rule engines. In: Bassiliades, N., Governatori, G., Paschke, A. (eds.) RuleML 2008. LNCS, vol. 5321, pp. 73–80. Springer, Heidelberg (2008). https://doi.org/10.1007/978-3-540-88808-6_10
17. Panagiotidi, S., Alvarez-Napagao, S., Vázquez-Salceda, J.: Towards the Norm-aware agent: bridging the gap between deontic specifications and practical mechanisms for norm monitoring and norm-aware planning. In: Balke, T., Dignum, F., van Riemsdijk, M.B., Chopra, A.K. (eds.) COIN 2013. LNCS, vol. 8386, pp. 346–363. Springer, Cham (2014). https://doi.org/10.1007/978-3-319-07314-9_19
18. Sensoy, M., Norman, T.J., Vasconcelos, W.W., Sycara, K.P.: OWL-POLAR: a framework for semantic policy representation and reasoning. J. Web Sem. **12**, 148–160 (2012)
19. Steyskal, S., Polleres, A.: Towards formal semantics for ODRL policies. In: Bassiliades, N., Gottlob, G., Sadri, F., Paschke, A., Roman, D. (eds.) RuleML 2015. LNCS, vol. 9202, pp. 360–375. Springer, Cham (2015). https://doi.org/10.1007/978-3-319-21542-6_23
20. Uszok, A., et al.: New developments in ontology-based policy management: increasing the practicality and comprehensiveness of KAoS. In: POLICY 2008, Palisades, New York, USA, 2–4 June 2008, pp. 145–152. IEEE Computer Society (2008)
21. von Wright, G.H.: Deontic logic. Mind New Ser. **60**(237), 1–15 (1951)
22. von Wright, G.H.: Norm and Action: A Logical Enquiry. Routledge and Kegan Paul, New York (1963)

Minimality and Simplicity of Rules
for the Internet-of-Things

Athanasios Panaretos[1], David Corsar[2], and Wamberto W. Vasconcelos[1]([🖂])

[1] Department of Computing Science, University of Aberdeen, Aberdeen, UK
`athanasios.panaretos.17@aberdeen.ac.uk`, `w.w.vasconcelos@abdn.ac.uk`
[2] School of Computing Science and Digital Media, Robert Gordon University,
Aberdeen, UK
`d.corsar1@rgu.ac.uk`

Abstract. Rule-based systems have been increasing in popularity in recent years. They allow for easier handling of both simple and complicated problems utilising a set of rules created in various ways (e.g., manually, or (semi-) automatically, via, say, machine learning or decision trees) depending on the situation. Despite their usefulness however, there are still improvements to be made. Knowledge representation technologies have been available for a long time and provide the means to represent domains formally and correlate entities in those domains. They also allow for ontological reasoning that can take advantage of such connections between entities. These techniques can be useful when applied on rule-based systems in order to improve the quality of rules and, hence, overall system performance. We describe and implement an approach to refine rules used in Internet-of-Things scenarios using knowledge representation and reasoning. The proposed solution uses ontological reasoning on the preconditions and postconditions of rules as it aims to reduce the total amount of rules in a system and simplify them.

Keywords: Rule-based systems · Internet-of-Things · Knowledge representation · Ontological reasoning

1 Introduction

The fast-spreading Internet-of-Things technology is creating massive changes in the way people interact with devices, but also devices interact with each other. In this quickly changing field, automation is becoming the key element, taking control from humans and giving it to machines when it comes to daily tasks.

Rule-based systems have been used for quite a while to regulate societies of agents. They are ideal for Internet-of-Things applications, however, they do have some issues. Firstly, the constant creation of rules to deal with different situations

---

This research is partially sponsored by the EPSRC grant EP/P011829/1, funded under the UK Engineering and Physical Sciences Council Human Dimensions of Cyber Security call (2016).

M. Lujak (Ed.): AT 2018, LNAI 11327, pp. 64–72, 2019.
https://doi.org/10.1007/978-3-030-17294-7_5

can lead to having far too many of them. Therefore, an issue of minimality of rules has arisen. Secondly, the attempt to minimize the rules in a system can result in a small set of rules that is however very complex and thus harder to maintain. Hence, there is a need for simplicity.

This paper presents a system which can tackle the issues at hand. The system is able to process events of Internet-of-Things scenarios and, along with a knowledge representation model of the domain, generate rules based on them. Furthermore, it refines these rules and through an exhaustive evaluation process it guarantees to maintain the system's accuracy while reducing the amount of rules residing in it. Explicit knowledge representation of all the required concepts is used to support the refinement process of the preconditions and postconditions of the rules.

2   Background and Related Work

Internet-of-Things has been identified as one of the emerging technologies in IT [4]. Despite the constant evolution of this technology, its main point, use of sensors and actuators based on knowledge without human intervention, remains the same [4]. This lack of solid definition of Internet-of-Things allows it to extend into multiple fields. The application of this technology ranges from personal to national making it quite efficient. Its current growth can be attributed to the adaptability of the technology itself and the many capabilities it grants its users.

Our approach makes use of explicit representation of knowledge. An ontology is an explicit specification of a conceptualization, that is the set of all the objects, entities and concepts and the relationships between them, of a domain [3]. Over time there have been a lot of successful attempts to generalize different situations and create ontological models that can satisfy a wide range of cases. The result is widely used models which greatly ease the process of inserting an ontology into any kind of system. Some relevant to Internet-of-Things are the Semantic Sensor Network[1], Open Digital Rights Language[2], Smart Appliances REFerence[3] and Smart Energy Aware Systems[4].

A closely related area of research is normative multi-agent systems. In human societies, norms have played an important role in governing the behavior of the individuals in a society [2]. Even though norms are essential in agent societies, they are not easy to synthesize. There are two approaches that deal with the problem of norm synthesis, offline and online. The offline approach tackles the problem by synthesizing all the norms required for a system during its design time. This technique however requires complete knowledge of the situation that the agents in the system will be facing.

---

[1] https://www.w3.org/TR/vocab-ssn/.

[2] https://www.w3.org/TR/odrl-model/.

[3] https://sites.google.com/site/smartappliancesproject/ontologies/reference-ontology.

[4] https://ci.mines-stetienne.fr/seas/index.html.

The online approach on the other hand synthesizes norms during runtime. This gives it the advantage of not requiring complete knowledge of the situation on design time which also implies that the norms that will be created over time will adjust to the conditions of the system as they keep changing [6]. It is worth mentioning that norm emergence has been gaining popularity lately. It is an online norm synthesis approach that allows agents to communicate with each other, synthesize norms themselves and decide on which ones will be used by the entire agent society. There are two related research work our project borrows from, namely IRON and its predecessor BASE. They both make use of a Case Based Reasoning mechanism to deal with conflict situations. Their differences are that IRON has a norm evaluation method and a norm generalization and specialization operator, which improve its performance.

3   Architecture and Implementation

The goal of the system is to process a log of events of Internet-of-Things scenarios and knowledge representation models in order to generate norms. The system will also have to be able to be integrated in different domains with only the input changing for each different adaptation. The rules, once generated, will be processed by the system and refined through generalizations and specializations of the ontological counterparts of the preconditions and postconditions. The output will be a set of rules that will be aiming to achieve minimality and simplicity.

Based on the system objectives, we can describe the several functional requirements that are inferred.

FR-1 The system will formulate rules based on an initial log of events and make them available in a specific format – The rules created will therefore be directly linked to the input log rather than abstract rules based on the Internet-of-Things scenario.

FR-2 The system will refine the rules by using a generalization and a specialization operator – These two operators will be able to make the rules move towards a more uniform form that will enable their merge.

FR-3 The system will evaluate the entire normative system after each operator action – This ensures that the norms that have been altered are kept only if they are efficient in their new form.

FR-4 The system will post-process the rules further to aim at achieving properties such as minimality and simplicity.

The scenario the system is applied on is a smart house that operates based on Internet-of-Things technology. All the sockets of the house have their voltage measured constantly which enables the complete knowledge of operation of every device. The system built, will be offering a set of norms to the occupants of the house that if followed will have beneficial effects to them such as reduced electricity cost and power conservation.

The data set[5] used is a result of a research project of the Distributed Systems Group of the Computing Science department of ETH in Zurich[6]. It is referred to as the ECO (Electricity Consumption and Occupancy) data set and it is a comprehensive open-source data set for non-intrusive load monitoring and occupancy detection research. It has information of 6 households for a period of 8 months with readings every second on all sockets of the house through smart meters. It additionally holds occupancy information through the use of a tablet computer in the households. [1] and [5] analyzed it in detail but due to its open-source nature it is useful to any other researcher on the field as well.

3.1 Architecture

It is important to distinguish the different components of the system so as to understand its functionality. We introduce all the main components as well as the initial inputs.

Input data – is the data on which the rules will be based and include tagged undesirable system states.

Ontologies – in the system refer to the knowledge representation of the devices as well as of the preconditions that define the rules.

Rules generator – generates rules according to data that has been given as input. The rules are created by picking at random elements from the ontologies that represent the preconditions and postconditions. If the generated rule can be applied to an undesirable state it is kept otherwise it is discarded.

Rules post-processor – receives the rules and generalizes or specializes them using the corresponding operator. Further aspects of ontological DL reasoning could be used to expand the concept hierarchies, this would give a richer set of generalisations/specialisations for use by the algorithm, but would not fundamentally alter the described approach.

Rules evaluator – evaluates the effectiveness of the generalized rules compared to their previous form. Specifically, it compares the amount of cases the rule got triggered before and after its generalization.

Rules merger – merges the generalized rules to reduce their total size.

3.2 Format of Rules

To understand our implementation better we introduce the format of the rules in the system:

`condition`:day/precondition_1/.../precondition_X;
`action`:device_1,action_1,...,device_X,action_X;
`group`:groupName

---

[5] http://rossa-prod-ap11.ethz.ch/delivery/DeliveryManagerServlet? dps_pid=IE594964.

[6] https://www.vs.inf.ethz.ch/.

In the condition part of the rule, the day refers to the day of the week while the preconditions refer to the time the rule will be applied. In the action part, the devices refer to any of the known devices in the house, while the actions, which have the value of 0 or 1 indicate whether the device should be turned off or on. Lastly, the groups, namely Cheap_Rate and Premium_Rate, are used to separate electricity cost depending on the time of the day. We also note that in our system we represent rules as trees and refer to nodes of these trees when performing actions between rules. For the sake of a simple example, let us assume that there are only 2 devices in the bedroom, a TV and a lamp. Accordingly, 2 rules have been generated:

    condition:Monday/2330;action:TV,0;group:Cheap_Rate
    condition:Monday/2335;action:Lamp,0;group:Cheap_Rate

When generalized and merged these 2 rules can be turned into a single one of the form condition:Monday/Late_Night;action:Bedroom,0;group:Cheap_Rate.

3.3   Ontologies in Our System

In the implementation we use as many ontologies as the preconditions and post-conditions we want to apply ontological reasoning on. In this case therefore, there is one ontology for the preconditions that is used to represent time and another for the postconditions which is used to represent devices. The time ontology splits up the time in different groups based on both the time of the day and the electricity cost. The devices ontology, separates the devices into groups based on their size and location in the house.

3.4   Functions and Operators

The most important functions amongst the many used in the system are the ones responsible for the merging of different rules. They are based on the criteria of the postcondition and precondition nodes being able to subsume other nodes of their type. This is detailed in Algorithm 1, establishing how we can merge nodes depending on preconditions and similarly for postconditions.

The generalization and specialization operators are the ones responsible for changing the form of the rules. There are two different kinds of operator sets as one deals with the preconditions of a rule while the other deals with the postconditions.

Data: current precondition node, list of all precondition and list of postcondition nodes
history← {};
get level of generalization of current node;
while *list of preconditions is not over* **do**
    if *the current node is in the same group as a preconditions node in the list* **then**
        get level of generalization of node in list;
        if *current node's postconditions subsume node's in the list postconditions* **then**
            compare their postconditions for contradictions;
            if *no contradictions* **then**
                add postconditions to current node;
                add node in list to history;
                delete node in list;
            end
        end
    end
end
return history;

Algorithm 1. Nodes merging based on preconditions

4 Evaluation

For the performance and scalability evaluation our system had to undergo, some adjustments were made. The system was set on a loop to generate a specific amount of rules and continuously refine their preconditions and postconditions. Afterwards, the rules were merged and the final number of the rules was stored in a text file. It is important to mention that we ran an extensive amount of experiments (100 times for every point that appears in the graph) so as to guarantee up to a point, the statistical significance of our solution given the random nature of the rules generation.

During the evaluation of our system we attempted to cover all the parameters that should be examined. The total number of rules in the normative system before and after it was processed was the first metric we observed. Scalability testing was included as well, measuring the time required for the system to complete one iteration based on the amount of rules in the normative system on one hand and the amount of data on the other.

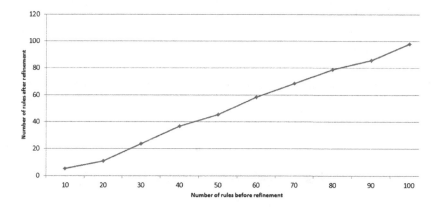

Fig. 1. Number of rules before and after refinement

One of the main components that had to be checked during the evaluation of our system was the improvement on the size of the modified normative system. It is worth noticing however that the randomness of the rules generation did not always allow for rules that could be merged. We display the statistics for this metric of evaluation in Fig. 1.

Scalability testing is used to evaluate the robustness of a system in situations of varying difficulty. As our system would have to be able to be integrated with Internet-of-Things scenarios that could incorporate a large set of rules or data, both of those parameters were tested.

The time required to process different amount of rules was recorded. This measurement indicates the toll multiple operations on rules can have on the system. The results are presented in Fig. 2.

Another important test to evaluate our implementation was the time it required to go through data of different sizes. For this test, the data input was changed from a full day to increments of 3 h and tested with 100 rules being generated. Figure 3 shows the results.

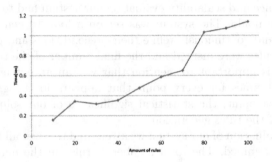

Fig. 2. Time required to process specific amount of rules

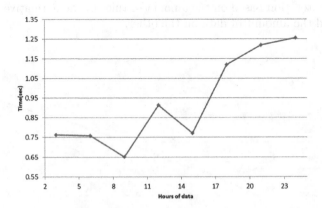

Fig. 3. Time required to process data

Besides the testing we carried out there are further experiments that could verify the consistency of our approach. Specifically, we were considering the formulation of two edge cases. The first would be an ideal, according to our understanding at least, initial set of rules with the intent of checking if our system can improve it further. The second, would be the worst possible initial set of rules in order to assess the system's performance when handling bad input of this kind. However, due to time limitations, we could not perform either evaluation.

5   Conclusions, Discussions and Future Work

We initially aspired to create a system that would post-process and refine rules and normative systems through constant evaluations. Our goal was then transformed into a specific architectural design and our system specifications were stated. We have achieved our set objectives and presented our implementation in detail. Our analysis of the system's performance was a thorough process that involved, due to the random factor in the rules creation, a large number of experiments. Through scalability testing as well, we have discovered that our solution is working as intended with little variation in time required, even if the amount of rules is increased.

We have achieved the functional requirements laid out in Sect. 3. In doing so we have made a contribution by extending and adapting an existing approach to address a specific scenario of Internet-of-Things.

In the implementation stage of the task at hand, we avoided integrating a Case-Based Reasoning mechanism into our system. This was done despite the improvement in the efficiency of the rules that it could provide for a few reasons. Firstly, the available free and open CBR systems are not easy to integrate with our system. Secondly, as our solution is focused on rule refinement rather than rule creation, we felt that it was beyond the scope of the paper to include a CBR system in the rule refinement machine.

During the development process of our system a lot of ideas were discussed and partially explored to enhance it. The enhancements can be split into system improvements and system extensions. The most significant improvement to our system would be an integration with available rule standards. This would enable our system to be easier to integrate with existing Internet-of-Things solutions. Ideally, instead of a specific technology and standard of rules, multiple options should be offered to whoever would want to incorporate our system, or parts of our system, into their own. Furthermore, additions to the system can be done to increase its capabilities. The easiest and most efficient would be a user-based rule insertion component. While the production of rules based on data is certainly as efficient as it can be, we need to consider the individual needs of every user. This would make the system more personalized and users would be more inclined to use it.

References

1. Beckel, C., Kleiminger, W., Cicchetti, R., Staake, T., Santini, S.: The eco data set and the performance of non-intrusive load monitoring algorithms. In: Proceedings of the 1st ACM Conference on Embedded Systems for Energy-Efficient Buildings (2014)
2. Durkheim, E., Simpson, G.: Emile Durkheim on the Division of Labor in Society/Being a Translation of His De La Division Du Travail Social, with an Estimate of His Work by George Simpson. Macmillan, London (1933)
3. Gruber, T.R.: Toward principles for the design of ontologies used for knowledge sharing. Int. J. Hum. Comput. Stud. - Special Issue: The Role of Formal Ontology in the Information Technology **43**(5–6), 907–928 (1995)
4. Gubbia, J., Buyyab, R., Marusic, S., Palaniswami, M.: Internet of Things (IoT): a vision, architectural elements, and future directions. FGCS **29**(7), 1645–1660 (2013)
5. Kleiminger, W., Beckel, C., Santini, S.: Household occupancy monitoring using electricity meters. In: Proceedings of the 2015 ACM International Joint Conference on Pervasive and Ubiquitous Computing (2015)
6. Morales, J., López-Sánchez, M., Rordriguez-Aguilar, J.A., Vasconcelos, W., Wooldridge, M.: Online automated synthesis of compact normative systems. ACM Trans. Autonom. Adapt. Syst. **10**(1), Article 2 (2015)

Stream-Based Perception for Agents on Mobile Devices

Jeremias Dötterl[1]([✉]), Ralf Bruns[1], Jürgen Dunkel[1], and Sascha Ossowski[2]

[1] Department of Computer Science,
Hannover University of Applied Sciences and Arts, Hannover, Germany
{jeremias.doetterl,ralf.bruns,juergen.dunkel}@hs-hannover.de
[2] CETINIA, University Rey Juan Carlos, Madrid, Spain
sascha.ossowski@urjc.es

Abstract. Multi-Agent Systems (MAS) lack advanced concepts for data stream processing, which inhibits their effective use in mobile ecosystems, where built-in smartphone sensors can provide valuable data about the current physical environment of the mobile user. With beliefs, plans, and goals, cognitive agent frameworks provide useful abstractions for the development of complex systems but do not contain effective mechanisms to sufficiently bridge the abstraction gap that exists between low-level streaming data and high-level percepts. The main contribution of this paper is an *enhanced perception* approach, which integrates two new abstractions, namely *expectations* and *interpretations*, into the commonly used perceive-deliberate-act cycle. Expectations and interpretations address the challenges of sensor data and provide higher-level knowledge to the agent's deliberation, which allows mobile agents to make situation-aware decisions in dynamically changing environments.

Keywords: Multi-Agent Systems · Data stream processing · Mobile computing · Agent perception

1 Introduction

Multi-Agent Systems (MAS) [27] support the engineering of complex distributed systems through the decomposition of problems into autonomous agents that perform high-level interactions [13,14]. In recent years, mobile devices have become mature computing platforms that are taking over an ever-increasing number of complex tasks. Agent-based abstractions can help to build complex systems on mobile devices [22]. Mobile systems can be designed and developed on an elevated abstraction level by making use of high-level agent concepts like *beliefs*, *plans*, and *goals*. Unfortunately, agent-based frameworks [4,5] lack satisfactory support for the processing of sensor data. Today's mobile devices are equipped with a rich set of sensors that can be exploited to achieve system behavior that adapts itself to the current situation of the mobile user. However, the processing of sensor data streams is not an explicitly addressed concern in agent-based systems.

© Springer Nature Switzerland AG 2019
M. Lujak (Ed.): AT 2018, LNAI 11327, pp. 73–87, 2019.
https://doi.org/10.1007/978-3-030-17294-7_6

The major problem is the existing *abstraction gap* between data streams and agent percepts [6,19,30]. Agents use their perception to obtain information from the environment. The agents expect to receive the information in form of high-level percepts, i.e. the percepts resemble actionable knowledge that the agents can understand and react to directly. However, sensor data is located on a lower level of abstraction: The individual data elements of the stream carry little informative value when observed in isolation and cannot be acted upon directly. To shift the low-level data stream to a higher-level percept stream, meaningful percept patterns have to be detected and encoded into meaningful situations. For example, a single GPS value in isolation merely allows conclusions about the location of an agent. Only by analyzing the patterns of multiple data elements, higher-level knowledge can be extracted: *Is the agent moving? Is it accelerating or slowing down? Is it moving faster or slower than other agents?* Without a dedicated stream processing component, agents cannot infer situational knowledge from complex data sequences. To achieve advanced situation awareness, agents have to analyze the relationships and patterns of multiple data elements and their relations in time.

In this paper, we propose two abstractions for the design and development of MAS in mobile ecosystems, namely *expectations* and *interpretations*. The agent's *expectations* narrow the agent's perception of the environment and control the agent's input. The agent's *interpretations* drive the agent's comprehension of the environment and allow to express how complex sequences of percepts should be interpreted by the agent to bridge the abstraction gap. Through enhanced perception, mobile agents[1] can perceive higher-level knowledge in low-level streaming data.

The rest of the paper is structured as follows. Section 2 describes related work. Section 3 presents the approach. In Sect. 4 we perform a case study. Section 5 evaluates and discusses our work. Section 6 terminates the paper with conclusions and final remarks.

2　Related Work

Our work occupies a niche between two lines of research: (i) agents on mobile devices, and (ii) data stream processing in agent-based systems.

There exist different frameworks and middleware for agent-oriented programming on mobile devices [3,22]. In the past, several agent-based systems have been proposed that operate on mobile devices: The approaches either present an agent-based mobile system for a specific application domain (e.g., e-health [7]) or aim to bring agent abstractions to mobile computing platforms [1,18,23]. However, none of these approaches uses advanced data processing to detect complex relationships between observed percepts.

There exists some work on advanced data processing in MAS. In many agent-based systems, reactive plans are triggered by the occurrence of a single event.

---

[1] We use the term *mobile agent* to refer to an agent that runs on a mobile device.

Buford et al. [6] extend the BDI agent architecture with event correlation to allow plans to be triggered by a (potentially complex) pattern of multiple events rather than only by a single, isolated event. Ziafati et al. [30] add advanced event processing to BDI agents in the context of autonomous robot programming. The robot's sensory information is processed in order to extract relevant knowledge that the robot's control component can use to make and execute appropriate plans. There are two approaches related to our work that make use of Complex Event Processing (CEP) [16] within the Jason [5] agent framework: Ranathunga et al. [20] use CEP within a global event processing component to interface Jason with the virtual *Second Life* platform. Ranathunga and Cranefield [19] integrate CEP into Jason agents to identify complex situations in the agent's environment. However, these approaches do not consider the characteristics of mobile ecosystems.

Weyns et al. [26] present a formal model for active perception, which allows agents to direct their attention to the most relevant occurrences in the environment. Active perception assumes that percepts are given on the knowledge level and narrows the agent's view. Our enhanced perception approach acknowledges that percepts can appear on a low abstraction level and widens the range of situations the agent can perceive.

Further related work can be found in the area of context-aware systems. Yılmaz and Erdur [29] present a context-aware MAS where mobile client agents can request context information from a server-side context agent. To infer the context, the context agent performs rule-based reasoning on a context ontology. Alfonso-Cendón et al. [2] let agents perform context-aware workflows in the ambient intelligence domain. The agents run on top of an existing context management system, which serves as the provider of context information. We are not aware of any context-aware multi-agent approach where data stream processing is integrated into a cognitive agent architecture to analyze mobile sensor data.

3   Agents with Enhanced Perception

3.1   Sensing the Environment

Modern smartphones have a wide range of data sources available through which they can capture the immediate environment [25]:

- *Internal sensors*: On-board sensors to measure acceleration, air pressure, GPS, humidity, temperature, rotation, etc.
- *External sensors*: Body sensors like bracelets or chest harness that are connected to the smartphone to measure blood pressure or heart rate.
- *Other apps*: Any other app on the device. For instance, the calendar app that informs about upcoming appointments.
- *Operating system*: Information about system events like low battery state or missed calls.
- *Communication interfaces*: Wireless communication, e.g. via WIFI, enables the access of web services or other data sources online.

Like Santi et al. [22], we consider these data sources artifacts of the environment, where the agent is situated and which the agent can sense to obtain data. In the A&A (agents & artifacts) meta-model [17], artifacts are the passive components of the MAS that are intended to *be used* by the agents. While agents constitute the pro-active and autonomous components of the system, artifacts can be understood as tools that provide functionality to the agents. Each artifact exposes a usage interface to the agents, which can consist of arbitrary operations. Artifacts are a generic mechanism to provide resources to the agents or to provide an interface for performing actions on the environment.

In our approach, we distinguish between two groups of artifacts.

1. *Device artifacts* provide access to the different sensors and services of the smartphone. Via these artifacts, the agent can obtain sensor data, check sensor availability, and activate or deactivate sensors.
2. *Domain artifacts* provide access to functionality that the agent needs to act in the given problem domain.

The artifacts provide the data in form of data streams. Streaming data has various properties that prevent its direct use in conventional agent architectures.

– *Low-quality* [15]: Data streams can be of low quality due to imperfect sensing; data can be missing or inaccurate.
– *Low-level* [28]: Due to the existing abstraction gap, it is often not possible to react to single isolated data elements as their meaning is not inherently clear.

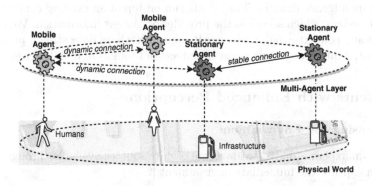

Fig. 1. Multi-Agent Systems with mobile agents

Other agents can also serve as data sources: Mobile agents can establish dynamic connections with nearby agents to engage in flexible interaction and data exchange, see Fig. 1. Interaction can take place with other mobile agents, which typically represent human actors, or with stationary, non-mobile agents, which can represent, e.g., shared infrastructure. As mobile agents can move freely, their connections are typically less stable and more dynamic than those of conventional, non-mobile agents.

3.2   Processing the Percept Stream

We propose AEP Architecture (**A**gents with **E**nhanced **P**erception) for agents on mobile devices, as shown in Fig. 2. The AEP architecture consists of three major components: The *belief base* and *deliberation* component originate in large parts from the conventional agent architecture [5,12,21]. *Enhanced perception* constitutes the proposed extension.

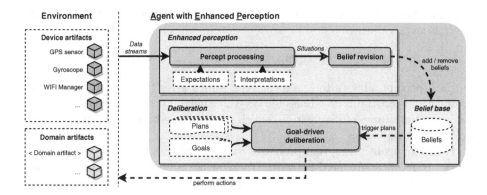

Fig. 2. AEP architecture: **A**gents with **E**nhanced **P**erception

Belief base: The belief base holds the agent's beliefs, which are pieces of information about the world that the agent believes to be true. Beliefs can change through external events in the environment (indicated by percepts) or through the agent's internal deliberation.

Deliberation: The agent deliberates over the world to decide which actions to perform. The agent's deliberation process is controlled by plans and is aimed at the achievement of the agent's goals.

In mobile environments, these two components are insufficient as the incoming percepts are mostly located on a low abstraction level, which prevents a direct understanding and reaction by the agent.

Enhanced perception: In AEP, the responsibility of handling low-level percepts is assumed by the enhanced perception component. Enhanced perception addresses the challenges introduced by data streams explicitly, which gives the agent greater control over the incoming percept stream and protects the agent's deliberation. In particular, low-level percepts are shifted to an appropriate abstraction level. (First steps towards such an enhanced perception approach were made in [10]).

As shown in Fig. 2, the agent acquires streaming data from several artifacts. The data arrives in form of percepts, which are processed by the two sub-components of the enhanced perception module:

1. *Percept processing* transforms the incoming percept stream according to the agent's expectations and interpretations and generates situations, which carry the higher-level knowledge that the agent was able to infer from the incoming percept stream.
2. *Belief revision* uses the situations to update beliefs in the agent's belief base. Belief revision manages the lifespan of beliefs according to the events the agent believes to have occurred in the environment.

Percept Processing. We consider each percept a structure with the following information:

$$(\text{percept-type}, \text{timestamp}, \text{key}_0 = \text{value}_0, ..., \text{key}_n = \text{value}_n)$$

Each percept adheres to a percept type, which gives the percept a semantic meaning and constrains its admissible key-value pairs. Furthermore, each percept holds the timestamp of its creation, which enables time-based pattern matching over percept sequences.

Hitherto, agent perception processes one percept at a time and neglects the history of recently observed percepts. To allow agents to perceive complex patterns in percept sequences, we extend the agent's perception by the following information flow concepts [8]:

- *Selection* of particular percepts that match certain conditions regarding percept type or attribute values.
- *Windows* that allow analysis of (i) the last N percept occurrences or (ii) the percept occurrences of the last T time units.
- *Aggregates* to combine multiple percepts and the data they carry to new information.

Therefore, we process the percept stream with the following information flow operators [8,16]:

p_1 and p_2	Conjunction
p_1 -> p_2	Sequence (followed by)
.window:time(t)	Time window
avg(x), max(x), min(x), sum(x)	Aggregation

In AEP, the agent holds expectations and interpretations, which make use of these operators to transform the percept stream.

Definition 1 (Expectations). *An agent's expectations characterize the agent's subjective attitude towards percepts. Expectations pose requirements for the data and information carried by the stream of observed percepts.*

Expectations limit the percept stream to those percepts that fulfill the agent's expectations. Percepts and percept sequences that violate the agent's expectations are purposefully ignored. This reduces the agent's computational load, prevents imperfect data manifesting itself in beliefs, and lets the agent gain control over the incoming data. Expectations address the problem of low data quality and allow to express data requirements regarding criteria like accuracy, consistency, and relevance. Expectations can be based on the agent's current beliefs.

Example 1 (Expectation). When the user is riding a bike, the agent might expect two consequent GPS measurements, which are measured within two seconds to each other, to be at most 20 m apart, which corresponds to a speed of 36 km/h ($\approx$22 mph). If the distance is larger than 20 m, the agent considers one of the data points to be erroneous and would drop at least one of the two for being inconsistent with the agent's expectations regarding the accuracy of the data.

We follow a rule-based approach, where the detection of a certain pattern in the percept stream triggers the forwarding of the percept instances that fulfill the expectations. Expectation rules have access to the agent's belief base.

```
_____ Example expectation rule _____
rule "forward plausible GPS data"
CONDITION: (every gps1=GPS -> gps2=GPS).window:time(2 seconds)
    where Agent.hasBelief(isCycling)
        and Geo.distance(gps1, gps2) < 20 meters
ACTION: forward gps2
```

Definition 2 (Interpretations). *An agent's* interpretations *form the agent's rapid recognition capabilities. Interpretations detect higher-level knowledge in low-level percept streams considering the relationships between multiple percept occurrences.*

Interpretations produce *situations*, i.e. higher-level information that is obtained by aggregating and correlating a multitude of percepts. Interpretations can be influenced by the agent's beliefs.

Example 2 (Interpretation). When the two latest GPS readings refer to different locations, the user must have moved.

Like expectations, interpretations can be expressed with pattern rules. The condition part describes meaningful percept occurrences (situations). Whenever a percept sequence matches the given pattern, a new situation is created. Interpretation rules can access the agent's belief base.

```
_____ Example interpretation rule _____
rule "detect movement"
CONDITION: every gps1=GPS -> gps2=GPS
    where Geo.isDifferent(gps1, gps2)
ACTION: create IsMoving
```

The situation is then either processed by (a chain of) subsequent interpretations yielding a possibly higher-level situation or passed to the belief revision component.

Belief Revision. Whenever a situation is detected, belief revision updates the belief base to reflect the agent's subjective view on the environment state. Belief revision activates and deactivates beliefs in the agent's belief base driven by revision rules. The detection of a situation can, under the consideration of the agent's current beliefs, result in the addition of new (temporary) beliefs or the removal of outdated beliefs that the agent believes to not be valid anymore.

As an example, consider the following revision rule which updates the agent's belief from *is standing still* to *is cycling.*

─────────────── Example revision rule ───────────────

```
CONDITION: IsMoving
   where Agent.hasBelief(hasBike)
   and not( Agent.hasBelief(hasCar) )
ACTION: Agent.addBelief(isCycling), Agent.removeBelief(standingStill)
```

Whenever the situation *isMoving* is detected and the belief *hasBike* exists in the belief base whereas the belief *hasCar* does not exist, the belief *isCycling* is added and the belief *standingStill* is removed.

The addition and deletion of a belief can trigger the execution of plans in the deliberation component of the AEP architecture. Triggered plans can then initiate actions, e.g., calling an operation provided by an artifact or sending a message to another agent. In cooperative settings, the agent can decide to share its beliefs with other agents to inform them about the current environment state. In competitive settings, the agent may enter into negotiations with other agents and negotiate on the basis of its inferred situations.

4   Case Study

4.1   Rebalancing of Bike Sharing Systems

In recent years, bike sharing systems [24] have become a viable transportation alternative in many cities but struggle with imbalanced station states [9]: When rentals and returns of bikes occur at different rates, a station becomes either completely empty or completely full, which prevents further rentals or returns.

In this case study, we describe an agent-based rebalancing approach that incentivizes users to return their bikes at destinations that are beneficial to the overall system balance [11]. Every user is represented by a *user agent*, which runs on the user's smartphone and analyzes the GPS data provided by the smartphone's integrated GPS sensor. Whenever the user agent detects that the user is cycling near a bike station, it contacts the corresponding *station agent* in order to request an incentive. If the station agent is interested in the user's currently rented bike, it responds with a corresponding incentive offer, i.e. a small discount. The station agents coordinate themselves to determine which of them should offer incentives to the user in order to achieve a balanced system state.

4.2   Situation-Aware Rebalancing with AEP

The user agent (UA) obtains GPS data from the GPS sensor artifact and processes the GPS data stream according to the following process, which is shown in Fig. 3.

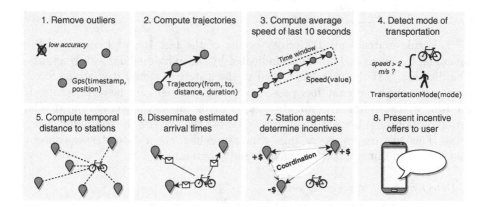

Fig. 3. AEP implementation of the dynamic rebalancing process

For the realization of the process with AEP, we decompose the process into two major parts: Steps 1–4 are realized with enhanced perception, whereas steps 5–8 are realized within the agent's deliberation component. The agent designer can implement the first four steps by formulating appropriate expectations, interpretations and revision rules.

1. Remove outliers The agent expects GPS data to be accurate. Therefore, the agent filters implausible GPS events with the expectation rule shown in Sect. 3.2.

2. Compute trajectories

```
——————————————— Interpretation Rule ———————————————
// 2. Compute trajectories
CONDITION: every gps1=Gps -> gps2=Gps
    where gps1.position as from
      and gps2.position as to
      and Geo.distance(from, to) as distance
      and (gps2.timestamp - gps1.timestamp) as duration
ACTION: create Trajectory(from, to, distance, duration)
```

The rule finds for every GPS-Event *gps1* its successor *gps2* and aggregates them to a new Trajectory event. This new Trajectory event carries the positions of the two GPS-Events, as well as their physical distance and the time that passed between the two GPS measurements. This information allows the agent to compute the user's speed.

3. Compute average speed of last 10 s

```
——————————————— Interpretation Rule ———————————————
// 3. Compute average speed of last 10 seconds
CONDITION: t=Trajectory.window:time(10 seconds)
    where sum(t.distance) as distanceSum
    and sum(t.duration) as durationSum
    and durationSum > 0
    and (distanceSum/durationSum) as speedValue
ACTION: create Speed(speedValue)
```

This rule matches all Trajectory events of the last 10 s and computes the sum of all distances and durations indicated by the individual Trajectory events. The distance that the user has moved in the last 10 s (stored in *distanceSum*) divided by the time that has passed between the first and last trajectory of the time window (stored in *durationSum*) yields the user's average speed. The action part of the rule creates a new Speed event that carries the computed speed value. This rule makes use of time windows, which are a data stream concept that is usually not available in agent-based programming.

4. Detect mode of transportation

```
——————————————— Interpretation Rule ———————————————
// 4. Detect mode of transportation
CONDITION: s=Speed
    where ( if( s.speedValue > 2m/s )
        then 'bike'
        else 'walk'
    end ) as mode
ACTION: create TransportationMode(mode)
```

The rule matches all Speed events and estimates depending on the given speed value whether the user is using a bike or walking. The action part of the rule creates a new TransportationMode event that indicates the estimated mode of transportation.

A revision rule updates the agent's belief base whenever the transportation mode changes.

```
——————————————— Revision Rule ———————————————
// Update beliefs
CONDITION: m=TransportationMode
    where m.mode = "bike"
    and Agent.hasBelief(isWalking)
ACTION: Agent.removeBelief(isWalking), Agent.addBelief(isCycling)
```

The rule reacts to all TransportationMode events by checking whether the appropriate belief exists in the agent's belief base: If the mode *bike* is detected and the agent holds the belief that the user is walking, the belief base is updated by removing the belief *isWalking* and adding the belief *isCycling*.

5.-8. Deliberation The addition of the *isCycling* belief triggers a plan in the agent that implements the steps 5–8 of the proposed rebalancing process. In this case study, we assume Jason as the underlying agent framework.

```
                         ——————— Jason AgentSpeak ———————
 1    // When belief isCycling is added:
 2    +isCycling : true <-
 3        !obtainIncentivesFromNearbyStations .
 4
 5    +!obtainIncentivesFromNearbyStations : true <-
 6        // iterate over all known stations:
 7        for( station(ID, LAT, LON) ) {
 8            !estimateArrivalTime(LAT, LON, ETA);
 9            if(ETA < 180) { // less than 3 minutes
10                .send(ID, tell, estimatedArrival(ETA));
11            }
12        } .
13
14    +!estimateArrivalTime(LAT, LON, ETA) : true
15        <- // ... (omitted for brevity)
16
17    // When incentive offer is received from station:
18    +incentiveOffer(Discount)[source(Station)] : true <-
19        displayOffer(Discount, Station) .
```

Whenever the user starts cycling, i.e. the belief *isCycling* is added (line 2), the UA adopts the goal to obtain incentives from nearby stations (line 3). When this goal is adopted (line 5), the UA estimates the arrival time for all stations that are stored in its belief base (lines 7 and 8). To the station agents of those stations, where the expected arrival time is lower than 3 min, the agent sends a message to inform them about the user's expected arrival (lines 9 and 10). The station agents (whose code is not shown here) then coordinate with each other to decide whether to offer an incentive to the user. When they have decided on a response, they send a corresponding message to the UA, which the UA reacts to by displaying it to the user (lines 18 and 19), who ultimately decides whether to accept or reject the offer.

If we implemented the same process without enhanced perception and passed percepts to the agent's deliberation directly, high-level knowledge such as *user is cycling* would not be available. Instead, the agent's deliberation would have to react to many single GPS events, which carry little information when observed in isolation. This high-level knowledge is made available through the presented sequence of event processing rules (expectation, interpretation, and revision rules). Using a dedicated event processing language, data stream processing concepts like sliding windows and information flow operators are available as first-class constructs, which allow expressing complex data patterns conveniently.

5   Evaluation and Discussion

To test our approach, we integrated the enhanced perception component into the Jason agent framework. Percepts are converted to event objects and pushed into a running event processing engine; in our prototype, we use the Esper engine[2]. The event processing engine processes the percepts with the registered processing rules. The Esper EPL (event processing language) supports the information flow

---

[2] https://www.espertech.com/esper/ (Accessed: 2018-08-06).

operators introduced in Sect. 3. In our prototype, the processing rules can access the agent's belief base to query, add, and remove beliefs.

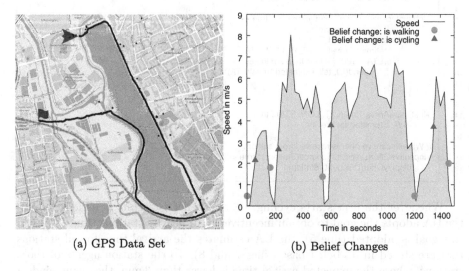

(a) GPS Data Set   (b) Belief Changes

Fig. 4. Case study implementation

We implemented the case study of Sect. 4 with our prototype. To test the expectation and interpretation rules with authentic data, we gathered GPS data from an Android device while riding a bike. To achieve the best possible accuracy, we used fine-grained location tracking and obtained GPS data from the device as frequently as possible. The GPS data is visualized in Fig. 4a. The data set consists of 1568 entries that were gathered over a time period of 25 min and contains noticeable outliers.

Using the rules of the case study, our approach accurately detects when the bike is cycling or walking; Fig. 4b shows the belief changes that occurred in the 25 min period. Whether a belief change occurs depends on the average speed of the last 10 s (see rule 3. in Sect. 4.2). When the speed value rises above the threshold value of 2 m/s, the belief *is cycling* becomes active; when the speed value drops below the threshold value, the belief *is walking* becomes active instead. Using a window size of 10 s, the belief is updated at most 10 s after the GPS event that signaled the significant speed change.

Smaller update delays could be achieved by lowering the window size. However, the shorter delay would come at the cost of false positives. If fewer trajectories are taken into account, small errors in the measured GPS locations have a greater impact on the estimated speed and might result in unwarranted belief changes.

In Table 1 we compare the number of low-level percepts that are processed by the agent's perception with the number of high-level situations that are provided to the agent's deliberation. The enhanced perception module receives 1568 raw

GPS events that are unfiltered and provide little actionable information. If the percepts were passed to the agent's deliberation directly, they would have to be filtered, correlated, and aggregated using exclusively the concepts available in Jason. With AEP, the deliberation receives no raw GPS events; instead, it gets provided by the enhanced perception module with 111 higher-level beliefs, which the deliberation is able to act upon directly.

Table 1. *Number of events* that were processed in our case study by the agent's (a) perception and (b) deliberation over a time span of 25 min.

Event	(a) Perception	(b) Deliberation
Gps	1568	0
IsWalking	0	5
IsCycling	0	4
ApproxSpeed[a]	0	51
ApproxPosition[a]	0	51
Total	1568	111

[a]The number depends highly on the chosen update rate. In our test, we updated the ApproxSpeed belief and the ApproxPosition belief every 30 s. In cases, were larger intervals are acceptable, the number of events is even lower.

6 Conclusion

Agent-based abstractions can facilitate the development of complex systems on mobile devices. Modern smartphones are equipped with a rich set of on-board sensors, which can provide valuable information about the user's environment. Unfortunately, traditional agent approaches provide insufficient support for the processing of sensor data streams.

In this paper, we have presented an enhanced perception approach to enable a more sophisticated data processing for agents on mobile devices. Enhanced perception is driven by the agent's expectations and interpretations, which integrate information flow concepts into the agent's perceive-deliberate-think cycle. The use of sliding windows and information flow operators allows detecting complex temporal percept patterns. An implementation with conventional agent abstractions (beliefs, plans, and goals) would be cumbersome and error-prone.

To demonstrate the feasibility of the approach, we integrated the Esper complex event processing engine into the Jason agent framework and implemented a case study in the bike sharing domain. Low-level GPS percepts are processed by enhanced perception; the agent's deliberation operates on the inferred higher-level knowledge.

Future work could investigate how multiple agents can cooperate to detect complex composite situations that a single agent cannot detect on its own due to missing data or interpretations.

References

1. Agüero, J., Rebollo, M., Carrascosa, C., Julián, V.: Does Android dream with intelligent agents? In: Corchado, J.M., Rodríguez, S., Llinas, J., Molina, J.M. (eds.) International Symposium on Distributed Computing and Artificial Intelligence 2008 (DCAI 2008). AINSC, vol. 50, pp. 194–204. Springer, Heidelberg (2009). https://doi.org/10.1007/978-3-540-85863-8_24
2. Alfonso-Cendón, J., de Alba, J.M.F., Fuentes-Fernández, R., Pavón, J.: Implementation of context-aware workflows with multi-agent systems. Neurocomputing **176**, 91–97 (2016). Recent Advancements in Hybrid Artificial Intelligence Systems and its Application to Real-World Problems
3. Bergenti, F., Caire, G., Gotta, D.: Agents on the move: JADE for Android devices. In: Santoro, C., Bergenti, F. (eds.) Proceedings of the XV Workshop "Dagli Oggetti agli Agenti", Catania, Italy, 25–26 September 2014. CEUR Workshop Proceedings, vol. 1260. CEUR-WS.org (2014)
4. Boissier, O., Bordini, R.H., Hübner, J.F., Ricci, A., Santi, A.: Multi-agent oriented programming with JaCaMo. Sci. Comput. Program. **78**(6), 747–761 (2013)
5. Bordini, R.H., Hübner, J.F., Wooldridge, M.: Programming Multi-agent Systems in AgentSpeak Using Jason, vol. 8. Wiley, Hoboken (2007)
6. Buford, J., Jakobson, G., Lewis, L.: Extending BDI multi-agent systems with situation management. In: 2006 9th International Conference on Information Fusion, July 2006
7. Chan, V., Ray, P., Parameswaran, N.: Mobile e-health monitoring: an agent-based approach. IET Commun. **2**(2), 223–230 (2008)
8. Cugola, G., Margara, A.: Processing flows of information: from data stream to complex event processing. ACM Comput. Surv. **44**(3), 15:1–15:62 (2012)
9. DeMaio, P.: Bike-sharing: history, impacts, models of provision, and future. J. Public Transp. **12**(4), 41–56 (2009)
10. Dötterl, J., Bruns, R., Dunkel, J., Ossowski, S.: Event-driven agents: enhanced perception for multi-agent systems using complex event processing. In: Belardinelli, F., Argente, E. (eds.) EUMAS/AT -2017. LNCS (LNAI), vol. 10767, pp. 463–475. Springer, Cham (2018). https://doi.org/10.1007/978-3-030-01713-2_32
11. Dötterl, J., Bruns, R., Dunkel, J., Ossowski, S.: Towards dynamic rebalancing of bike sharing systems: an event-driven agents approach. In: Oliveira, E., Gama, J., Vale, Z., Lopes Cardoso, H. (eds.) EPIA 2017. LNCS (LNAI), vol. 10423, pp. 309–320. Springer, Cham (2017). https://doi.org/10.1007/978-3-319-65340-2_26
12. Georgeff, M.P., Lansky, A.L.: Reactive reasoning and planning. In: Proceedings of the Sixth National Conference on Artificial Intelligence - Volume 2, AAAI 1987, pp. 677–682. AAAI Press (1987)
13. Jennings, N.R.: On agent-based software engineering. Artif. Intell. **117**(2), 277–296 (2000)
14. Jennings, N.R.: An agent-based approach for building complex software systems. Commun. ACM **44**(4), 35–41 (2001)
15. Khaleghi, B., Khamis, A., Karray, F.O., Razavi, S.N.: Multisensor data fusion: a review of the state-of-the-art. Inf. Fusion **14**(1), 28–44 (2013)

16. Luckham, D.C.: The Power of Events: An Introduction to Complex Event Processing in Distributed Enterprise Systems. Addison-Wesley Longman Publishing Co., Inc., Boston (2001)

17. Omicini, A., Ricci, A., Viroli, M.: Artifacts in the A&A meta-model for multi-agent systems. Auton. Agent. Multi-Agent Syst. **17**(3), 432–456 (2008)

18. Rahwan, T., Rahwan, T., Rahwan, I., Ashri, R.: Agent-based support for mobile users using AgentSpeak(L). In: Giorgini, P., Henderson-Sellers, B., Winikoff, M. (eds.) AOIS -2003. LNCS (LNAI), vol. 3030, pp. 45–60. Springer, Heidelberg (2004). https://doi.org/10.1007/978-3-540-25943-5_4

19. Ranathunga, S., Cranefield, S.: Improving situation awareness in intelligent virtual agents. In: Dignum, F., Brom, C., Hindriks, K., Beer, M., Richards, D. (eds.) CAVE 2012. LNCS (LNAI), vol. 7764, pp. 134–148. Springer, Heidelberg (2013). https://doi.org/10.1007/978-3-642-36444-0_9

20. Ranathunga, S., Cranefield, S., Purvis, M.: Interfacing a cognitive agent platform with second life. In: Beer, M., Brom, C., Dignum, F., Soo, V.-W. (eds.) AEGS 2011. LNCS (LNAI), vol. 7471, pp. 1–21. Springer, Heidelberg (2012). https://doi.org/10.1007/978-3-642-32326-3_1

21. Rao, A.S.: BDI agents: from theory to practice. In: Proceedings of the 1st International Conference of Multiagent Systems, July 1995

22. Santi, A., Guidi, M., Ricci, A.: JaCa-Android: an agent-based platform for building smart mobile applications. In: Dastani, M., El Fallah Seghrouchni, A., Hübner, J., Leite, J. (eds.) LADS 2010. LNCS (LNAI), vol. 6822, pp. 95–114. Springer, Heidelberg (2011). https://doi.org/10.1007/978-3-642-22723-3_6

23. Sartori, F., Manenti, L., Grazioli, L.: A conceptual and computational model for knowledge-based agents in ANDROID. In: Proceedings of the 14th Workshop "From Objects to Agents" co-located with the 13th Conference of the Italian Association for Artificial Intelligence (AI*IA 2013), Torino, Italy, 2–3 December 2013, pp. 41–46 (2013)

24. Shaheen, S., Guzman, S., Zhang, H.: Bikesharing in Europe, the Americas, and Asia: past, present, and future. J. Transp. Res. Rec. **2143**(1), 159–167 (2010)

25. Stipkovic, S., Bruns, R., Dunkel, J.: Pervasive computing by mobile complex event processing. In: 2013 IEEE 10th International Conference on e-Business Engineering, pp. 318–323, September 2013

26. Weyns, D., Steegmans, E., Holvoet, T.: Towards active perception in situated multi-agent systems. Appl. Artif. Intell. **18**(9–10), 867–883 (2004)

27. Wooldridge, M.: An Introduction to MultiAgent Systems, 2nd edn. Wiley Publishing, Chichester (2009)

28. Ye, J., Dobson, S., McKeever, S.: Situation identification techniques in pervasive computing: a review. Pervasive Mob. Comput. **8**(1), 36–66 (2012)

29. Yılmaz, Ö., Erdur, R.C.: iConAwa - an intelligent context-aware system. Expert Syst. Appl. **39**(3), 2907–2918 (2012)

30. Ziafati, P., Dastani, M., Meyer, J.J., van der Torre, L.: Event-processing in autonomous robot programming. In: Proceedings of the 2013 International Conference on Autonomous Agents and Multi-agent Systems, AAMAS 2013, pp. 95–102. International Foundation for Autonomous Agents and Multiagent Systems, Richland (2013)

Argumentation and Negotiation

Distributed Ledger and Robust Consensus for Agreements

Miguel Rebollo$^{(\boxtimes)}$, Carlos Carrascosa, and Alberto Palomares

Universitat Politècnica de València, Camino de Vera s/n, 46022 Valencia, Spain
{mrebollo,carrasco,apalomares}@dsic.upv.es

Abstract. This work proposes the application of consensus processes to ensure the consistency of the data stored in distributed ledgers. Consensus allows a group of agents to reach agreements about the value of common variables or, in this case, data structures such as Merkle trees or chains of blocks. Nevertheless, the consensus algorithm requires for all the participants to apply the same equation. A malicious agent can interfere in the process just by introducing some deviation from the expected value. In this work, the authors propose a method to detect when the information has been modified and, under certain assumptions, it can recover the original data.

Keywords: Consensus · Agreement · Complex networks ·
Failure tolerance · Applications · Distributed Ledger Technology ·
Blockchain

1 Introduction

This work proposes an extension of a consensus process, which belongs to the family of gossiping algorithms, to keep a distributed ledger. Interest in blockchain grows because the strengthening in privacy protection [1], and it can be applied to diverse areas such as food tracking systems [2], administrative contracts [3], distributed voting [4], or power grid management [5]. Its usage in the IoT requires certain adaptations, but blockchain technology provides secure and optimized protocols [6,7]. Security concerns are one of the most important ones in this technology, and the main protocols implement different defenses against byzantine attacks, which can compromise the stability of the system [8,9].

Consensus process in networks allows calculating in a distributed way the value of some common function. Each agent uses only its value and the value from its direct neighbors to recalculate the value of the function and to propagate the new value to its neighbors. This iterative process converges to one unique, final value for the function that is being calculated. Agents have no further knowledge about the size, the topology of the network, nor any other characteristic.

This work is supported by the PROMETEOII/2013/019 and TIN2015-65515-C4-1-R projects of the Spanish government.

Let be $G = (V, E)$ an undirected graph formed by a set of vertexes V and a set of links $E \subseteq V \times V$ where $(i, j) \in E$ if exists a link between nodes i and j. A vector $x = (x_1, \dots, x_n)^T$ contains the initial values of the variables associated with each one of the nodes of the network. Olfati-Saber and Murray [10] propose the algorithm described by Eq. 1, and that is executed until the difference between two consecutive iterations is under some limit.

$$x_i(t+1) = x_i(t) + \varepsilon \sum_{j \in N_i} [x_j(t) - x_i(t)] \tag{1}$$

To follow precisely the algorithm is mandatory for all the nodes. A well-known misbehavior is the follow-the-leader one [11], in which one of the nodes remains unchanged or changes arbitrarily. The complete network converges to the value of this node. Another case appears when some nodes fake the transmitted value. In any case, the network converges to a value different from the average. Therefore, is too easy for a node to alter the final result of the consensus.

This work proposes a method to detect failures in the consensus process in a distributed way. It is applied to the Distributed Ledger Technology (DLT) to avoid malicious agents alter the contents of the ledger. The rest of the paper is structured as follows. Section 2 extends the consensus algorithm to include malicious nodes that try to fake the result of the process. Section 3 shows the application of consensus to maintain a distributed ledger among a set of agents and, finally, Sect. 4 resumes the main conclusions of this work.

2   Consensus with Malicious Agents

A deviation in the consensus process can be easily modeled as follows.

$$x_i(t+1) = x_i(t) + \sum_{j \in N_i} [x_j(t) - x_i(t)] + u_i(t) \tag{2}$$

where $u_i(t)$ is the error introduced by node i in the iteration t. Some models allow detecting the failure, but they need the global knowledge of the network structure since they are based on the use of an observation matrix that is calculated from the adjacency matrix [12].

Figure 1 shows an example of the process. The random network has 10 agents with initial values $x = (1, 2, \dots, 10)^T$. Agent 5 introduces 4 extra units in iteration $t = 3$, so $u_5(3) = 4$. The network converges to the new average, as if agent 5 had $x_5(0) = 9$ from the beginning, instead of the original value $x_5(0) = 5$. The main problem that this work address is how to detect this failure and if it is possible to correct it.

2.1   Cheat Detection

In the example shown in Fig. 1(left), agent 5 introduces a deviation in the consensus value. We can clean Eq. 1 and obtain the following expression.

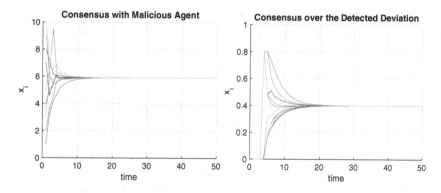

Fig. 1. (Left) Agent 5 adds 4 units in iteration $t = 3$, so the result converges to 5.9 instead of 5.5 (Right) the consensus over the detected deviation converges to $dv_i(t) = 0.4$, and applying the formula in Eq. 6 we obtain $c_i = 4$ that is the deviation introduced by agent 5

$$x_i(t+1) = x_i(t) + \varepsilon \left[\sum_{j \in N_i} x_j(t) - \sum_{j \in N_i} x_i(t) \right]$$

$$x_i(t+1) = x_i(t) + \varepsilon \sum_{j \in N_i} x_j(t) - \varepsilon d_i x_i(t)$$

$$0 = \underbrace{x_i(t+1) + (\varepsilon d_i - 1)x_i(t) - \varepsilon \sum_{j \in N_i} x_j(t)}_{dv_i(t)}. \tag{3}$$

being d_i the degree of node i. Each iteration must fulfill

$$dv_i(t) = 0 \; \forall t > 0 \tag{4}$$

Each agent compares the newly calculated value with the corresponding one calculated from the values in the previous iteration. If the difference is not zero, then the agent can suspect about the validity of the obtained result. The only constraint that the method must fulfill is that the first exchange must be trustful. Depending on the domain and how the problem is modeled, in most of the cases, this condition is satisfied. Therefore, we can detect that the result that we have obtained has been somehow manipulated. The next step is to correct it.

2.2 Cheat Correction

Let's assume for clarity that the deviation is positive it is added at once in one of the iterations by one agent. The process is the same for multiple deviations in several iterations. When a deviation from the expected value is detected, $dv_i(t)$ is the value the agent has to compensate. From Eq. 3 we can see how the excess

$u_i(t)$ is spread among the neighbors. In each iteration, the malicious agent keeps $(1 - \varepsilon d_i)u_i(t)$ for itself and spreads $\varepsilon u_i(t)$ to each one of its neighbors:

$$dv_i(t) = \varepsilon \sum_{j \in N_i} u_j(t), \quad \rightarrow \quad \frac{dv_i(t)}{\varepsilon} = \sum_{j \in N_i} u_j(t) \tag{5}$$

and dividing the deviation by the value of ε, any agent knows the alteration that has been introduced in the process. Note that, as the values of $\sum_{j \in N_i} u_j(t)$ are aggregated, it is not possible to know which agent has been the one that has cheated. This solution allows the neighbors of the malicious agent to know that something is wrong in the consensus process and even correct it. However, it is needed for the correction to be also propagated through all the network. Therefore, a parallel consensus over the deviation $dv_i(t)$ is performed.

Let's create a vector by extending the cumulated deviation detected by agent i until instant t, $D_i(t) = \sum_{s=0}^{t} dv_i(s)$, with $w_i(t) = w_i(t-1) + 1$ if $dv_i(t) \neq 0$. That is, $w_i(t)$ counts how many times agent i has detected a deviation. The same consensus process is performed over $(D_i(t)|w_i(t))$ in parallel with the consensus over $x_i(t)$, but only by the trustful agents[1]. When the process converges, the fake result obtained in $x_i(t)$ can be corrected as follows

$$\hat{x}_i(t) = x_i(t) - \frac{D_i(t)/\varepsilon}{w_i(t)} = x_i(t) - \underbrace{\frac{D_i(t)}{\varepsilon w_i(t)}}_{c_i(t)} \tag{6}$$

Equation 6 is the result of the application of a cumulative consensus over the deviations $dv_i(t)$ and the correction with Eq. 5.

Figure 1(right) shows the evolution of $dv(t)$. The initial values were $x(0) = (1, 2, \ldots, 10)$; agent 5 includes a deviation of $u_5(3) = 4$ to obtain a final average value of 5.9, but the compensation propagated through $dv(t)$ converges to $dv(t) = 0.4$. Applying Eq. 6, $c(t) = 4$, so $x(t) - c(t)/n$ give us the correct result of consensus process. Algorithm 1 describes the process that each node has to execute.

3   Consensus for Distributed Ledger

We'll show the application of the detection of failures in the consensus process to a real-world scenario: the Distributed Ledger Technology (DLT). Distributed ledgers record, replicate, share and synchronize data without a central administrator and over the basis of peer-to-peer networks. Blockchain is one possible utility of the DLT. The database is spread among a set of nodes in a network. Each one of them keeps an identical copy of the ledger. When one node generates a new block of data, it is spread to the complete network and the nodes vote to decide which copy is the correct one.

---

[1] If a malicious agent keeps cheating many times, it can be detected by its neighbors. The demonstration is out of the scope of this work.

Algorithm 1. Consensus algorithm with cheat detection

1: set initial value $x_i(0)$
2: **while** $x_i(t)$ not converge **do**
3:     $x_i(t+1) = x_i(t) + \sum_{j \in N_i} [x_j(t) - x_i(t)] + u_i(t)$
4:     $dv_i(t) = x_i(t+1) + (\varepsilon d_i - 1)x_i(t) - \varepsilon \sum_{j \in N_i} x_j(t)$
5:     **if** $dv_i(t) > 0$ **then**
6:         accumulate $dv_k i(t)$ in $D_i(t)$
7:         $w_i(t) = w_i(t-1) + 1$
8:     **end if**
9:     $D_i(t+1) = D_i(t) + \varepsilon \sum_{j \in N_i} [D_j(t) - D_i(t)]$
10:    $w_i(t+1) = w_i(t) + \varepsilon \sum_{j \in N_i} [w_j(t) - w_i(t)]$
11: **end while**
12: $c_i(t) = \frac{D_i(t)}{\varepsilon w_i(t)}$
13: corrected result is $x_i(t) - c_i(t)/n$

To apply the consensus process presented in this paper, we assume that only one agent has the authority to emit blocks with the information the agent generates. For example, for IoT, only the sensor creates a block with its readings, or an academic institution generates certificates from their students, or an agency is who signs contracts. The problem that arises in those scenarios is how to ensure that the participants exchange the data as is.

The chosen structure that stores the blocks of data in each agent is Merkle trees. In this trees, the terminal nodes (leaves) are the blocks that contain the data, and the internal nodes hashes calculated from the hashes of their children. For our proposal

- each agent keeps a copy of the Merkle tree,
- each agent emits blocks with its generated information (e.g., sensor readings),
- the rest of the nodes spread the block and stores it in their own Merkle tree.

Let's consider a sensor network with agents that keep the record of the readings and uses DLT with Merkle trees to distribute and synchronize the data among the sensors using a consensus process.

1. agent i creates a block with all the readings s
2. it calculates the hash corresponding to the string with the readings
3. insert the block to its copy of the Merkles tree
4. obtain the updated hash of the root h_r
5. it composes a vector formed by $(s|h_r|y_i = 1)$
6. all the other agents sets their initial state to $(''|''|y_i = 0)$.

After that, a consensus process begins, and when it converges, all the nodes obtain the original string and hash value doing s/y_i and h/y_i (Fig. 2).

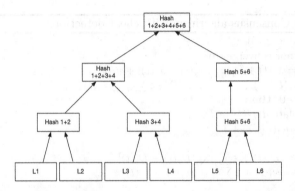

Fig. 2. Merkles tree to store the blocks of DLT. Leaves are the blocks that contain the data. Internal nodes contain hashes calculated from the hashes of their children.

For example, let's consider that agent 4 generates the following block

```
{ "device": 4,
  "readings": [
    {"value": 0.45469, "time": "04-Oct-2018 23:36:16"},
    {...} ]
}
```

The hash for the root once it has been added to the tree is

CC327F8CE3D88E1D7279894089BBD5C9D47BFBC5C735CD0D7ECC02A4DF417A46

When the consensus process finishes, all the agents have received the same block of data and the hash for the root. Each one of them adds the block to its tree and retrieves the new hash for the root, who must match with the received one. Figure 3 shows the convergence of such a consensus process. The plot represents the sum of all the characters of the block. When the consensus converges, it means that the block has arrived at all the agents and they can extract the data and add it to their trees.

This process works as expected and keeps identical copies of the Merkles trees in all the agents. A malicious node that tries to modify the block needs a block that can pass as valid, so it has to

1. modify the block with a new reading s'
2. insert the modified block in the tree
3. retrieve the new hash from the root h'_r
4. compose the message $(s'|h'_r|y_i(t))$ and sent it to its neighbors.

However, in this case, the modification is automatically detected by the neighbors, and it can be corrected over the received blocks using the deviation value dv_i propagated through the network and Eq. 6 (see Fig. 3).

To complete the approach to the DLT with consensus, a set of experiments analyzes how the solution degrades as the number of malicious agents increases.

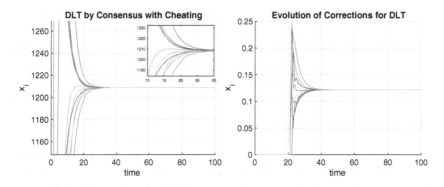

Fig. 3. Consensus process over a DLT. The values are the sum of all characters of the readings and the hash. (Left) One node introduces a modified block in $t = 20$. (Right) Convergence of the dv value for the correction.

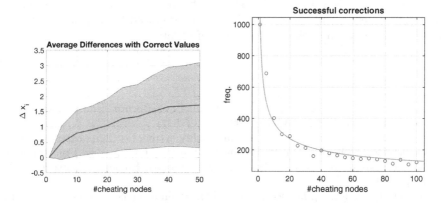

Fig. 4. (Left) Deviation without correction in networks with 100 agents, varying the number of traitors. The central line is the mean value and the area the standard deviation. (Right) Number of complete successful corrections for 1,000 executions. The distribution follows a power law with parameter $\alpha = -0.44$

The tests have been executed over networks with 100 agents, varying the number of malicious agents from 5 to 50 (which are the 50% of the size of the network). In each case 20 networks have been generated with 50 repetitions in each one of them, changing which are the traitor agents. Therefore, 1,000 executions provide the data for each case. Figure 4(left) shows the mean value (the central line) and the standard deviation (the shadowed area). The presence of a residual deviation is due to the position of the traitors in the network. Figure 4(right) reveals how the number of corrections are distributed. The distribution follows a power law with parameter $\alpha = -0.44$.

The solutions of Sundaram [12] to the BGP require that less than one-third of the agents were traitors, and at least half of the neighbors of each agent must be loyal. Since the networks generated for the experiments are random, without any control about the loyalty of the agents or their connectivity, and the tests arrive at a proportion of 50-50 among loyal and traitor generals, there are cases in which the network can not compensate the deviation. It is interesting to see that the consensus process still works even when the one-third bound is overpassed. It is something that needs a more in-depth study for future works.

4   Conclusions

This work proposes a modification of the Olfati–Saber and Murray consensus algorithm that can recover from byzantines failures. In the general case, it is not possible to detect which agent fails, but at least their direct neighbors can detect when appears a deviation from the consensus process. Tis deviation can be corrected over the final result, once the consensus has finished. The model has been applied to a real-world domain in which the Byzantine Generals' Problem arises: the Distributed Ledger Technology (DLT). The proposed solution works appropriately, and detect and correct the deviations produced by malicious agents if they are less than 1/3 of the total number of agents.

References

1. Kshetri, N.: Blockchain's roles in strengthening cybersecurity and protecting privacy. Telecommun. Policy **41**(10), 1027–1038 (2017)
2. Tian, F.: An agri-food supply chain traceability system for China based on RFID a blockchain technology. In: Proceedings of the 13th International Conference on Service Systems and Service Management (ICSSSM), Kunming, China, pp. 1–6, June 2016
3. Wright, A., De Filippi, P.: Decentralized blockchain technology and the rise of Lex Cryptographia (2015). https://ssrn.com/abstract=2580664
4. Rebollo, M., Benito, R.M., Losada, J.C., Galeano, J.: Robust distributed voting mechanism by consensus. In: 2018 IEEE/ACM, ASONAM 2018 (2018)
5. Pop, C., Cioara, T., Antal, M., Anghel, I., Salomie, I., Bertoncini, M.: Blockchain based decentralized management of demand response programs in smart energy grids. Sensors **18**(162), 1–21 (2018)
6. Fernandez-Carames, T.M., Fraga-Lamasa, P.: Review on the use of blockchain for the Internet of Things. IEEE Access **6**, 32979–33001 (2018)
7. Moinet, A., Darties, B., Baril, J.-L.: Blockchain based trust and authentication for decentralized sensor networks arXiv.1706.01/730v1 (2017)
8. Toulouse, M., Le, H., Phung, C.V., Hock, D.: Defense strategies against byzantine attacks in a consensus-based network intrusion detection system. Informatica **41**, 193–207 (2017)
9. Jesus, E.F., Chicarino, V.R.L., de Albuquerque, C.V.N., Rocha, A.A.D.A: A survey of how to use blockchain to secure Internet of Things and the stalker attack. Secur. Commun. Netw. **2018**, 1–27 (2018). Article ID 9675050
10. Olfati-Saber, R., Murray, R.M.: Consensus problems in networks of agents with switching topology and time-delays. IEEE TAC **49**(9), 1520–1533 (2004)

11. Orlov, Y., Pilloni, A., Pisano, A., Usai, E.: Consensus-based leader-follower tracking for a network of perturbed diffusion PDEs via local boundary interaction. IFAC **49**(8), 228–233 (2016)
12. Sundaram, S., Hadjicostis, C.N.: Distributed function calculation via linear iterative strategies in the presence of malicious agents. IEEE TAC **56**(7), 1495–1508 (2011)

The Challenge of Negotiation
in the Game of Diplomacy

Dave de Jonge[1,2]([✉]), Tim Baarslag[3], Reyhan Aydoğan[4], Catholijn Jonker[5], Katsuhide Fujita[6], and Takayuki Ito[7]

[1] IIIA-CSIC, Bellaterra, Spain
davedejonge@iiia.csic.es
[2] Western Sydney University, Sydney, Australia
[3] Centrum Wiskunde & Informatica, Amsterdam, The Netherlands
[4] Özyeğin University, Istanbul, Turkey
[5] Delft University of Technology, Delft, The Netherlands
[6] Tokyo University of Agriculture and Technology, Fuchu, Japan
[7] Nagoya Institute of Technology, Nagoya, Japan

Abstract. The game of Diplomacy has been used as a test case for complex automated negotiations for a long time, but to date very few successful negotiation algorithms have been implemented for this game. We have therefore decided to include a Diplomacy tournament within the annual Automated Negotiating Agents Competition (ANAC). In this paper we present the setup and the results of the ANAC 2017 Diplomacy Competition and the ANAC 2018 Diplomacy Challenge. We observe that none of the negotiation algorithms submitted to these two editions have been able to significantly improve the performance over a non-negotiating baseline agent. We analyze these algorithms and discuss why it is so hard to write successful negotiation algorithms for Diplomacy. Finally, we provide experimental evidence that, despite these results, coalition formation and coordination do form essential elements of the game.

1   Introduction

Automated negotiations have been studied extensively, but traditionally most work has focused on the strategy to determine which deals to propose *given* the utility values of those deals. A point that has received less attention is the fact that in many real-world negotiation settings, for any given proposal, a negotiator would need to spend considerable effort on estimating its value. Only recently, more attention has been given in the literature to negotiation domains where the calculation of utility is a highly non-trivial and time-consuming task. For example, [9] treated a problem in which determining the value of a deal was NP-hard and in [11] an algorithm was presented for negotiations applied to non-zero-sum General Game Playing.

The Automated Negotiating Agents Competition (ANAC) is an annually returning competition that aims to improve the state-of-the-art in automated

© Springer Nature Switzerland AG 2019
M. Lujak (Ed.): AT 2018, LNAI 11327, pp. 100–114, 2019.
https://doi.org/10.1007/978-3-030-17294-7_8

negotiations [3]. It was first held in 2010 and has been steadily growing in popularity. The setup of this competition has been updated each year to reflect the advancements made in the field of research. While ANAC started with small contract spaces and linear utility functions [4], it has featured increasingly complex scenarios, involving very large agreement spaces [8], multilateral negotiations [1], human-agent interactions [13], and non-linear utility functions [2,8].

However, in all of these editions, the process of evaluating a proposal was abstracted away. The agents would know the value of any potential proposal almost instantaneously because it could be calculated with a simple linear formula (this was true even in the editions with non-linear utility functions). Furthermore, the agents were not required to have any background knowledge of the negotiation domains and did not need to apply any form of reasoning to obtain the utility value of a proposal. The utility functions of the agents' opponents, on the other hand, were assumed to be completely unknown.

We argue that in real negotiations it is important to have knowledge of the domain and one should be able to reason about it. One cannot, for example, expect to make profitable deals in the antique business without having any knowledge of antique, no matter how good one is at bargaining. Moreover, a good negotiator should also be able to reason about the desires of its opponents. A good car salesman, for example, would try to find out what type of car best suits his client's needs to increase the chances of making a profitable deal. Therefore, we envisioned a need to add a new league to ANAC that does involve this kind of complex reasoning.

The game of Diplomacy forms an excellent test case for this type of complex negotiations, as it is a game that includes many of the difficulties one would also have to face in real-life negotiations [6]. It involves constraint satisfaction, coalition formation, game theory, trust, and even psychology. Now that modern Chess and Go computers are already far superior to any human player [15], we expect that Diplomacy will start to draw more attention as the next big challenge for computer science.

Although the game of Diplomacy has already been under attention of the Automated Negotiations community for a long time, to date very few successful negotiating Diplomacy players have been developed. Some of the earliest work on this game, for example, was presented in [14], but they only managed to play a very small number of games, because they had to play them with humans.

An informal online community called DAIDE exists which is dedicated to the development of Diplomacy playing agents.[1] Many agents have been developed by this community but only very few are capable of negotiation. One of the main non-negotiating bots developed on this framework is called the DumbBot.

In [6] a new platform called DipGame was introduced to make the development of Diplomacy agents easier for scientific research. This platform was later extended into the BANDANA platform [10]. Several negotiating agents have been developed using DipGame such as DipBlue [7] which consists of a negotiation algorithm built on top of the DumbBot. Unfortunately, its negotiation

---

[1] http://www.daide.org.uk.

algorithm did not result in a very strong increase in performance with respect to the non-negotiating DumbBot. An entirely new agent was presented in [10], called D-Brane, which can play with or without negotiations. Again, it turned out that when applying negotiations it is only slightly stronger than when it plays without negotiating. In 2015 the non-negotiating version of D-Brane won the Computer Diplomacy Challenge[2] which was organized as part of the ICGA Computer Olympiad.

On the other hand, another negotiation algorithm was implemented on top of DumbBot [5], which did strongly outperform the non-negotiating DumbBot. Unfortunately, this agent required a supercomputer to run.

Another negotiating agent, called AlphaDip, was presented in [12], which was largely based on D-Brane. Although it did improve over D-Brane, the authors still concluded that adding negotiations to their agent only had a very small influence on its overall performance.

This paper presents the setup and results of the ANAC 2017 Diplomacy Competition and the ANAC 2018 Diplomacy Challenge and provides an analysis of the proposed negotiation strategies for Diplomacy. The rest of the paper is organized as follows: Sect. 2 introduces the game of Diplomacy while Sect. 3 explains the negotiation protocol used in this game. Sections 4 and 5 present the setup and results of the 2017 and 2018 editions respectively. In Sect. 6 we present an experiment we conducted to show the importance of cooperation in Diplomacy. Finally, in Sect. 7, we conclude the paper with the lessons learned.

2 Diplomacy

Diplomacy is a widely played game for seven players. Just like chess it is completely deterministic (i.e. there are no dice, cards, or any other source of randomness) and there is no hidden information.[3] Players make their moves simultaneously. It is designed in such a way that each player needs to negotiate with the other players in order to have a chance of winning. It can be played as a classical board game, or it can be played online.[4]

The game takes place on a map of Europe in the year 1901, which is divided into 75 *Provinces*. Each player plays one of the seven great *Powers* of that time: *Austria* (AUS), *England* (ENG), *France* (FRA), *Germany* (GER), *Italy* (ITA), *Russia* (RUS) and *Turkey* (TUR) and each player starts with three or four units (armies or fleets) which are placed in fixed initial positions on the map. In each round of the game, each player must '*submit an order*' for each of its units, which tells those units how to move around the map and allows them to conquer the map's provinces.

---

[2] https://icga.leidenuniv.nl/?page_id=987.

[3] One might argue that Diplomacy does have hidden information, because players make secret agreements. However, these agreements have no formal meaning, and form part of the players' strategies rather than of the rules of the game. Therefore, *formally* speaking there is no hidden information.

[4] http://www.playdiplomacy.com/.

Some of the Provinces are so-called *Supply Centers* and the goal for the players is to conquer those Supply Centers. A player is eliminated when he or she loses all his or her Supply Centers and a player wins the game when he or she has conquered 18 or more of the 34 Supply Centers (a *Solo Victory*). However, the game may also end when all surviving players agree to a draw.

The game iterates through five types of rounds (or 'phases'), in the following order: *Spring, Summer, Fall, Autumn, Winter.* The first round of the game is referred to as Spring 1901, followed by Summer 1901, etcetera. After Winter 1901 follows Spring 1902, Summer 1902, and so on.

The main difference between Diplomacy and other deterministic games like Chess and Go, is that in Diplomacy players are allowed to negotiate with each other and form coalitions. At each round, before the players submit their orders, the players are given time to negotiate with each other and make agreements about the orders they will submit. Negotiations take place in private, and each agreement that is made is only known to the players involved in that agreement.

Typically, players may agree not to invade certain provinces, or they may agree that one player will help the other player to invade a certain province. In this way, players essentially form coalitions. These coalitions are not given beforehand. Instead, during the course of the game players may form and break coalitions as they like.

3   The Negotiation Protocol

In a real Diplomacy game there are no formal rules for the negotiations. Players are allowed to negotiate anything and there is no guarantee that players will obey their agreements. However, for our competition we needed to establish a well-defined negotiation language and protocol so that the agents could understand each other. Furthermore, in order to simplify the game and eliminate the issue of trust, we imposed the rule that the players are always obliged to obey their agreements. This means that our negotiation language needed to have well-defined formal semantics, which are explained below.

As the negotiation protocol, we used the Unstructured Negotiation Protocol [9], because it most closely resembles how negotiations in real games of Diplomacy take place. In this protocol, the agents do not take turns, but instead are allowed to propose or accept a deal whenever they want. A deal may involve any number of agents. Once all players involved in the deal have accepted it, a special *Notary* agent checks whether it is consistent with earlier made agreements. If this is indeed the case then the Notary will send a confirmation message to all agents involved in the deal. Once the Notary has sent this confirmation message the deal is considered officially binding. Players may propose and accept as many deals as they wish and negotiations continue after a deal has been confirmed.

If an agent has proposed or accepted a deal, but then changes its mind, and the deal has not yet been confirmed by the Notary, it can send a reject message to withdraw from the proposal and hence prevent it from becoming confirmed. However, once the deal is confirmed by the Notary the agents involved must always obey it.

Since each proposal is only sent to those players that are involved in it the other players will never be aware that this deal was proposed. Also, the Notary sends its confirmation message only to the players involved in the deal, so the agreement remains secret.

3.1 Allowed Proposals

In this section we define the set of deals that agents may propose to each other. A deal may consist of any number of *Order Commitments* and any number of *Demilitarized Zones*.

Definition 1. *An **Order Commitment** oc is a tuple: $oc = (y, \phi, o)$, where y is a 'year' (an integer greater than 1900), $\phi \in \{Spring, Fall\}$ is a 'phase' and o is any legal order for any unit.*

An Order Commitment represents a promise that a power will submit a certain order during a certain phase and year. For example: *"In the Spring of 1902 the army in Holland will move to Belgium"*. Formally, an Order Commitment (y, ϕ, o) is obeyed if Power P submits the order o during phase ϕ of year y, where P is the owner of the unit defined by the details of the order o.

Definition 2. *A **Demilitarized Zone** dmz is a tuple: $dmz = (y, \phi, A, B)$ with y and ϕ as in Definition 1, A is a nonempty set of Powers and B is a nonempty set of Provinces.*

A Demilitarized Zone is an agreement between the specified Powers that none of them will invade (or stay inside) any of the specified Provinces during the specified phase and year. For example, the Demilitarized Zone

$$(1903, Fall, \{FRA, GER, ENG\}, \{NTH, ECH\})$$

has the interpretation *"In the Fall of 1903 France, Germany, and England will keep out of the North Sea and the English Channel"*. Formally, a Demilitarized Zone is obeyed if none of the powers in A submits any order during phase ϕ of year y to move any unit into any of the provinces in B.

Definition 3. *A **Deal** d is a non-empty set:*

$$d = \{oc_1, \ldots oc_n, dmz_1, \ldots dmz_m\}$$

where each oc_i is an Order Commitment, each dmz_i is a Demilitarized Zone, and where n and m can be any non-negative integers.

When a deal is confirmed by the Notary it means that all Order Commitments and all Demilitarized Zones in it must be obeyed.

A proposed deal can only be accepted or rejected in its entirety. If an agent wishes to accept only a part of the deal, it can simply propose a new deal which only consists of the subset of Order Commitments and Demilitarized Zones it desires.

Apart from proposing this type of deals, agents are also allowed to propose a draw to all other players. The game ends in a draw if all agents that have not been eliminated propose a draw in the same round of the game.

4   The ANAC 2017 Diplomacy Competition

4.1   Submission Rules and Tournament Setup

The assignment for the participants was to implement a negotiation algorithm using the BANDANA framework. This negotiation algorithm would then be combined with the tactical module of D-Brane to form a complete agent. This tactical module would then choose which moves the agent makes, while obeying the agreements made by the negotiation algorithm. The participants were not allowed to implement a complete Diplomacy playing agent from scratch. They were only allowed to implement a negotiation algorithm so that the competition focused purely on the negotiation aspect of Diplomacy.

In order to determine whether to accept a proposal or not, the participants' negotiation algorithms had the possibility to consult D-Brane's Tactical Module to see which moves would be played if that proposal was accepted.

The tournament was run using the Parlance game server.[5] We let all agents participating in the competition play 110 games together. Since a game requires 7 players and we only had 4 participants, we supplemented the agents with 3 instances of the non-negotiating D-Brane. In each game the players were randomly assigned to the 7 Powers.[6] Every round of each game had a deadline of 30 s. In order to prevent the games from continuing forever a draw was declared automatically in any game that advanced to the Winter 1920 phase. The agents' overall score for the tournament was determined by the number of Supply Centers they conquered.

4.2   Submissions

We received the following submissions:

- **Frigate**, by Ryohei Kawata and Katsuhide Fujita, *Tokyo University of Agriculture and Technology*, Japan
- **Agent Madoff**, by Tan Hao Hao, *Nanyang Technological University*, Singapore
- **DDAgent**, by Daichi Shibata, *Nagoya Institute of Technology*, Japan
- **NaiveThinkerG**, by Giancarlo Nicolo, *Universitat Politècnica de València*, Spain

Due to lack of space we cannot give a description of all of these agents. Therefore, we will only discuss the winner and the runner-up.

---

[5] https://pypi.python.org/pypi/Parlance/1.4.1.

[6] It would have been better to assign each agent to each Power an equal number of times, because some Powers are stronger than others. Unfortunately, however, the Parlance game server does not provide this option.

Frigate. Frigate only proposes bilateral deals, and only to Powers that own at least 3 and at most 10 Supply Centers. Furthermore, it does not deal with any Power that forms a direct threat to any of Frigate's own Supply Centers. For each Power that does qualify Frigate constructs a proposal by consulting the D-Brane Tactical Module to find the best plans for itself and the other agent, under the restriction that they do not invade each others' Supply Centers. The proposal will then consist of the union of these plans.

Frigate randomly chooses a deal from the proposals it found, where the probability depends on the strength of the other agent (the weaker the agent, the higher the probability) and the number of Supply Centers that Frigate expects to gain from it. Furthermore, the probability is multiplied by 5 if the other agent is considered an ally. An agent is considered an ally if it was involved in the last confirmed deal that Frigate was involved in.

Although Frigate does implement an acceptance strategy, due to a bug in the code, it never accepts any incoming proposals.

Agent Madoff. In order to generate proposals Agent Madoff first tries to predict the opponents' orders using the D-Brane Tactical Module under the assumption that the opponents have not made any agreements. Then, it identifies which orders are in conflict with its own interests, namely orders for units to invade any of Agent Madoff's own Home Supply Centers, or any province that Agent Madoff is also trying to invade. It then tries to find alternative orders for such units and proposes them. If it cannot find any suitable alternative order then Agent Madoff will try to ask a third party for support to defend or attack the province in question.

Agent Madoff does not really apply a coalition formation strategy. However, it does keep track of each opponent's 'hostility'. Initially, it assigns to each Power has a *hostility value* of 0. This value is decreased whenever a Power steals a Supply Center from Agent Madoff, and is increased whenever a Power agrees to give support to Agent Madoff. This value is then used by Agent Madoff's acceptance strategy. The higher this value, the more likely it is that Agent Madoff will accept a proposal from this opponent.

When Agent Madoff receives a proposal it calculates for each component of this deal a value between 0 and 1 which depends on various heuristics, such as the value of the province that is the destination of the order (in case of a move order commitment), or the hostility of the supported power (in case of a support order commitment). It then calculates the average value over these components. The higher this average value, the higher the probability that Agent Madoff will accept it.

4.3 Results

Initially, we ran the competition according to the setup announced to the participants. Unfortunately, no agent performed significantly better than the non-negotiating D-Brane, which means that the ability to negotiate did not really improve the results of the agents. We then played 50 games with 4 instances of each agent versus 3 instances of D-Brane. The idea behind this was that it might be easier for the agents to negotiate with a copy of themselves, rather than with a different agent. Unfortunately, this setup also did not result in any of the players significantly outperforming the others.

Therefore, to decide a winner, we counted the number of proposals made by each agent that were accepted by every other agent involved in them, and considered that value as the final score of each agent. The idea being that if an agent's proposals are accepted by the other agents, this can be seen as a measure of quality, even though the agreement did not in the end result in a higher number of Supply Centers. The results are displayed in Table 1. We see that Frigate was proclaimed the winner of the competition and Agent Madoff was awarded the second prize.

Table 1. Final results of the 2017 Diplomacy Competition. We counted the number of proposals made by each agent that were eventually accepted by all the other agents involved in it.

	Confirmed proposals
Frigate	**372**
Agent Madoff	170
DDAgent	61
NaiveThinkerG	30

5 The 2018 Diplomacy Challenge

Because the 2017 Diplomacy Competition did not end with one agent being significantly better than any of the other agents, or even better than the non-negotiating agent, we decided to change the setup for 2018. Instead of a 'Competition' we turned it into a 'Challenge', meaning that a winner would only be proclaimed if its results are significant.

5.1 Tournament Setup

Most of the setup for 2018 was identical to the setup of 2017. We used exactly the same negotiation protocol, and the participants were again required to implement a negotiation algorithm on top of D-Brane. The main difference was that the 2018 Challenge consisted of two rounds.

In the first round for each agent we ran 100 games with 4 instances of that agent against 3 instances of the non-negotiating D-Brane agent. We say an agent *passed* the first round if the instances of that agent conquered a statistically significant higher number of Supply Centers on average than the D-Branes. The agents that did not pass the first round were eliminated from the Challenge.

For the second round we then let all agents that passed the first round play together. Since it was likely that there would be less than 7 such agents, we stated the rule that the field would be supplemented with as many agents that did not pass the first round as necessary, even though such agents were not eligible to win the challenge. Furthermore, if there still would not be enough agents, we would supplement the field with instances of the non-negotiating D-Brane agent. We played 100 games and the agent that conquered the highest number of Supply Centers would be the winner of Round 2.

In order to win the Challenge an agent had to win the second round, as well as pass the first round. This means that if the winner of the second round did not pass the first round there would be no winner at all.

5.2   Motivation

The motivation behind this setup is that in Round 2 the real negotiation skills of the agents are tested. In theory, if an agent makes purely selfish proposals, it will not succeed, because its proposals will not be accepted by the other agents. On the other hand, if it makes purely altruistic proposals or accepts any proposal it receives, it will not succeed either, because it will be exploited by its opponents. In practice, however, a bad negotiator could still be able to win Round 2, because its opponents are not perfect either and therefore it might purely benefit from bad proposals made by the other agents. In order to prevent such 'freeloading' behavior we demanded that each agent was also able to successfully negotiate with only copies of itself. For this reason we have included Round 1 in this challenge. One could also roughly say that Round 1 tests the agents' 'proposing strategy', while Round 2 tests their 'acceptance strategy'.

5.3   Submissions

We received the following submissions:

- **CoalitionBot**, by Ido Westler, Yehuda Callen, Moche Uzan, Arie Cattan, Avishay Zagury *Bar Ilan University*, Israel
- **M@sterMind**, by Jonathan Ng, *Nanyang Technological University*, Singapore
- **Gunma**, by Ryohei Kawata and Katsuhide Fujita, *Tokyo University of Agriculture and Technology*, Japan
- **GamlBot**, by Michael Vassernis, *Bar Ilan University*, Israel
- **DDAgent2**, by Daichi Shibata, *Nagoya Institute of Technology*, Japan

Unfortunately, it turned out that DDAgent2 was too slow to participate, because in many rounds it was not able to submit its orders before the deadline.

Again, due to space constraints we will only discuss the two best agents of the two respective rounds.

CoalitionBot. CoalitionBot is a very passive player. It only proposes demilitarized zones and it accepts any incoming proposal. In the first turn, it proposes a bilateral deal to every other Power. This deal proposes that the other Power will not invade any of the CoalitionBot's own supply Centers during the current turn, and in return the CoalitionBot will not invade the other power's Supply Centers during the same turn. Any agent that accepts this proposal will be considered an ally for the rest of the game. In all other turns, CoalitionBot proposes to all its allies that they will not attack each others' Supply Centers.

We will see below that CoalitionBot was able to perform strongly in the first round, but not in the second round. This is not surprising, given that it always accepts any incoming proposal and does not try to exploit its opponents. Its implementation seems to be based on the idea that it can always completely trust its opponents. Clearly, this works well when playing against copies of itself, but not when playing against less altruistic opponents.

Gunma. Gunma proposes two types of deals, which the authors call a 'Mutual Support' and a 'Combined Attack', respectively. A Mutual Support is a deal in which one unit of Gunma supports an opponent's unit to hold, and the opponent's unit supports Gunma's unit to hold in return. A Combined Attack is a deal in which one of Gunma's units attacks a province owned by an enemy, with support from as many units from allies as possible. Whenever Gunma can find a Combined Attack, it will propose it. On the other hand, it will only propose a Mutual Support if it finds one for which it is sure it can gain a Supply Center.

For any received proposal Gunma predicts how many Supply Centers it would gain from it. It accepts the deal that yields the highest gain, but if there are multiple such deals, it uses the current number of supply centers owned by the proposer as a tie-breaker. In that case it will accept the deal from the currently weakest Power.

Note that Gunma's proposing strategy is rather greedy. It only proposes deals that yield benefit to himself, and never considers the needs of its negotiation partners. When it comes to accepting, however, it is less selfish. If no deal yields any gain, than it is willing to accept a deal that does not cause Gunma to lose any Supply Centers.

5.4 Results

The Results of Round 1 are displayed in Table 2. We see that only CoalitionBot and Gunma were able to outperform D-Brane. However, a one-sided Student-t test[7] revealed that the results of Gunma were not significant (p-value 0.23). Therefore, only CoalitionBot managed to pass Round 1 (p-value $9.7 \cdot 10^{-9}$).

The results of Round 2 are shown in Table 3. As explained above, we needed to include all the agents in this round, as well as 3 instances of D-Brane, in order to

---

[7] With respect to the null-hypothesis that each agent has a mean score of $\frac{34}{7}$ Supply Centers per game.

Table 2. Results of the 2018 Diplomacy Challenge, Round 1. Displayed are the average number of conquered supply centers per game, with their standard errors.

	Sup. Centers	Result
CoalitionBot	5.528 ± 0.110	PASS
D-Brane	3.963 ± 0.146	
Gunma	4.950 ± 0.128	FAIL
D-Brane	4.733 ± 0.171	
D-Brane	4.930 ± 0.164	
M@sterMind	4.803 ± 0.123	FAIL
D-Brane	5.440 ± 0.184	
GamlBot	4.420 ± 0.138	FAIL

Table 3. Results of the 2018 Diplomacy Challenge, Round 2. Gunma scores highest, but the results are not significant.

	Supply Centers
Gunma	5.69 ± 0.300
GamlBot	5.31 ± 0.334
CoalitionBot	4.94 ± 0.289
D-Brane	4.54 ± 0.157
M@sterMind	4.44 ± 0.290

have 7 players, even though CoalitionBot was the only agent that passed Round 1 and therefore the only candidate to win the challenge.

We see that Gunma performed best, although the difference between the first three agents is non-significant. Since the CoalitionBot did not beat the other agents in Round 2, and it was not able to clearly outperform the D-Brane in this round either, the 2018 Diplomacy Challenge ended with no winner.

6   Is Cooperation Even Possible?

One question that may come to mind when looking at the results, is whether it is really possible at all to improve performance by means of negotiation. Any experienced Diplomacy player would answer this question with a definite 'yes', but we would like to back this claim up with scientific evidence.

The question is then how we could show that it is possible to negotiate successfully, without having any algorithm that can do this to our disposal. Fortunately, we have managed to design an experiment that allows us to show the benefit of cooperation, without actually using a negotiation algorithm.

It worked as follows. We first let 7 instances of the non-negotiating D-Brane play 200 games and recorded how many Supply Centers each Power conquered on average. The results are displayed in Table 4. Next, we repeated this experiment, but with only 6 instances of D-Brane while one of those agents was playing two Powers at the same time. For each possible combination of two Powers we played 200 games (there are $\binom{7}{2} = 21$ such combinations, so we played $21 \cdot 200 = 4200$ games) and recorded the number of Supply Centers conquered by the agent playing two Powers.

In this way we have been able to show that if one agent plays the role of two Powers at once, it scores more Supply Centers than if two agents individually play the same two Powers. In other words, when two Powers work together as a team, they have a clear advantage. These results are displayed in Table 5. For example, in the first row we see that when AUS and ENG are played by one agent, then that agent scores on average 6.99 Supply Centers. However, we see in Table 4 that when these Powers are played by individual agents, they only score 1.60 and 4.39 Supply Centers respectively, yielding a total score of $1.60 + 4.39 = 5.99$, which is also displayed in the first row of Table 5.

The combination of AUS and ENG only yields a small advantage, but for many other coalitions we see much stronger synergy effects. For example, FRA and GER together score 22.1 Supply Centers when played by a single agent, while when playing individually they only score[8] $4.98 + 4.11 = 9.09$.

In general, we see a clear advantage in 12 out of the 21 possible combinations (more than 4 Supply Centers difference, indicated with $++$) and a small advantage in 4 of those combinations (indicated with $+$). When we calculate the average over all combinations we find that the agent playing two Powers scores around 14 Supply Centers, which is clearly more than the $\frac{2}{7} \cdot 34 = 9.71$ Supply Centers that two individual agents would conquer on average.

Although it is clear that players have an advantage when cooperating, we also conclude that this highly depends on *which* two Powers are forming a coalition. FRA and GER, for example, form a much stronger coalition than AUS and ENG. This is an important observation, because this may also explain why it is hard for the submitted agents to negotiate successfully. In many games the negotiating agents may be assigned to Powers that do not form strong combinations, making it hard to benefit from negotiation.

The fact that some coalitions are stronger than others is well-known among experienced Diplomacy players, and is a consequence of the topology of the map. For example, Russia and Turkey are two bordering Powers, which means that if they form a coalition at the beginning of the game then each of them does not have to worry about being attacked by the other, and can therefore completely focus on its other direct neighbors. Furthermore, the fact that they are located next to each other means they can easily give support to one another.

On the other hand, Turkey and England form a weak coalition because they are positioned on opposite ends of the map, so they cannot attack each other in early stages of the game, which means they would not benefit from any mutual peace agreement, and they cannot give each other support either.

For some coalitions we even see a detrimental effect. Although in most cases they are relatively small, they cannot be attributed to statistical fluctuations. We suspect that this results from the fact that they play different opening moves when playing together, which coincidentally happen to be worse.

Finally, we should note that the difference in strength between the various coalitions may not only be caused by the topology of the map, but may also partially be a consequence of the strategy applied by D-Brane. Therefore, we expect these results to be different, but not radically different, if we repeated this experiment with a different agent.

---

[8] Table 5 shows a value of 9.08 instead of 9.09. This difference is due to rounding errors.

We conclude from these experiments that it should definitely be possible for two agents to benefit from negotiations. Interestingly, these results also suggest *how* such a negotiation algorithm could be implemented. The idea is that if our agent is playing, for example, FRA, then it could consult the D-Brane Tactical module to ask which moves it should play if it were playing as both FRA and GER. Then, it could propose those moves to GER.

Table 4. The number of Supply Centers conquered by each Power, when 7 instances of D-Brane are playing without negotiations

Power	Supply Centers
AUS	1.60 ± 0.16
ENG	4.39 ± 0.17
FRA	4.98 ± 0.20
GER	4.11 ± 0.24

Power	Supply Centers
ITA	2.41 ± 0.16
RUS	10.44 ± 0.42
TUR	6.09 ± 0.17

Table 5. The number of Supply Centers conquered by each combination of two Powers played by one agent, compared to their score when played by two agents. Differences greater than 4 Supply Center are indicated with ++ or − −, while smaller differences are indicated with + or −. In all cases except AUS+ENG, AUS+GER and GER+TUR the p−value was smaller than 10^{-4}.

Coalition of 2 Powers	Score by 1 agent	Score by 2 agents	
AUS + ENG	6.99	5.99	+
AUS + FRA	9.91	6.57	+
AUS + GER	4.11	5.7	−
AUS + ITA	12.91	4.01	++
AUS + RUS	17.61	12.03	++
AUS + TUR	17.95	7.69	++
ENG + FRA	17.95	9.37	++
ENG + GER	17.78	8.50	++
ENG + ITA	8.88	6.8	+
ENG + RUS	20.37	14.83	++
ENG + TUR	8.82	10.48	−

Coalition of 2 Powers	Score by 1 agent	Score by 2 agents	
FRA + GER	22.1	9.08	++
FRA + ITA	13.43	7.39	++
FRA + RUS	9.91	15.41	− −
FRA + TUR	8.71	11.07	−
GER + ITA	11.7	6.52	++
GER + RUS	21.27	14.54	++
GER + TUR	8.99	10.20	−
ITA + RUS	19.21	12.85	++
ITA + TUR	11.92	8.5	+
RUS + TUR	24.34	16.53	++
Overall	14.04	9.71	++

7   Discussion and Conclusions

From these two competitions we have learned that it is still very hard for the Automated Negotiations community to implement algorithms for domains as complex as Diplomacy. So far, no submission has been able to significantly out-perform a non-negotiating agent, even though we have experimentally shown that it is definitely possible for agents to benefit from cooperation.

However, it is important to understand that we are not expecting the Diplomacy Challenge to have a winner any time soon. We regard it as a long term challenge which might take several years to tackle. After all, in the cases of Chess, Go, and Poker it also took many years to develop strong programs.

Diplomacy is a very complex game and it is hard for participants to write a strong algorithm in the few months they have between the call for participation and the submission deadline. Before they could even start implementing they first needed to learn the rules of the game (which are fairly complex), learn the rules of the competition, and learn to work with the BANDANA framework. After that, they needed to come up with a smart algorithm, implement it, debug it, and optimize it.

Studying the source codes of the agents, we made two important observations:

1. Most agents never make any proposals for any of the future turns. They only make proposals for the current turn.
2. Many of the agents seem to have bugs in their code.

We think that both of these observations play an important role in the reason why the agents fail to negotiate successfully.

Any experienced Diplomacy player would agree that it is essential to plan several steps ahead. An important reason for this is that one does not often encounter a situation in which two players can both directly benefit from cooperation. Although it often happens that one player can give support to another player, it may then take several turns before a situation occurs in which the other player can return the favor. Therefore, it is essential that, in the short term, players are not purely selfish. They should be willing to help another player, while only expecting the favor to be returned at a later stage. Currently, none of the submitted agents seem to exhibit this kind of long term negotiation strategy.

Similarly, we think that the second observation is a very important one. As explained, the participants only have a limited amount of time to implement their agents, so perhaps we can only expect any participant to win the challenge after participating for several years. We noticed, for example, that due to a bug Frigate never accepted any proposals, even though it did implement an acceptance strategy. Also, Agent Madoff was more likely to accept a proposal if it involved a unit invading a province currently occupied by a Power that is considered a friend. We think that this is an error and that the author intended the opposite. Luckily, we see that two participants from 2017 have continued to participate in 2018, so the necessary drive seems to exist to commit to this long-term challenge.

In future editions of the Diplomacy Challenge, whenever negotiating agents play together with non-negotiating agents, we may need to make sure the negotiating agents play Powers that are more likely to form successful coalitions, as indicated by our experiments in Sect. 6.

Acknowledgments. This work is part of the Veni research programme with project number 639.021.751, which is financed by the Netherlands Organisation for Scientific Research (NWO), and project LOGISTAR, funded by the E.U. Horizon 2020 research and innovation programme, Grant Agreement No. 769142.

References

1. Aydoğan, R., Fujita, K., Baarslag, T., Jonker, C.M., Ito, T.: ANAC 2017: repeated multilateral negotiation league. In: The 11th International Workshop on Automated Negotiation, ACAN 2018 (2018)
2. Aydoğan, R., et al.: A baseline for nonlinear bilateral negotiations: the full results of the agents competing in ANAC 2014, pp. 96–122. Bentham Science Publishers (2017)
3. Baarslag, T., Aydoğan, R., Hindriks, K.V., Fuijita, K., Ito, T., Jonker, C.M.: The automated negotiating agents competition, 2010–2015. AI Mag. **36**(4), 115–118 (2015)
4. Baarslag, T., Hindriks, K., Jonker, C., Kraus, S., Lin, R.: The first Automated Negotiating Agents Competition (ANAC 2010). In: Ito, T., Zhang, M., Robu, V., Fatima, S., Matsuo, T. (eds.) New Trends in Agent-Based Complex Automated Negotiations. SCI, vol. 383, pp. 113–135. Springer, Heidelberg (2012). https://doi.org/10.1007/978-3-642-24696-8_7
5. Fabregues, A.: Facing the challenge of human-aware negotiation. Ph.D. thesis, Universitat Autònoma de Barcelona (2012)
6. Fabregues, A., Sierra, C.: DipGame: a challenging negotiation testbed. Eng. Appl. Artif. Intell. **24**(7), 1137–1146 (2011)
7. Ferreira, A., Lopes Cardoso, H., Reis, L.P.: DipBlue: a diplomacy agent with strategic and trust reasoning. In: ICAART 2015 - Proceedings of the International Conference on Agents and Artificial Intelligence, Lisbon, Portugal, 10–12 January 2015, vol. 1, pp. 54–65. SciTePress (2015)
8. Fujita, K., Aydoğan, R., Baarslag, T., Ito, T., Jonker, C.: The fifth Automated Negotiating Agents Competition (ANAC 2014). In: Fukuta, N., Ito, T., Zhang, M., Fujita, K., Robu, V. (eds.) Recent Advances in Agent-based Complex Automated Negotiation. SCI, vol. 638, pp. 211–224. Springer, Cham (2016). https://doi.org/10.1007/978-3-319-30307-9_13
9. de Jonge, D., Sierra, C.: NB3: a multilateral negotiation algorithm for large, nonlinear agreement spaces with limited time. Auton. Agent. Multi-Agent Syst. **29**(5), 896–942 (2015)
10. de Jonge, D., Sierra, C.: D-Brane: a diplomacy playing agent for automated negotiations research. Appl. Intell. **47**(1), 158–177 (2017)
11. de Jonge, D., Zhang, D.: Automated negotiations for general game playing. In: Proceedings of the 16th Conference on Autonomous Agents and MultiAgent Systems, AAMAS 2017, São Paulo, Brazil, 8–12 May 2017, pp. 371–379. ACM (2017)
12. Marinheiro, J., Lopes Cardoso, H.: Towards general cooperative game playing. In: Nguyen, N.T., Kowalczyk, R., van den Herik, J., Rocha, A.P., Filipe, J. (eds.) Transactions on Computational Collective Intelligence XXVIII. LNCS, vol. 10780, pp. 164–192. Springer, Cham (2018). https://doi.org/10.1007/978-3-319-78301-7_8
13. Mell, J., Gratch, J., Baarslag, T., Aydoğan, R., Jonker, C.: Results of the first annual human-agent league of the automated negotiating agents competition. In: Proceedings of the 2018 International Conference on Intelligent Virtual Agents (2018)
14. Ephrati, E., Kraus, S., Lehman, D.: An automated diplomacy player. In: Levy, D., Beal, D. (eds.) Heuristic Programming in Artificial Intelligence: The 1st Computer Olympia, pp. 134–153. Ellis Horwood Limited, Chicester (1989)
15. Silver, D., et al.: Mastering the game of go with deep neural networks and tree search. Nature **529**(7587), 484–489 (2016)

Automated Negotiations Under User Preference Uncertainty: A Linear Programming Approach

Dimitrios Tsimpoukis[1,2(✉)], Tim Baarslag[1,3], Michael Kaisers[1], and Nikolaos G. Paterakis[2]

[1] Centrum Wiskunde & Informatica,
Science Park 123, 1098 XG Amsterdam, The Netherlands
{D.Tsimpoukis,T.Baarslag,M.Kaisers}@cwi.nl
[2] Technische Universiteit Eindhoven,
De Zaale, 5600 MB Eindhoven, The Netherlands
N.Paterakis@tue.nl
[3] Department of Information and Computing Sciences, Utrecht University,
Princetonplein 5, 3584 CC Utrecht, The Netherlands
T.Baarslag@uu.nl

Abstract. Autonomous agents negotiating on our behalf find applications in everyday life in many domains such as high frequency trading, cloud computing and the smart grid among others. The agents negotiate with one another to reach the best agreement for the users they represent. An obstacle in the future of automated negotiators is that the agent may not always have a priori information about the preferences of the user it represents. The purpose of this work is to develop an agent that will be able to negotiate given partial information about the user's preferences. First, we present a new partial information model that is supplied to the agent, which is based on categorical data in the form of pairwise comparisons of outcomes instead of precise utility information. Using this partial information, we develop an estimation model that uses linear optimization and translates the information into utility estimates. We test our methods in a negotiation scenario based on a smart grid cooperative where agents participate in energy trade-offs. The results show that already with very limited information the model becomes accurate quickly and performs well in an actual negotiation setting. Our work provides valuable insight into how uncertainty affects an agent's negotiation performance, how much information is needed to be able to formulate an accurate user model, and shows a capability of negotiating effectively with minimal user feedback.

1 Introduction

Negotiation between two or more different parties is the joint decision making process towards a satisfactory outcome for all sides. If such an outcome is achieved, it constitutes an agreement.

© Springer Nature Switzerland AG 2019
M. Lujak (Ed.): AT 2018, LNAI 11327, pp. 115–129, 2019.
https://doi.org/10.1007/978-3-030-17294-7_9

In recent years there have been significant advancements in automating the negotiation process meaning that human negotiators are being represented by computer agents. Fully computerized negotiation offers a lot of benefits such as achieving better (win-win) deals for all sides, reduction in negotiation duration, and of course much reduced users' stress and frustration due to participation in the negotiation process [4]. *Automated negotiation* finds application in many areas, some of which are high frequency trading, cloud computing and the smart grid. Such settings can be very dynamic, and as a result automating the negotiation process becomes imperative, considering that it is very uncomfortable for the user having to participate in negotiations so frequently, especially in domains in which they are not knowledgeable.

A major obstacle in the future of representative automated negotiation is the agent's level of knowledge about the preferences of the user it represents [6]. Preference elicitation is a tedious procedure to the users since they have to interact with the system repeatedly and participate in lengthy queries. To address this challenge, the agents should be able to accurately represent the users under minimal information about their preferences. Therefore, the agent must strike a balance between *user model* accuracy and user interference. Even though research in the field of automated negotiations has made progress on opponent modeling, in most cases the agents themselves were operating under fully specified preference profiles (see Sect. 2). The major questions that arise from the above problem are:

- How can we model the incomplete information about the users' preferences supplied to the agent in cases of uncertainty?
- How can we estimate user preferences from incomplete information?
- How does uncertainty about the user's preferences affect an agent's negotiation performance?

In this work we address the problems associated with negotiation under uncertainty and test the results in a scenario inspired from the smart grid. The contributions are threefold:

- We propose a way of representing user preference information, based on categorical data, showing preference relations between different possible outcomes.
- We present a method of estimating preference information from the incomplete information model based on linear optimization.
- We test the proposed method while negotiating on a smart grid cooperative scenario, examining the accuracy of the generated preference profile as well as actual negotiation performance.

The rest of this work is organized as follows: Sect. 2 discusses related work in the field of negotiation under uncertainty. Section 3 presents the problem setting, the key components in automated negotiation, as well as the new proposed ordinal data based incomplete information model. Section 4 describes the two proposed preference estimation methods. In Sect. 5 we are presenting the results of our strategies in terms of user model accuracy and negotiation performance, and in Sect. 7 we make suggestions for future work.

2   Related Work

The subject of modeling partial information about a user's preference profile, as well as the process of trying to formulate an accurate model of the user's real preferences given incomplete information has been a topic of research through the years, but not a lot of it has been applied in the negotiation domain.

A key area of research in the field of user-preference modeling is *Multi-Attribute Utility Theory*. Many strategies have been proposed in this field, with the target of creating a preference profile under incomplete information of the user preferences. A large family of such strategies are the UTA (Utilité Additives) methods, originally proposed by Jacquet-Lagreze and Siskos in 1982 [16]. The UTA method and its extensions [14,21], obtain a ranked set of outcomes as input and formulate a new piecewise linear utility function through the use of linear programming. An application of the UTA method on the negotiation domain has been presented by Roszkowska [22]. The main limitation of the method is that the input outcome set needs to be a complete ranking of outcomes, meaning a total ordering (even though it might not include the whole outcome space). Even though the method we propose also utilizes a ranking as input in the experimental implementation, it can also work with any arbitrary set of partial orders.

Automated negotiation research has focused mostly on opponent preference modeling rather than on the user preference elicitation [7,8]. However, several techniques in opponent modeling are of interest to our case. Jonker et al. present an agent architecture that uses heuristics based on the opponent's bidding sequence to elicit opponent preference information [17]. Even though the user's preference profile is considered known in these methods, opponent modeling strategies could also be applied in user preference modeling.

Aside from multi-attribute utility theory, another option for representing user information was proposed by Boutilier et al. [10] and studied in the negotiation domain [6,20]. CP-nets provide a graphical representation of conditional and qualitative preference relations. Cornelio et al. extend the CP-net concept to incorporate uncertainty in the networks including probabilistic elements [11], and Aydoğan et al. [1,3] apply CP-nets theory in the negotiation domain using heuristics on the partial ordering of attribute values to generate a total ordering of outcomes. While CP-nets prove an effective way of representing partial information, our method is able to make the transition to utility-based negotiation based on ordinal data on full negotiation outcomes.

Our proposed decision model is inspired mainly by the work of Srinivasan and Shocker [24], who proposes a strategy for estimating the weights of different attributes given a set of pairwise comparisons of outcomes by using linear programming. The main limitation of this model, apart from the fact that it is limited to weight estimation, is that the evaluations of the stimuli values that appear on the comparison set need to be known. We extend this model to propose a different formulation of the problem using categorical data that estimates complete preference profiles based on the outcome set. We also formulate a simplified version of related work [24] for estimating the different negotiation issue weights.

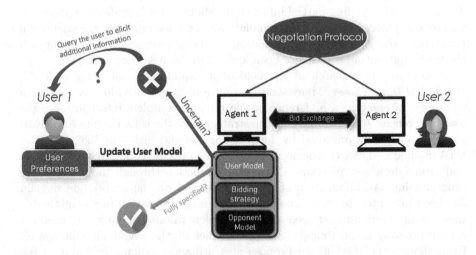

Fig. 1. Negotiation setting

3   Problem Setting

3.1   Problem Description

Let us consider a setting where a computer *agent* is negotiating with an opponent agent on behalf of a *user* it is supposed to represent. The agents are exchanging bids (offers) to reach an agreement. The user that an agent represents has a set of preferences towards particular outcomes and the agent tries to achieve a negotiation outcome that satisfies these preferences as best as possible. This is schematically illustrated in Fig. 1.

In a typical setting, an agent representing the user is assumed to have a *utility function* that fully describes the user's preference profile and translates every possible outcome to marginal values. However, the agent in a negotiation setting dost not necessarily have a priori, a fully specified user preference model, which we will call *user model*. Part of the reason is the user's discomfort to engage with the system continuously.

Consider a typical example in a smart grid domain where a user would have to interact with the energy management system in his residence to update his preferences. This is a tedious procedure to the user, which requires lengthy queries and on occasion even the user himself might not be sure about his preferences due to lack of negotiation domain knowledge. As a result, agents have to be able to negotiate on partial information about the user preferences, whilst also querying the user for additional information as little as possible.

In cases of uncertainty an agent might be provided with an initial set of information that might be known to it from domain knowledge, previous inter-actions with the user, past negotiation data etc. The information obtained from querying the user is another important concept when an agent needs to elicit information about the user's preferences. It may be difficult to query the user for precise utility information, but, on the other hand, it could be much easier for a user to compare outcomes. To that regard, we will propose a partial infor-mation model based on ranked outcomes by the user which will be the initial information supplied to the agents.

Our goal is to formulate a strategy, where an agent will be able to generate a utility function that will approximate the real utility function as best as possible given a partial information model based on a set of ranked outcomes that are obtained from queries.

3.2   Formal Model

We present the key elements of a negotiation model architecture under preference uncertainty. These are: *the negotiation protocol, the negotiation scenario*, the users' *preference profiles*, the agents' *negotiation tactics*, presented below.

Negotiation Domain. During a negotiation, the participants are trying to reach an agreement over m issues which we denote as $I = \{1, ..., m\}$. For example, in the case of a smart grid collective these can include the price at which the energy is traded, the need for green energy utilization, the willingness to share, etc. Every issue i is discrete; i.e. each issue can take a finite number of n_i values which we denote as:

$$V_i = \left\{ x_1^{(i)}, x_2^{(i)}, ..., x_{n_i}^{(i)} \right\}. \tag{1}$$

The *negotiation domain* $\Omega = V_1 \times V_2 \times \ldots \times V_m$ is the set of all possible negotiation outcomes. A negotiation outcome $\omega \in \Omega$ is thus an m–tuple that assigns a single value $\omega_i \in V_i$ to every issue i, such as "0.15 €/kWh" for the issue "price of energy to be traded".

Negotiation Protocol. The *negotiation protocol* dictates the actions that can be performed by an agent at any given moment. We will be using the widely used *Alternating Offers Protocol*, where each participant gets a *turn* per round [8]. On each turn, the agent can accept or propose a counter-offer (or *bid*) to the last offer by the opponent.

A negotiation *deadline* can be specified as the maximum number of negoti-ation *rounds*, or in real time quantities. If an agreement has not been achieved within the time-frame specified by the deadline, the negotiation ends and all participants obtain utility zero. We assume the negotiation deadline is universal and known to all participating agents [8,13].

Preference Profile. Every user participating in a negotiation has a specific set of preferences regarding the possible outcomes. The preference profile is given by an ordinal ranking over the set of possible outcomes: an outcome ω is said to be weakly preferred over an outcome ω' if $\omega \succeq \omega'$ where $\omega, \omega' \in \Omega$, or strictly preferred if $\omega \succ \omega'$.

Under mild assumptions [18], preference profiles can be expressed in a cardinal way through the use of a *utility function* such that:

$$\omega \succeq \omega' \iff u(\omega) \geq u(\omega'). \tag{2}$$

There is an outcome of minimum acceptable utility which is called *reservation value* [5,12].

We will focus on *linear additive utility functions*, in which every issue i's value is calculated separately according to an evaluation function v_i as follows:

$$u : \Omega \mapsto [0,1] \subseteq \mathbb{R} \quad \text{with} \quad u(\omega) = \sum_{i=1}^{m} w_i \cdot v_i(\omega_i), \tag{3}$$

$$\text{where} \quad \sum_{i=1}^{m} w_i = 1. \tag{4}$$

Here, w_i are the normalized weights that indicate the importance of each issue to the user, and $v_i(\omega_i)$ is the evaluation function that maps the ith issue value to a utility. Note that the linear utility function does not take dependencies between issues into account. Alternatively, non-linear utility functions can be incorporated to describe such dependencies [2,15,19].

Agent. The agent's *bidding strategy* defines the agent's structuring of the bids during a negotiation [4], mapping negotiation states to an action (*Acceptance*, or a *Counter-offer* in the Alternating Offers Protocol). The agent can perform better with an idea of the opponents' preferences and bidding strategy through *opponent modeling* techniques to propose bids which are more likely to be accepted [7,23].

Well-known bidding strategies include the *time-dependent bidding tactics* where the result of the decision functions is based on the time passed in the negotiation [9,13] as follows:

$$u(t) = P_{min} + (P_{max} - P_{min}) \cdot (1 - F(t)), \tag{5}$$

$$F(t) = k + (1 - k) \cdot (1 - k) \cdot t^{\frac{1}{e}}, \tag{6}$$

where P_{min}, P_{max} are the minimum and maximum accepted offers, t is the normalized[1] time $t \in [0,1]$ and $k \in [0,1]$ is the utility of the first offer. If $0 < e < 1$ the agent does not reduce its target utility in the early stages of the negotiation and concedes at the end of the deadline [9,13]. The agent that follows this type of strategy is called *Boulware*. In the opposite case of $e \geq 1$, the agent is called Conceder as it concedes to its reservation value (P_{min}) very quickly.

---

[1] The time range of a negotiation usually is $[0, D]$ where D is the deadline in rounds or time units and is normalized to the values $[0, 1]$.

User Model. The representative agent has a *user model*, which consists of the agent's beliefs about the user's preferences. We assume the agent is supplied with an initial set of answers to queries to the user, in the form of a user *ranking* $\mathcal{O} \subseteq \Omega$ of d different negotiation outcomes [24]:

$$\mathcal{O} = \left\{ o^{(1)}, o^{(2)}, \ldots, o^{(d)} \right\}, \tag{7}$$

$$\text{where } o^{(1)} \succeq o^{(2)} \cdots \succeq o^{(d)}, \quad o^{(i)} \in \Omega.$$

This set will usually only contain a fraction of all outcomes Ω and hence determines its level of uncertainty. Note that this notation allows us to denote the ith issue value of an outcome $o^{(j)} \in \mathcal{O}$ with $o_i^{(j)}$ as before. The ranking $\mathcal{O}$ can alternatively be expressed as a set of $d - 1$ pairwise comparisons:

$$\mathcal{D} = \{ (o^{(j)}, o^{(j+1)}) \mid o^{(j)} \in \mathcal{O} \text{ and } 0 < j \leq d - 1 \}. \tag{8}$$

Given the outcome ranking $\mathcal{O}$, the agent's goal is to formulate its own estimated utility function $\hat{u}(\omega)$ that approximates the real utility function $u(\omega)$ as much as possible. Establishing 'the most likely' utility function from a ranking of outcomes $\mathcal{O}$ is complicated, as there is far less information available in $\mathcal{D}$ than in $u(\omega)$. Furthermore, $\mathcal{O}$ might not contain any information about particular outcomes, especially in large domains, requiring completion of the ordering.

4   Estimating a Utility Function from a User Model

If an agent is to operate under a non-fully specified preference profile, it needs to formulate a strategy that will be able to derive a utility function from a set of pairwise comparisons of outcomes. To do so, we will extend an approach followed in [24].

Consider a ranking $\mathcal{O}$ of negotiation outcomes and the set $\mathcal{D}$ of corresponding pairwise comparisons. Given the pairwise comparisons, the same inequality should hold for the utility function of the agent (2). From the definition of the utility function (2), we can integrate the weight and each evaluator value in one variable and we rewrite (3) as:

$$u : \Omega \mapsto [0, 1] \subseteq \mathbb{R} \quad \text{with} \quad u(\omega) = \sum_{i=1}^{m} \phi_i(\omega_i), \tag{9}$$

$$\text{with} \quad \phi_i(\omega_i) = w_i \cdot v_i(\omega_i). \tag{10}$$

This results in a new discrete set of variables

$$Y = \left\{ \phi_1(x_1^{(1)}), \ldots, \phi_1(x_{n_1}^{(1)}), \phi_2(x_1^{(2)}), \ldots, \phi_2(x_{n_2}^{(2)}), \phi_m(x_1^{(m)}) \ldots, \phi_m(x_{n_m}^{(m)}) \right\}. \tag{11}$$

With one additional piece of information, estimating the utility function can be translated into a linear optimization problem with the set Y as the set of unknown variables. For each pairwise comparison between outcomes $(o, o') \in \mathcal{D}$ we derive from (2) and (9) that:

$$\sum_{i=1}^{m} \left(\phi_i(o_i) - \phi_i(o'_i) \right) \geq 0, \quad \text{with} \quad \phi_i(o_i), \phi_i(o'_i) \in Y. \tag{12}$$

We denote the above term as $\Delta u_{o,o'}$ so

$$\Delta u_{o,o'} = \sum_{i=1}^{m} \left(\phi_i(o_i) - \phi_i(o'_i) \right), \quad \Delta u_{o,o'} \geq 0. \tag{13}$$

Now, we can translate the above inequalities into a linear optimization problem using standard linear programming techniques. For this, we need to consider a set of 'slack variables' namely z. The number of slack variables $z_{o,o'}$ is equal to the number of comparisons (o, o') in $\mathcal{D}$. The linear program is formulated as:

$$\text{Minimize:} \quad F = \sum_{(o,o') \in \mathcal{D}} z_{o,o'}, \tag{14}$$

subject to the constraints (Table 1):

$$z_{o,o'} + \Delta u_{o,o'} \geq 0, \tag{15}$$

$$z_{o,o'} \geq 0, \text{ for } (o, o') \in \mathcal{D}, \tag{16}$$

$$\phi_i(x_j^{(i)}) \geq 0, \text{ for } i \in I, \ j \in \{1, 2, ..., n_i\}. \tag{17}$$

Table 1. Summary of the linear program that estimates the new utility functions parameters.

Objective function	Decision variables	Constraints
F	$Y \cup \{z_{o,o'} \mid (o, o') \in \mathcal{D}\}$	(15), (16), (17), (18)

In its current form the optimization problem yields the *trivial solution* where all $\phi_i(x_j^{(i)}) = 0, z_{o,o'} = 0$. To tackle this problem an additional constraint is required. Hence, arises the need for some additional piece of information about the preferences of the user. In our solution, the additional information is the *best* outcome for the user, i.e. the outcome of maximum utility ω^*. Note that this does not mean that we know the importance of each separate issue, but only that particular outcome that is the most desired from the user. This translates into our final constraint for the optimization problem:

$$u(\omega^*) = 1 \quad \Rightarrow \quad \sum_{i=1}^{m} \phi'_i(\omega_i^*) = 1. \tag{18}$$

From the constraints (15) and (16) we can see that

$$z_{o,o'} \geq \max\{0, \ -\Delta u_{o,o'}\}. \tag{19}$$

Given that the goal is to minimize F, **the optimal solution** will be

$$z_{o,o'}^* = \max\{0, \ -\Delta u_{o,o'}\}. \tag{20}$$

We should note at this point that, in the case that the initial judgment about the comparisons in $\mathcal{D}$ is correct, Δu_{jk} will always be positive. As a result all $z_{o,o'}$ will equal 0. This is an interesting attribute of this method, since it can determine and pinpoint errors in user judgment as well. If all the $z_{o,o'}$ are not zero after solving the linear program, there is no solution set that satisfies all the comparisons in $\mathcal{D}$. This means that at lease one stated judgment regarding the preference of two or more outcomes is wrong. This can prove very important when the agent queries the user for information, in cases where the user is not entirely sure about their preferences or does not have complete knowledge of the negotiation domain and might give wrong feedback about their own preferences. With our method these errors in user feedback can be pinpointed and addressed.

5   Experiments and Results

5.1   Setup

Scenario. To show that our proposed model is applicable in a real negotiation setting we conducted experiments in a simulation of a negotiation scenario. The scenario is inspired by the smart grid domain and refers to a fictitious energy cooperative, where different residents participate in energy exchanges. The issues of negotiation consist of the amount of energy bought or sold in different periods of time, which in electrical energy systems are called *Programme Time Units* (PTUs), and the type of energy exchanged (Green, Conventional). The possible issue values for every PTU are $\{-3\,\mathrm{kWh}, -2\,\mathrm{kWh}, \ldots, +2\,\mathrm{kWh}, +3\,\mathrm{kWh}\}$. The sign of the value corresponds to whether the user buys or sells the given amount of energy. After an agreement is reached, for every PTU the amount sold by one user is bought by the opponent. We created different preference profiles based on different energy requirements patterns.

Measures. We selected two metrics to evaluate our model: *accuracy* towards the real preference profile and *negotiation performance*.

To evaluate our model in terms of accuracy we compare the estimated weights and evaluator values compare to the real preference profile. The comparison was made in terms of 3 different accuracy measures: the *Pearson Correlation Coefficient*, the *Spearman Ranking Coefficient* of bids between the entire resulting utility space and the real utility space, and the maximum single bid utility distance in the set. The Pearson Correlation Coefficient assesses linear relationships between the two utility functions, while the Spearman Correlation assesses monotonic relations based on their rank. The accuracy measures experiments were performed on two scenarios with 3 (2 PTUs & Type of Energy) and 5 (4 PTUs & Type of Energy) issues respectively. In practice, the outcome space of the 5 issue domain is 5000 times bigger than the 3 issue one. The calculations were the result of averaging after 100 iterations for each uncertainty level.

Apart from the accuracy measures, we also investigate the influence of preference uncertainty in an actual negotiation and how well an agent performs in this setup using our utility estimation strategies. To do so, we examined the trace of the target utilities throughout a negotiation session of the *Conceder* agent, presented in Sect. 3.2. To monitor the complete negotiation trace, we pitted the Conceder agent against a *never-accepting agent*. The deadline was set at 180 rounds and the negotiation domain only on a 5-issue smart grid scenario (4 PTUs & Type of Energy).

Baseline Strategy. We tested our strategy against a simple preference estimation method called *Benchmarking Strategy*, based on the intuition that the more desired outcomes appear in the high positions of the ranked outcome set $\mathcal{O} = \left\{ o^{(1)}, o^{(2)}, \ldots, o^{(d)} \right\}$. According to this method, all issue values occurring in $o^{(i)}$ are awarded $d - i$ points (for example, the values that make up the most preferred outcome $o^{(1)}$ all receive maximum points). These scores are summed for every i and then renormalized to values between 0 and 1 to determine the final score for each value of every issue.

Weight Estimation Strategy. In some negotiation scenarios the preferences for each issue might be known but the importance of each issue to the user is not. For this case we created a simpler strategy based on our Linear Programming model where the evaluator functions are known but the weights are not. The solving strategy is exactly the same to the one presented in Sect. 4, with the difference that the unknown variables are the issue weights only, since the evaluator values are known. Hence, we replace the final constraint (18) with (4), which states that the sum of the weights must equal 1.

5.2   Results

Accuracy Measures. Figure 2 presents the accuracy of the model compared to the real preferences for 2 different domain sizes: 3 and 5 issues. The level of uncertainty is expressed as the number of outcomes that appear on the ranked set that is supplied to the agent. The first thing that we infer from the accuracy result figures is that our model becomes very accurate even with very few comparisons (less than 1% of the $d - 1$ required for a perfect ranking of the outcomes). Both our models outperform the *benchmark strategy* significantly. Especially in the Weight Estimation case, all measures rapidly converge to the desired values. This is reasonable if we consider the fact that in this case the evaluator functions are considered known, which is already a very large amount of information about the user preferences. To verify this claim, we ran a test case

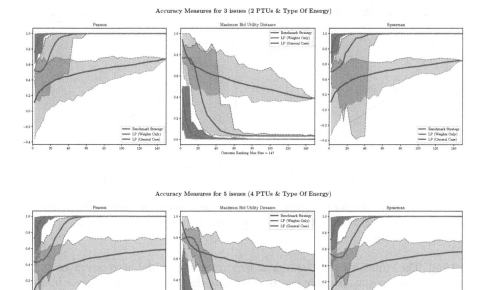

Fig. 2. Accuracy measures of simulations. The horizontal axis represents the size of the outcome ranking that is supplied to the agent and the vertical axis the different metric values.

for the 5 issue domain where the agent was supplied with 0 comparisons and the weights were set to 0.2. The results yielded Pearson and Spearman coefficient values above 0.7, which indicates relatively high accuracy even when the weights are off.

We present the results up until 150 comparisons for each experiment since all metrics converge to their final values by then. However, we need to remark that only the Spearman correlation coefficient reaches its target value of 1 in the case of a total ranking of outcomes ($d - 1$ comparisons). This means that although the actual values of the weights and corresponding utilities might not be exactly the same the ranking of outcomes is correct.

Negotiation Performance: The accuracy results suggest that our models should perform well in an actual negotiation setting. To visualize the performance of our models in an actual negotiation, we visualize the Conceder agents traces for different amounts of comparisons for a whole negotiation session (180 rounds). That is, we observe the *target utilities* that are proposed at any given round of negotiation according to the conceder strategy. Figure 3 shows these traces for different amounts of preference information when following the Benchmark Strategy and our proposed Linear Programming Strategy as an estimation

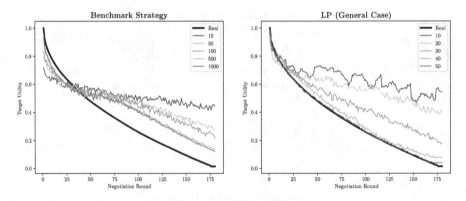

Fig. 3. Target utilities for a Conceder agent strategy under different levels of uncertainty using the *Benchmark Strategy* and the *Linear Programming Strategy*

method. The superiority of the Linear Programming model becomes evident, as with a small amount of comparisons ($d \leq 50$) the real trace is followed almost perfectly, whereas the Benchmark model does not even for a much higher amount of comparisons ($d = 1000$). For 50 comparisons, the sum over all rounds of the average bid distances (averaged over 100 iterations) of the trace compared to the real trace was 2.564 following the Baseline strategy, compared to 0.120 following the Linear Programming strategy.

The negotiation results mirror the knowledge we obtained from the accuracy experiments. Given that at around 50 outcomes our method yields a Spearman's rank coefficient of $\rho \simeq 1$, the user model becomes fully accurate, hence the negotiation performance is not be affected. For the benchmark strategy on the other hand, the trace never converges to the real profile. This is explained by the fact that the benchmark method takes only the evaluator values into account during its reasoning and not the issues' importance (weights) at all. This can result at wrong issue weights, which in turn affects the performance negatively.

6   Conclusion

We presented an information model that is based on categorical data and has the form of a partial order of outcomes. This form of information may be readily elicited by asking a user to compare outcomes. Given this input, the agent needs to find the best sequence of queries that elicits as much preference information as possible while minimizing user bother.

We created a decision model that utilizes the pairwise comparison information, and through the use of linear programming we estimated a linear additive utility function, which the agent will use to negotiate. The proposed decision model was tested in terms of user-model accuracy and negotiation performance. The accuracy results showed that even with a very small numbers of comparisons (less than 1% of a total ranking of outcomes), the agent can reach high levels of accuracy (Spearman $\rho \simeq 1.0$). We achieved similar results in performance tests, with negotiation agreement utilities reaching no-uncertainty levels. Finally, our proposed Linear Programing model outperformed a baseline model both in terms of accuracy, as well as performance.

In a nutshell, we created a model that obtains incomplete ordinal preference data in the form of rankings and through the use of linear programming approximates the preferences of the user as best as possible. The results show that even given a few outcome comparisons (i.e. user queries), together with the knowledge of the overall best bid, an agent can improve the user model accuracy significantly, and negotiates well as a result.

7   Discussion and Future Work

Computerized agents poised to represent users in negotiations should do so under incomplete information about the preferences of the users they represent. This work is a first step towards a reliable way of implementing such automated negotiation under preference uncertainty.

In this work, we present a method of representing incomplete user-preference information and a decision model that utilizes rankings of outcomes to elicit as much information as possible. We focus on bilateral negotiation, but pave the way for future work to examine how uncertainty affects an agent against multiple opponents. It is reasonable to expect that when facing more opponents the margin of error for an uncertain agent is smaller given that mistakes are more likely to be exploited.

Furthermore, our model allows the incorporation of error in user feedback and is able to pinpoint inconsistencies in user judgment, which could prove useful in cases where the agent does not have enough knowledge about the domain or is not certain about the user fidelity. The effect of judgment error could also be further examined, e.g., on a total ranking of outcomes.

One last avenue for future work would be to test the model's performance in more heterogeneous scenarios. The results show small differences in the amount of comparisons needed for high user model accuracy levels for various domains sizes. This is explained by the fact that there is only a small increase in the number of linear utility function parameters relative to the size of the outcome space. This finding may change for real-life domains without the linear attributes that we assume in our model. Possible interdependencies between negotiation issues would require non-linear optimization techniques and new and more complex preference elicitation strategies.

Acknowledgment. This work is part of the Veni research programme with project number 639.021.751, which is financed by the Netherlands Organisation for Scientific Research (NWO).

References

1. Aydoğan, R., Baarslag, T., Hindriks, K.V., Jonker, C.M., Yolum, P.: Heuristics for using CP-nets in utility-based negotiation without knowing utilities. Knowl. Inf. Syst. **45**(2), 357–388 (2015). https://doi.org/10.1007/s10115-014-0798-z

2. Aydogan, R., et al.: A baseline for non-linear bilateral negotiations: the full results of the agents competing in ANAC 2014. In: Intelligent Computational Systems: A Multi-Disciplinary Perspective, pp. 1–25. Bentham Science, July 2016. https://eprints.soton.ac.uk/399235/

3. Aydoğan, R., Yolum, P.: Learning opponent's preferences for effective negotiation: an approach based on concept learning. Auton. Agent. Multi-Agent Syst. **24**(1), 104–140 (2012)

4. Baarslag, T.: Exploring the Strategy Space of Negotiating Agents: A Framework for Bidding, Learning and Accepting in Automated Negotiation. ST. Springer, Cham (2016). https://doi.org/10.1007/978-3-319-28243-5

5. Baarslag, T., et al.: Evaluating practical negotiating agents: results and analysis of the 2011 international competition. Artif. Intell. **198**, 73–103 (2013). https://doi.org/10.1016/j.artint.2012.09.004

6. Baarslag, T., Gerding, E.H.: Optimal incremental preference elicitation during negotiation. In: Proceedings of the Twenty-Fourth International Joint Conference on Artificial Intelligence, IJCAI 2015, pp. 3–9. AAAI Press (2015). http://dl.acm.org/citation.cfm?id=2832249.2832250

7. Baarslag, T., Hendrikx, M.J.C., Hindriks, K.V., Jonker, C.M.: Learning about the opponent in automated bilateral negotiation: a comprehensive survey of opponent modeling techniques. Auton. Agent. Multi-Agent Syst. **30**(5), 849–898 (2016). https://doi.org/10.1007/s10458-015-9309-1

8. Baarslag, T., Kaisers, M.: The value of information in automated negotiation: a decision model for eliciting user preferences. In: Proceedings of the 16th Conference on Autonomous Agents and MultiAgent Systems, AAMAS 2017, pp. 391–400. International Foundation for Autonomous Agents and Multiagent Systems, Richland, SC (2017). http://dl.acm.org/citation.cfm?id=3091125.3091185

9. Baarslag, T., Kaisers, M., Gerding, E.H., Jonker, C.M., Gratch, J.: Computers that negotiate on our behalf: major challenges for self-sufficient, self-directed, and interdependent negotiating agents. In: Sukthankar, G., Rodriguez-Aguilar, J.A. (eds.) AAMAS 2017. LNCS (LNAI), vol. 10643, pp. 143–163. Springer, Cham (2017). https://doi.org/10.1007/978-3-319-71679-4_10

10. Boutilier, C., Brafman, R.I., Domshlak, C., Hoos, H.H., Poole, D.: CP-nets: a tool for representing and reasoning withconditional ceteris paribus preference statements. ArXiv e-prints, June 2011

11. Cornelio, C., Goldsmith, J., Mattei, N., Rossi, F., Venable, K.B.: Updates and uncertainty in CP-nets. In: Cranefield, S., Nayak, A. (eds.) AI 2013. LNCS (LNAI), vol. 8272, pp. 301–312. Springer, Cham (2013). https://doi.org/10.1007/978-3-319-03680-9_32

12. Fatima, S.S., Wooldridge, M., Jennings, N.R.: Optimal negotiation strategies for agents with incomplete information. In: Meyer, J.-J.C., Tambe, M. (eds.) ATAL 2001. LNCS (LNAI), vol. 2333, pp. 377–392. Springer, Heidelberg (2002). https://doi.org/10.1007/3-540-45448-9_28.   http://dl.acm.org/citation.cfm?id=648208.757345

13. Fatima, S.S., Wooldridge, M., Jennings, N.R.: Multi-issue negotiation under time constraints. In: Proceedings of the First International Joint Conference on Autonomous Agents and Multiagent Systems: Part 1, AAMAS 2002, pp. 143–150. ACM, New York (2002). https://doi.org/10.1145/544741.544775
14. Greco, S., Kadziński, M., Mousseau, V., Słowiński, R.: Robust ordinal regression for multiple criteria group decision: UTAGMS-GROUP and UTADISGMS-GROUP. Decis. Support Syst. **52**(3), 549–561 (2012). https://doi.org/10.1016/j.dss.2011.10.005
15. Ito, T., Klein, M., Hattori, H.: A multi-issue negotiation protocol among agents with nonlinear utility functions. Multiagent Grid Syst. **4**(1), 67–83 (2008)
16. Jacquet-Lagreze, E., Siskos, J.: Assessing a set of additive utility functions for multicriteria decision-making, the UTA method. Eur. J. Oper. Res. **10**(2), 151–164 (1982). https://doi.org/10.1016/0377-2217(82)90155-2
17. Jonker, C.M., Robu, V., Treur, J.: An agent architecture for multi-attribute negotiation using incomplete preference information. Auton. Agent. Multi-Agent Syst. **15**(2), 221–252 (2007). https://doi.org/10.1007/s10458-006-9009-y
18. Keeney, R., Raiffa, H.: Decisions with Multiple Objectives: Preferences and Value Trade-Offs. Wiley Series in Probability and Mathematical Statistics. Applied Probability and Statistics. Cambridge University Press (1993). https://books.google.nl/books?id=GPE6ZAqGrnoC
19. Marsa-Maestre, I., Lopez-Carmona, M.A., Velasco, J.R., Ito, T., Klein, M., Fujita, K.: Balancing utility and deal probability for auction-based negotiations in highly nonlinear utility spaces. In: IJCAI, vol. 9, pp. 214–219 (2009)
20. Mohammad, Y., Nakadai, S.: FastVOI: efficient utility elicitation during negotiations. In: Miller, T., Oren, N., Sakurai, Y., Noda, I., Savarimuthu, B.T.R., Cao Son, T. (eds.) PRIMA 2018. LNCS (LNAI), vol. 11224, pp. 560–567. Springer, Cham (2018). https://doi.org/10.1007/978-3-030-03098-8_42
21. Nguyen, D.V.: Global maximization of UTA functions in multi-objective optimization. Eur. J. Oper. Res. **228**(2), 397–404 (2013). https://doi.org/10.1016/j.ejor.2012.06.022
22. Roszkowska, E.: The application of UTA method for support evaluation negotiation offers. Optimum Stud. Ekonomiczne **2**(80), 144–162 (2016). https://doi.org/10.15290/ose.2016.02.80.11
23. Sanchez-Anguix, V., Aydoğan, R., Baarslag, T., Jonker, C.M.: Can we reach pareto optimal outcomes using bottom-up approaches? In: Aydoğan, R., Baarslag, T., Gerding, E., Jonker, C.M., Julian, V., Sanchez-Anguix, V. (eds.) COREDEMA 2016. LNCS (LNAI), vol. 10238, pp. 19–35. Springer, Cham (2017). https://doi.org/10.1007/978-3-319-57285-7_2
24. Srinivasan, V., Shocker, A.D.: Estimating the weights for multiple attributes in a composite criterion using pairwise judgments. Psychometrika **38**(4), 473–493 (1973). https://doi.org/10.1007/BF02291490

An Adversarial Algorithm for Delegation

Juan Afanador[✉], Murilo Baptista, and Nir Oren

University of Aberdeen, Aberdeen AB24 3UE, Scotland
{r01jca16,m.baptista,n.oren}@abdn.ac.uk

Abstract. Task delegation lies at the heart of the service economy, and is a fundamental aspect of many agent marketplaces. Research in computational trust considers which agent a task should be delegated to for execution given the agent's past behaviour. However, such work does not consider the effects of the agent delegating the task onwards, forming a chain of delegations before the task is finally executed (as occurs in many human outsourcing scenarios). In this paper we consider such delegation chains, and empirically demonstrate that existing trust based approaches do not handle these situations as well. We then introduce a new algorithm based on quitting games to cater for recursive delegation.

1 Introduction

Agents seeking to achieve some goal may delegate tasks to others. Such delegations seek to increase the likelihood of the task being successfully executed, given the presumption that the agent receiving the task (the *delegatee*) is willing and capable to do so, on the part of the agent delegating the task (the *delegator*). While this is the commonly adopted view, the delegatee may actually not be the best suited agent for executing the task, but rather be able to further delegate (due to its knowledge or connections) to others who are. This type of *recursive delegation* has—to our knowledge—rarely been considered in the multi-agent systems community, though it captures a common situation where, e.g., projects are repeatedly contracted and subcontracted within organisations.

We believe that existing approaches to trust are ill-suited to making delegation decisions in domains where recursive delegation is possible. This arises due to several factors, namely that (1) agents within such a system are faced with a choice of whether to execute a task, or delegate it onwards; (2) delegators must learn about the competencies of their neighbours with respect to both delegation and execution; and (3) the topology of the network of possible interactions may change. The likelihood of a task being successfully executed thus depends on multiple conditions, resulting in potentially large changes in the likelihood of successful task execution, which are difficult to handle.

In this work, we propose an algorithm that explicitly considers recursive delegation by building on quitting games [15]. We then compare the performance of this algorithm to several existing techniques, empirically demonstrating its improved behaviour. Critically, we do not consider reputation, but only direct

M. Lujak (Ed.): AT 2018, LNAI 11327, pp. 130–145, 2019.
https://doi.org/10.1007/978-3-030-17294-7_10

trust observations, meaning that evaluating our algorithm against many existing trust and reputation based approaches would be inappropriate. Instead, our evaluation concentrates on trust-based approaches for partner selection based on multi-armed bandits, namely an ϵ-greedy approach [17], UCB1 [2], Thompson Sampling [5], and the Gittins Index [7]. We describe these approaches in Sect. 2. In Sect. 3, we present our new quitting game based algorithm, providing an empirical comparison between the various approaches in Sect. 4. We discuss our results and situate them within existing work in Sect. 5, before concluding in Sect. 6.

2 Background

The problem of task delegation among partners with unknown competencies can be viewed as an exploitation/exploration problem, where partners should have tasks delegated to them (exploitation), while unknown agents should occasionally have tasks delegated to them so as to determine their competence (exploration). A common framework for modelling, precisely, this class of problems is offered by multi-armed bandit models, or multi-armed bandits (MABs) for short; an overview of which will be provided in what follows, accompanied by the algorithms used to solve them.

2.1 Multi-armed Bandits

A multi-armed bandit problem depicts a scenario where a single agent must repeatedly select one among several courses of action, obtaining a reward from this action. The repeated occurrence of an action can affect the rewards it yields, an effect modelled by a random variable which—whenever the action is performed—can cause a change to occur in the reward state underpinning the action. In the MAB model, each potential action is referred to as an *arm*, while choosing the action is referred to as *pulling an arm*.

Definition 1 (Multi-Armed Bandits—Arms). *An arm A is a tuple $\langle X, r, h, f \rangle$ where X is an ordered list of possible states of the arm, and r is a probability distribution over possible rewards, parameterised by X.*

The history *of the arm, h, is a set of pairs (x_h, l_h) where $l_h \in \mathbb{Z}$ is the number of times the arm was pulled while in the state indexed by x_h. The* current state *of the arm is the state associated with the largest index of the arm's history with a non-zero l_h.*

Denoting the set of all possible histories as H, and the index of the current state of the arm as x, f is a probability distribution over the states $[x_h, x_{h+1}]$ parameterised over H.

Definition 2 (Multi-Armed Bandits—Pulling an arm). *Pulling an arm with current state x_i and history $h = [(x_1, l_1), \ldots, (x_i, l_i), (x_{i+1}, 0), \ldots (x_n, 0)]$ will update the arm's history to h' as follows:*

$$h' = \begin{cases} [(x_1, l_1), \ldots, (x_i, l_i + 1), (x_{i+1}, 0), \ldots (x_n, 0)] & \text{if } f(h) = x \\ [(x_1, l_1), \ldots, (x_i, l_i), (x_{i+1}, 1), \ldots (x_n, 0)] & \text{otherwise} \end{cases}$$

A multi-armed bandit is then a set $\mathcal{A}$ of arms. The number of times each arm was pulled starts at zero. Pulling an arm updates the arm as described above, and—given that the arm is in state x—yields a reward R with likelihood $r(x, R)$.

A policy is a function $\mathcal{S} : [a_1, \ldots, a_n] \times [r_1, \ldots, r_n] \to \mathcal{A}$. In other words, given a sequence of arm-pulls and the rewards thus obtained, the policy specifies which arm should be pulled next. The main problem considered by the MAB literature involves identifying a policy which is in some sense optimal, e.g., which maximises rewards, or minimises regret. It has been long established that if the states of the MAB and the probability distribution of its rewards are known, the Gittins Index can be used to identify the optimal arm to pull [7].

Formally, the Gittins Index for arm i in state x_i, with a discount factor for future rewards of β, is defined as follows:

$$G(x_i) = \sup_{\sigma > 0} \frac{E[\sum_{t=0}^{\sigma-1} \beta^t r(x_i) | \text{ initial state of arm}]}{E[\sum_{t=0}^{\sigma-1} \beta^t | \text{ initial state of arm}]}$$

The Gittins Index computes the expected reward of pulling arm x_i against the cost of not pulling it, and thus identifies the arm with the highest expected reward as the one that should be pulled. Calculating the Gittins Index is computationally prohibitive [7], in response to which various numerical approximations have been proposed in the literature [3,8].

More importantly, in practice, the probability distribution of the rewards and the states of each arm may not be known. In this case, the Gittins Index may be used as a heuristic based on beliefs about rewards and arm states, which means that different ways of calculating these beliefs will result in different procedures with very distinct properties. We now describe several such heuristics addressing the MAB problem, namely UCB1 [2], ϵ-greedy [17], and Thompson Sampling [5]. We will compare the performance of our approach to these heuristics in Sect. 4.

2.2 MAB Heuristics

We begin this section by briefly describing several well-known MAB heuristics in the context of standard MABs. In Sect. 3 we detail how these heuristics must be modified to deal with recursive delegation.

UCB1. Rather than simply maximising rewards, *upper confidence bound* (UCB) algorithms, exemplified by UCB1 [2], attempt to minimise decision-theoretic regret—the difference between the expected reward obtained had the optimal arm been pulled, and the expected reward of some other arm pulling policy.

UCB1 is simple to implement and works well in practice, while guaranteeing that the achieved regret will grow only logarithmically with the number of arm-pulls that occur.

For an arm j, UCB1 tracks the average reward obtained from that arm (μ_j), and the number of times the arm has been pulled (n_j), as well as the total number of times that the MAB's arms have been pulled (n). It then picks arm j, so as to maximise an upper bound on the mean expected reward given by the following equation [2]:

$$\mu_j + \sqrt{\frac{2\ln n}{n_j}},$$

This choice guarantees that the probability of deviating from the population mean decays exponentially through time, in accordance with the Chernoff-Hoeffding inequality [10]. Once the arm has been pulled, μ_j, n_j and n are updated to identify the next arm to pull.

Thompson Sampling. This is another simple approach to selecting an arm, and does so by sampling an expected reward based on the arm's history, before selecting the arm whose sample reward is maximal. To perform such sampling, a probability distribution over the arms is required [1]. In this work we consider binary rewards, and we therefore perform our sampling using a Beta distribution, whose parameters record the number of times the arm returned a reward, and the number of times it did not. Thompson Sampling then samples each arm using this probability distribution, and selects the arm which—again, using this sampling—has the highest expected reward.

ϵ-Greedy. This heuristic selects the arm which will yield the highest expected reward with likelihood $1 - \epsilon$ [17], otherwise picking an arm at random. It is important to note that this heuristic differs from Thompson Sampling in that no sampling over the arms takes place, meaning that the best arm (in the sense of the expected reward) is always picked, unless a random arm is chosen (with likelihood ϵ).

All of the heuristics described above seek to balance exploitation (that is, selecting the arm most likely to give a high reward) with exploration (that is, learning more about the likelihood that the arms will give a reward). If the distribution governing the reward an arm provides is stationary, then these heuristics work well, and give well-understood convergence guarantees. However, in the case of recursive delegation, agents at each level learn simultaneously, meaning that the stationary distribution assumption is—until the learning stage ends—violated. It is for this reason that these heuristics function poorly when applied to recursive delegation. We conclude this section by briefly describing how we adapted the heuristics to operate in the domain of recursive delegation.

2.3   Applying MAB Heuristics to Recursive Delegation

Agents able to delegate to others must make two choices when tasked with an action, namely whether to execute the action themselves, or delegate it onwards (and in the latter case, must also decide who to delegate to). Each agent has a list of *delegatees* to which they can delegate a task. By viewing the delegatee agents as neighbours of the *delegator*, we obtain a directed graph over which a path represents a sequence of delegations.

We unify the execution/delegation decision for an agent by associating a *dummy agent* with each agent in the system, allowing the actual agent to delegate to the dummy agent, and ensuring that the dummy agent has no delegatee agents that they can pass the task onto. A task reaching the dummy agent must therefore be executed (by the agent associated with the dummy agent). Figure 1 illustrates a sample delegation network consisting of 6 agents $(a, \ldots, f)$, together with dummy agents $(a', \ldots, f')$. In this scenario, one possible sequence of delegations (also referred to as a *delegation chain*) is a, b, c, f, f'.

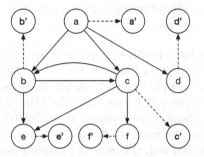

Fig. 1. A network of agents illustrating possible delegation links. Dotted lines indicate links to dummy agents which, when delegated to, execute the task.

To use the heuristics described above in a recursive context, agents make a *local* delegation decision, choosing who to pass the task to based only on their neighbours' potential to become delegatees. If a dummy agent receives the task, then it is executed, and feedback on success or failure is provided to every agent in the delegation chain. From thereon, each agent updates the statistics relevant to its delegation decision with respect to its neighbours, and the process repeats. Clearly, this approach prevents an agent from considering how others within the chain make decisions, and we claim that this affects the effectiveness of MAB heuristics in recursive delegation scenarios.

2.4 Quitting Games

We formulate an alternative approach to delegation which explicitly considers the actions available to agents through a game-theoretic mechanism based on quitting games [15]. Quitting games are multi-player stochastic games where players are faced with two choices, namely to *continue* (c) or to *quit* (q). The game ends and the players obtain rewards in two situations, whenever a *quit* action occurs, or the game reaches some terminal time. If the game does not end after the players have selected a move, i.e. simultaneous *continue* actions, then it enters another iteration where players act again, repeating this process until termination. Figure 2 illustrates a generic two-player quitting game between agents a and b.

The first entry in each terminal node appearing in Fig. 2 corresponds to the reward accrued to a, the other denotes b's reward. Whenever (c_a, q_b) is played, a receives r_{c_a} and b obtains r_{q_b}, whereas (c_a, c_b) leads to yet unrealised rewards denoted by "$\circlearrowleft$". Agents a and b plan future moves by formulating *strategies* based on the anticipation of potential $\varepsilon - equilibria$.

Definition 3 (Quitting Game—Strategies). *At every iteration t within a time horizon T, each player i is provided with a set of actions $A_i = \{c_i, q_i\}$. A strategy is a probability measure $x_t^i : T \rightarrow [0, 1]$ denoting the likelihood of playing c_i at iteration t.*

Definition 4 (Quitting Game—ε-equilibrium). *A profile or vector of strategies $\boldsymbol{x}_t$, produces a stream of rewards r_{S_t}, contributed by those players S_t who have chosen not to quit the game, giving rise to an expected reward $v_t^i(\boldsymbol{x}_t) := \boldsymbol{E}_x[r_{S_t} I_{t<\infty}]$. A solution concept states the criteria for playing a particular profile. ε-equilibrium is the solution concept employed when solving a quitting game. A profile $\boldsymbol{x}_t$ is an ε-equilibrium if the expected reward it yields plus an overhead $\varepsilon_t > 0$, is at least that of any other strategy y_t^i for every player i:*

$$v_t^i(\boldsymbol{x}_t) \geq v_t^i(\boldsymbol{x}_t^{-i}, y_t^i) - \varepsilon_t.$$

Note that if $\varepsilon_t = 0$, the above expression produces a Nash equilibrium. ε-equilibria can be further qualified as *cyclic* if there exists a point in time $\tau \in T$ when $x_t^i = x_{t+\tau}^i$, or *stationary* if $x_t^i = x_0^i$ for each $t \in T$. For instance, given $r_{q_a} > 0$, $r_{c_a} < r_{q_b}$, $r_{q_a} < r_{c_a}$, and $r_{c_b} \geq r_{q_b}$, the stationary profile $(\mathbf{x}^a, c_b)$, $x_t^a \ll 1$ is an ε-equilibrium of the game in Fig. 2. More generally, every quitting game where players prefer unilateral termination to indefinite continuation, has

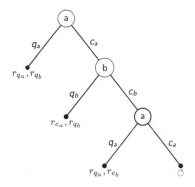

Fig. 2. Quitting game in extensive form

a cyclic subgame perfect ε-equilibrium [15], while every two and three players quitting game has a stationary ε-equilibrium [16].

To use these ideas in the context of recursive delegation, a *delegator* playing a quitting game may never see the task executed, depending on the periodicity of the cyclic equilibrium, unless the delegation process unfolds either as a recursive negotiation with the same *delegatee*, or every delegation chain is constrained to no more than two *delegatees*. While most quitting games have more than three players in the context of recursive delegation—and we therefore have no guarantees regarding ε-equilibria—these games appear to capture an important aspect of recursive delegation. Therefore, the algorithm for recursive delegation which we propose in the next section builds on quitting games and, as discussed in Sect. 4, appears to outperform other MAB based approaches in this context.

3   Approach

As indicated in Sect. 2.1, the problem of task delegation may be seen as an exploitation/exploration problem in the spirit of MABs, where *delegators* waver between delegating the task to competent partners (exploitation) and delegating the task to unknown partners (exploration). It is also apparent from Sect. 2.4 that recursive delegation has a natural predisposition to a game-theoretical treatment, due precisely to its explicit approach to recursion. In this section we present an algorithm for recursive delegation based on quitting games. Details on the corresponding adaptation of MAB heuristics, and the Gittins Index in particular, will be briefly addressed by the end of this section, procuring a comparable benchmark for Sect. 4.

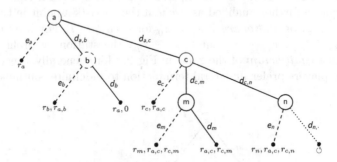

Fig. 3. Delegation game in extensive form

3.1   Delegation as a Quitting Game

Quitting games are readily adaptable to recursive delegation. They typify the occurrence of self-embedded instances of strategic interaction, resembling the replication of delegation requests along a delegation chain. That is, if a *delegator* (a) and a potential *delegatee* (b) were to play a quitting game, to determine whether to delegate a task or not, the profile (c_a, c_b) would take them both to a new iteration of the same delegation request. Unlike a standard quitting game, however, a delegation process requires distinct strategic scenarios, where, e.g., b becomes a *delegator* facing a new *delegatee*. For this reason we have adjusted quitting games to this type of interactions, preferring instead the term *delegation games* when referring to them.

The players of a *delegation game* have a *delegate* (d) action and an *execute* (e) action, and their rewards depend on future *delegate* actions. Every pair of agents populating each instance of the game consists of one former *delegatee* acting as *delegator*, and one new agent serving as potential *delegatee*. *Delegation games* can only be prolonged by (d_i, d_j) profiles for every *delegator* i and *delegatee* j—provided there are available *delegatees* and sufficient time—, and are brought to an end whenever an *execute* action occurs. Future actions are formulated in terms of *strategies* and the pursue of *ε-equilibria*.

Definition 5 (Delegation Game). *A delegation game is a tuple* $\langle N, (A_i, u^i, r^i)_{i \in N} \rangle$. *All N agents, or players, pair up with one another. A player generating a delegation request will be referred to as* delegator, *while a player at the receiving end of the delegation request will be termed* delegatee. *Potential delegatees within the reach of a* delegator *are said to be the latter's* neighbours.

Every iteration of the game comprises several instances of strategic interaction. There are as many instances in a single iteration, as available delegatees can be found. At every iteration t within a time horizon T, each player i is provided with a set of actions $A_i = \{d_i, e_i\}$.

Definition 6 (Delegation Game—Strategies and Expected Rewards). *A strategy is a probability measure* $x_t^i : T \to [0, 1]$ *indicating the likelihood of playing d_i at iteration t. Vectors of strategies $\boldsymbol{x}_t$ are termed profiles.* $r_{D_t}^i$ *is a random variable representing the rewards obtained from delegation by each player i, given the set of* delegatees D_t *at iteration t.* $u_t^i : \boldsymbol{x}_{t-1} \times \mathbb{R} \to \Delta(A_i)$ *is a measurable set-valued function that updates each player's strategies once an action e_j occurs or a terminal node is reached. Profiles induce a probability distribution which permits the computation of the expected rewards* $v_t^i(\boldsymbol{x}_t) := \boldsymbol{E}_{\boldsymbol{x}}[r_{D_t} I_{t < \infty}]$.

Figure 3 depicts one iteration of a (deterministic) *delegation game*. Agents a, b, c, m and n are arranged in a tree-like structure, where b and c are a's *neighbours*, m and n are c's *neighbours*, while b and m have no *neighbours*, and n is linked to another unspecified tree which allows delegation to continue. a has to decide between choosing a *delegatee* from $\{b, c\}$ or executing the task itself i.e. it has to decide whether to play $d_{a,b}$, $d_{a,c}$ or e_a.

Each one of the three branches radiating from a, in Fig. 3, exemplifies an absorbing state of a *delegation game*. a can play e_a and perform the task itself. It can also delegate the task to b, in which case b might accept the task by playing e_b, or not by playing d_b, thus returning the task to a and forcing the occurrence of e_a. In each case, a and b receive $(r_a, 0), (r_{a,b}, r_b)$ and $(r_a, 0)$, respectively. Alternatively, a could delegate to c. If n decides to play e_n, it receives r_n, while

c and a obtain $r_{c,n}$ and $r_{a,c}$. The rewards of any agent in the delegation chain emanating from n's *neighbour*, will not be realised until some agent plays an *execute* action, the delegation process reaches a terminal node like b, or the time horizon is exhausted.

When rewards are subject to stochastic processes, the selection of an action has to be expressed in terms of strategic profiles $(\mathbf{x}_t)$, as in Definition 6. The probability distribution these profiles induce is then used to calculate the expected rewards (v_t^i). By contrasting expected rewards in the manner of an ε-equilibrium, *delegators* and *delegatees* select a particular strategy, which once played provokes the respective information states to update (u_t^i). These ideas on how a *delegation game* operates, are presented in Algorithm 1.

Algorithm 1. Delegation Game (DIG)

Input: $P := \{a_i, ad_i\}_{i \in N}$: Tuple of agents and their neighbours, r: Array of sampled rewards.

Output: S: Sequence of agents receiving a delegation request, x: Array of mixed strategies.

1: **function** DIG(P_i)
2:     $S \leftarrow \{S_i\}_{i \in N},\ x \leftarrow \{x_i\}_{i \in N},\ r \leftarrow \{r_i\}_{i \in N}$
3:     **for** j=1$\rightarrow N$ **do**
4:         $ad_j \leftarrow \{a_k\}_{k \neq j \in B \subset N},\ r_j \leftarrow \{\mathcal{U}(r_{j,0}, r_{j,T})\}_{j \in B \subset N},\ S_j \leftarrow \emptyset, x_j \leftarrow 0$
5:         **for** $a_k \in ad_j$ **do**
6:             $x_{j,k} = \frac{r_{j,1} - r_{j,0}}{r_{j,k} - r_k}$
7:             $x \leftarrow x \cup \{x_{j,k}\}$
8:         **while** $(x \neq \emptyset) \wedge (\exists j [S_j == \emptyset])$ **do**
9:             $m \leftarrow argmax_{j \in ad_j}(r)$
10:             **if** $(random() < x_{j,m})$ **then**
11:                 **if** $a_m \in S_j$ **then**
12:                     Update $x_{j,m}, r_{j,m}$
13:                 **else** $a_m \notin S_j$
14:                     $S_j \leftarrow S_j \cup \{a_m\}$
15:                     **return** LEARN$(P_m; r_m, x_m)$
16:             **else**
17:                 a_j executes the task
18:                 $S_j \leftarrow \emptyset$
19:     **return** (S, x)

1: **function** LEARN$(P_i; r_i, x_i)$
2:     **if** $r_{i,0} \leq r_{i,1}$ **then**
3:         a_i executes the task
4:         Update $x_{k,i}, r_{k,i}$
5:     **else**
6:         **return** DIG(P_i)

In Algorithm 1, a set $B \subset N$ of neighbours is assigned to each of the N agents, and their respective rewards sampled from an uniform distribution (line 4). The resulting initial state allows the computation of individual mixed strategies i.e. the probabilities of delegating, whenever pairs of agents and neighbours engage in a delegation request (line 6). Note that the notation is preserved except for $r_{.,1}$ and $r_{.,0}$, denoting the rewards of executing the task given a *delegatee's* willingness to further delegate or not. As long as there are neighbours who have not received such a request, despite holding a positive probability of delegating, the selection of the one with the highest expected pay-off will take place (lines 8 and 9), seeking a Nash equilibrium. If capable of executing the task, as given by a random "state of nature" (line10), this latter agent will have to weigh up the possibility of passing the task down the delegation chain or attempting its completion, thereby triggering a learning process (lines 11–15).

3.2   Delegation as Nested MABs

We now specify a second heuristic which treats recursive delegation as a set of nested MABs, and where each agent makes a local decision regarding how to delegate based on an approximation to the Gittins Index. This heuristic is described in Algorithm 2.

Algorithm 2 is initialised in the same manner as Algorithm 1. It implements the Gittins Index through a beta reputation mechanism captured in lines 16–19, which feeds the numerical approximation to the index as specified in lines 8–10. The former is but a counter of successful delegation events, acting as a wrapper of the latter over recursive calls. In this way, monitoring behaviour is accounted for with a binary random variable keeping track of successful and failed choices.

The main procedure in Algorithm 2 is Brezzi and Lai's proposal of a MAB optimal policy. For a large number of trials, and a time-discounting rate $c \in [0.8, 1]$—as calibrated by Brezzi and Lai [3] for efficient performance—, the following closed-form function is used to approximate the Gittins Index [3]:

$$G(T) \approx \mu + \sqrt{\frac{\mu(1-\mu)}{T+1}} \psi \left(\frac{1}{(T+1)^c} \right);$$

where μ is the mean of the compound distribution of the random variable indicating a successful delegation, and

$$\psi(t) = \begin{cases} \sqrt{t/2} & , t \leq 0.2 \\ 0.49 - (0.11t)^{-1/2} & , t \in (0.2, 1] \\ 0.63 - (0.26t)^{-1/2} & , t \in (1, 5] \\ 0.77 - (0.58t)^{-1/2} & , t \in (5, 15] \\ \{2log(t) - loglog(t) - log(16\pi)\}^{1/2} & , otherwise \end{cases}$$

approximates the boundary of the continuation region, delineating the set of iterations for which it is suboptimal to stop the exploration of potential delegatees.

Algorithm 2. Dynamically Indexed Delegation (DID)

Input: $P := \{a_i, ad_i\}_{i \in N}$: Tuples of agents and their neighbours, δ: Array of time-discounting parameter.

Output: S: Sequence of agents receiving a delegation request, μ: Array of probabilities of successful delegation.

1: **function** DID$(P_i; \delta_i)$
2:     $S \leftarrow \emptyset, \mu \leftarrow \{\mu_i\}_{i \in N}, \mu_i \sim Beta(1,1)$
3:     **for** i=1$\rightarrow N$ **do**
4:         $ad_i \leftarrow \{a_j\}_{j \neq i \in K}, \delta_i \leftarrow [0.8, 1),$
5:         $CountSuccess_{a_i} \leftarrow 0, CountFailure_{a_i} \leftarrow 0$
6:         $\alpha_i \leftarrow CountSuccess_{a_i}, \beta_i \leftarrow CountFailure_{a_i}$
7:     **for** i=1$\rightarrow N$ **do**
8:         $\mu_i \leftarrow \frac{1}{(1+\beta_i/\alpha_i))}$
9:         $G_{i,j} \leftarrow \mu_j + (\frac{\mu_j(1-\mu_j)}{\alpha_j+\beta_j+1})^{1/2}\psi(1/(\alpha_j + \beta_j + 1)log(\delta_i^{-1}))$
10:        $m \leftarrow argmax(\{G_{i,k}\}_{k \in ad_i})$
11:        **if** $a_m \neq a_i$ **then**
12:            $S \leftarrow S \cup \{a_m\}$
13:            **return** $DID(P_m; \delta_m)$
14:        **else**
15:            Self-execute
16:        **if** $Outcome == True$ **then**
17:            $CountSuccess_{a_m} \leftarrow CountSuccess_{a_m} + 1$
18:        **else**
19:            $CountFailure_{a_m} \leftarrow CountFailure_{a_m} + 1$
20:        **return** $Outcome$

---

4 Evaluation

Having described our MAB and quitting game based heuristics, we now turn to evaluating their effectiveness. We begin this section by detailing our experimental setup, following which we describe our experiments and results.

4.1 Experimental Setup

Our evaluation consisted of running the various heuristics over 1000 delegation requests, each run over 100 different graphs representing different possible initial states. The algorithms were tested on two types of structures: 4-level directed trees (as in Fig. 2), and networks of randomly formed neighbourhoods (as in Fig. 1). The trees have a branching factor of 5 neighbours per node, with a final population of 156 agents. The random networks have a fixed population of 100 agents, some of which may not be reachable. Agents in random networks also possess 5 neighbours each, sampled from all available nodes excluding their immediate predecessor and the root.

We experimented with different parameters for each of the heuristics. For ϵ-greedy, ϵ takes on values between 0.05 and 0.1 [17]. Thompson Sampling was recovered from a Bayesian variation of the same algorithm with no exploration.

The discount factor in DID ranged within [0.8, 1), as to remain consistent with the closed-form approximation to the Gittins Index [7]. The initial probabilities of delegation were sampled from an uninformative Beta distribution.

For each heuristic we measured the probability that a delegation would be successful after the nth iteration (averaged over the 100 runs), as well as the regret value for the action. This latter value is computed as the difference between the probability that a task would be successfully executed if the optimal delegation path was followed, and the final likelihood of successful execution.

4.2   Results

Figure 4a shows the performance of the various heuristics over directed trees. We observe that the DIG heuristic significantly increases the chance of successful delegation when compared to other approaches. Thompson Sampling appears to outperform the remaining approaches, but takes longer to approach its optimal value than other techniques.

With regards to regret, we observe (Figs. 4b and 5a) that DIG by maximising the likelihood of successful delegation also minimises its regret, and that this relationship holds for the remaining algorithms. Furthermore, none of the algorithms obtain levels of regret greater than UCB1's theoretical upper regret bound (Fig. 4b and Table 1).

Turning to random networks, Fig. 6a demonstrates that DIG and DID outperform all other approaches. It appears that the rate of convergence for Thompson sampling significantly lags behind the other approaches. Our results for regret (Fig. 6b) are similar to those for directed trees.

If we consider the length of the resulting delegation chains, we observe that in directed trees (Fig. 5b) all algorithms occasionally create chains which span the height of the tree, though ϵ-greedy algorithms usually converge to a single delegation instance. We believe that the latter is due to the algorithm's focus on exploitation over exploration. In the case of random networks, this behaviour changes, with ϵ-greedy exploring the network at length, while other approaches quickly converge to different delegation chain lengths.

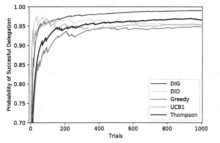

(a) Probabilities of Successful Delegation

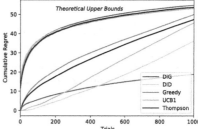

(b) Regret Metrics and Upper Bounds

Fig. 4. Comparative performance over directed trees

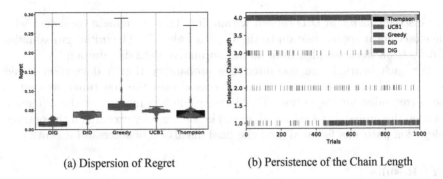

(a) Dispersion of Regret   (b) Persistence of the Chain Length

Fig. 5. Comparative performance over directed trees

On account of the difference in the number of neighbours, and the presence of cycles, the variance of marginal regret is less uneven, but larger on average in the random graph case. There are more pronounced differences in the levels of regret as new agents are discovered every trial, as shown in Fig. 7b. Indeed, DIG settles at a 2-agent long chain, leading to exceptional levels of successful delegation. In this sense, DIG can be considered the most efficient algorithm.

Table 1. Relative performance over Directed Trees (D.T.) and Random Networks (R.N.)

Algorithm	Network structure	Probability of successful delegation	Mean rate of convergence[a]	Mean regret
DIG	D.T.	**0.975**	*0.498*	**4.60**
	R.N.	**0.985**	*0.434*	**10.821**
DID	D.T.	0.958	0.363	7.766
	R.N.	0.974	0.324	15.842
ϵ-Greedy	D.T.	0.927	0.437	31.352
	R.N.	0.931	**0.608**	17.596
Thompson Sampling	D.T.	0.947	**0.731**	21.281
	R.N.	0.906	0.227	21.779
UCB1	D.T.	0.948	0.387	13.995
	R.N.	0.858	0.172	33.689

[a]The mean rate of convergence was approximated by the error of deviating from a probability of delegating equal to 1 (e_t), over the first 175 trials i.e., $q \approx \frac{log(e_{t+1}/e_t)}{log(e_t/e_{t-1})}, t \in \{1,\ldots,175\}$. The cut-off point was obtained through the Welch method [19].

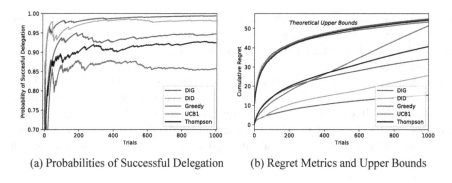

(a) Probabilities of Successful Delegation   (b) Regret Metrics and Upper Bounds

Fig. 6. Comparative performance over random networks

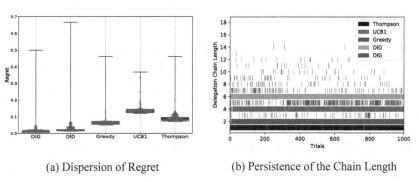

(a) Dispersion of Regret   (b) Persistence of the Chain Length

Fig. 7. Comparative performance over random networks

5 Discussion and Future Work

Our results demonstrate that the DIG strategy outperforms other approaches when dealing with recursive delegation problems. As future work, we intend to investigate the theoretical properties of the heuristic to further understand its salient features and the conditions behind its performance.

We believe that our approaches operate better than existing heuristics due to the violation of the stationarity assumption in our domain. Our DID heuristic has similarities to the manner in which the generalised Gittins Index is computed under weaker forms of stationarity [11], suggesting the incorporation of evolutionary algorithms into future research in the domain of recursive delegation.

By construction, delegation in our MAB framework conforms to a multilevel linear program, where new delegation problems lie embedded in the constraints restricting every agent's objective. We intend to validate a similar mapping between DIG and multilevel bilinear programs against recent work on (stochastic) multilevel optimisation problems [6], tracing back to questions on stationarity and the pertinence of evolutionary, hierarchical, and genetic algorithms [9].

Another strand of future work which we are actively pursuing involves increasing the empirical faithfulness of our approach. This means introducing resource constraints, explicit rewarding schemes, and potential costs to the delegation problem, by borrowing ideas from the principal-agent theory literature [20], and results from coalitional game theory [14].

There is little work in the computational trust community dealing with recursive delegation. To our knowledge, the only publications which address these issues are [13] and [4]. In the former, the authors consider a supply chain problem and model it via recursive MABs, but focus on budget constraints for each arm, solving local bandit problems in parallel to identify trustworthy suppliers. In [4] the authors evaluate how simple algorithms to assign responsibilities for task delegation failures across delegation chains, may affect the performance of the system.

6   Conclusions

In this paper we described the recursive delegation problem, and empirically demonstrated that a heuristic based on quitting games outperforms different multi-arm bandit based techniques, namely UCB1, ϵ-greedy, Thompson Sampling, and Lai and Brezzi's numerical approximation to the Gittins Index. Our heuristic outperforms these approaches both with regards to regret, and the probability of successful delegation over different graph topologies.

Our results are directly applicable to multi-agent system marketplaces, and address an oft-ignored issue in computational trust research, which usually considers only non-recursive task delegation. In this regard, extensions to include explicit rewarding schemes and resource constrains seem a fruitful direction of future research. We believe they will give rise to decisive contributions to computational trust theory and AI, if further pursued along the lines of hierarchical reinforcement learning in non-stationary environments [12,18].

References

1. Agrawal, S., Goyal, N.: Analysis of Thompson sampling for the multi-armed bandit problem. In: Conference on Learning Theory, pp. 39–1 (2012)
2. Auer, P., Fischer, P.: Finite-time analysis of the multiarmed bandit problem. Mach. Learn. **47**, 235–256 (2002)
3. Brezzi, M., Lai, T.L.: Optimal learning and experimentation in bandit problems. J. Econ. Dyn. Control. **27**(1), 87–108 (2002)
4. Burnett, C., Oren, N.: Sub-delegation and trust. In: AAMAS, pp. 1359–1360. IFAAMAS (2012)
5. Chapelle, O., Li, L.: An empirical evaluation of Thompson sampling. In: Advances in Neural Information Processing Systems, pp. 2249–2257 (2011)
6. Franke, S., Mehlitz, P., Pilecka, M.: Optimality conditions for the simple convex bilevel programming problem in banach spaces. Optimization **67**(2), 237–268 (2018)
7. Gittins, J., Glazebrook, K., Weber, R.: Multi-Armed Bandit Allocation Indices. Wiley, Hoboken (2011)

8. Gutin, E., Farias, V.: Optimistic Gittins indices. In: Advances in Neural Information Processing Systems, pp. 3153–3161 (2016)
9. He, X., Zhou, Y., Chen, Z.: Evolutionary bilevel optimization based on covariance matrix adaptation. IEEE Trans. Evol. Comput. (2018)
10. Hoeffding, W.: Probability inequalities for sums of bounded random variables. J. Am. Stat. Assoc. **58**(301), 13–30 (1963)
11. Koulouriotis, D.E., Xanthopoulos, A.: Reinforcement learning and evolutionary algorithms for non-stationary multi-armed bandit problems. Appl. Math. Comput. **196**(2), 913–922 (2008)
12. Kulkarni, T.D., Narasimhan, K., Saeedi, A., Tenenbaum, J.: Hierarchical deep reinforcement learning: integrating temporal abstraction and intrinsic motivation. In: Advances in Neural Information Processing Systems, pp. 3675–3683 (2016)
13. Sen, S., Ridgway, A., Ripley, M.: Adaptive budgeted bandit algorithms for trust development in a supply-chain. In: Proceedings of the 2015 International Conference on Autonomous Agents and Multiagent Systems, AAMAS 2015, pp. 137–144. International Foundation for Autonomous Agents and Multiagent Systems, Richland (2015). http://dl.acm.org/citation.cfm?id=2772879.2772900
14. Skibski, O., Michalak, T.P., Rahwan, T., Wooldridge, M.: Algorithms for the shapley and myerson values in graph-restricted games. In: Proceedings of the 2014 International Conference on Autonomous Agents and Multi-agent Systems, pp. 197–204. International Foundation for Autonomous Agents and Multiagent Systems (2014)
15. Solan, E., Vieille, N.: Quitting games. Math. Oper. Res. **26**(2), 265–285 (2001)
16. Solan, E., Vieille, N.: Quitting games-an example. Int. J. Game Theory **31**(3), 365–381 (2003)
17. Sutton, R.S., Barto, A.G.: Reinforcement Learning: An Introduction. MIT Press, Cambridge (2011)
18. Vezhnevets, A.S., et al.: Feudal networks for hierarchical reinforcement learning. arXiv preprint arXiv:1703.01161 (2017)
19. Welch, P.D.: The statistical analysis of simulation results. In: The Computer Performance Modeling Handbook, vol. 22, pp. 268–328 (1983)
20. Zhang, H., Zenios, S.: A dynamic principal-agent model with hidden information: sequential optimality through truthful state revelation. Oper. Res. **56**(3), 681–696 (2008)

Policies to Regulate Distributed Data Exchange

Samuel R. Cauvin(✉), Nir Oren, and Wamberto W. Vasconcelos

Department of Computing Science, University of Aberdeen, Aberdeen, UK
{r01src15,n.oren,w.w.vasconcelos}@abdn.ac.uk

Abstract. Data sharing is becoming an integral part of many aspects of our daily lives. We propose a method for controlling access to data and knowledge through fine-grained, user-specified explicitly represented policies. We present an overview of a policy formalism and mechanisms to facilitate distributed data sharing. We provide a breakdown of how our approach defines compliance and violation, specifically providing a new outlook on violation of permissions within the context of data sharing. We also examine how our mechanisms have been adapted to support socially responsible interactions between participants, whilst still providing them with control over their own data. We also explore a series of planned experiments investigating how users understand and interact with policies in a simplified version of our formalism.

1 Introduction

Data sharing is becoming an integral part of many aspects of our daily lives. With the emergence of data-driven technologies that employ intelligent sensor devices in an environment, such as smart cities [5,45] and smart homes [18], data exchange and data sharing has to be addressed. While data sharing can provide benefits and services to users, it is important to regulate it to allow users to retain control of their data, addressing issues related to information governance. Not only is it important to give control to individual users, but to maximise the benefit to all users in data-sharing ecosystems.

Usually, data sharing is specified (and constrained) through the use of data access policies. These policies specify how data may (or may not) be accessed, changed and used. The traditional management of typical access policies tends to be centralised [1,11,14,40]. This poses a number of problems, such as information ownership and reliance on a central authority that may allow the manipulation of these policies, and which answers queries regarding current policy settings for data. A counter proposal to such a centralised form of policy management is provided in [37] which describes a distributed architecture for normative regulations.

This research is partially sponsored by the EPSRC grant EP/P011829/1, funded under the UK Engineering and Physical Sciences Council Human Dimensions of Cyber Security call (2016).

© Springer Nature Switzerland AG 2019
M. Lujak (Ed.): AT 2018, LNAI 11327, pp. 146–161, 2019.
https://doi.org/10.1007/978-3-030-17294-7_11

We envisage a data-sharing economy where data can be safely exchanged between participants. In addition to data, we also consider participants sharing data access policies amongst themselves. To achieve this, we present the following elements: an information model to support fine-grained policies, and a proposal for a distributed data-sharing infrastructure.

We present a language to specify data access policies that is based on deontic concepts such as prohibition, permission and obligation. We equipped this language with fully distributed mechanisms to support participants making decisions on how they should go about sharing data in a socially responsible manner. That is, we enable participants to anticipate consequences and minimise their negative effects where possible.

In this paper we present a language and associated mechanisms which are sufficiently expressive to capture many data exchange scenarios but that can also be presented at a higher level that we hope will aid users with less technical experience in creating and interpreting policies. This language draws on existing proposals, selecting some of their features and adding others where required, to build a minimal but sufficient feature set to address data exchange scenarios.

We aim to answer the following research questions:

Q1 What information/knowledge is needed to represent policies to regulate data sharing in a machine-processable fashion?
Q2 What mechanisms can we provide, using the information model and their representations (from Q1), to enable rational decisions about data sharing and policy-compliance?
Q3 Can our information model and their representations (from Q1) and mechanisms (from Q2) be sufficient to support data sharing in a distributed and secure fashion?

In this paper we will primarily focus on Q1, but some detail will be provided on how we are addressing Q2 and Q3.

In Sect. 2, we present an outline of our approach, including details of its important distributed aspects. In Sect. 3 we provide details of our policy language designed to regulate data exchange between peers. Section 4 introduces the mechanisms that drive our solution and how they are adapted to maximise social welfare. Section 5 discusses related work and in Sect. 6 we conclude with a discussion of what we have achieved and what we plan to do as future work.

2   A Data Exchange Economy

Our approach builds on work on peer-to-peer networks [4,34], in which participants (whether sensors, individuals, or companies) are peers, and where each of them is a self-interested party taking part in an economy where data is being exchanged. Peers hold a unique identifier, which is distributed by a central authority. This central authority also provides peers with neighbours to communicate with.

As we work in a fully distributed environment, each of our peers holds their own (possibly incomplete) information about other peers. Peers collect information as they interact with other peers, storing records of all interactions they take part in. As our peers gather additional information about the peer-to-peer network (e.g., data, goals, and policies of other peers), we allow them to exchange this information, in addition to just exchanging data.

Every peer defines a set of policies that determine how they will interact with other peers. These policies can be updated as time passes to reflect changes in the peers' goals or knowledge about other peers. Our policies may express general regulatory statements such as for example, "no drug records and medical records can be obtained by the same party", or more specific, such as "I will only provide 10 records to each person". Our peers function autonomously, exchanging data with respect to their policies, and any goals (get this piece of data, send this piece of data to as many peers as possible, etc.) they have been given. Users do not influence the data exchange process directly, which is one way we ensure that all participants follow our mechanisms/transaction protocol.

Since our peers function independently of any central authority, it is important that our solution has a secure way to determine what events occurred in the past. For instance, to ensure no more than ten records of data are provided, we have to be able to verify how many records were provided in previous interactions. Without a central storage location, we turn to distributed storage. We considered current distributed ledger technologies, such as Blockchain [16,25], but concluded that these would provide too many unnecessary features. For simplicity, we created a solution where peers maintain a set of records, accessible only to themselves, of any transaction they had been a part of. These transaction records cannot be tampered with and do not need to be synchronised amongst peers. Moreover, records can only be accessed through our mechanisms.

Another challenge is how to apply and enforce penalties without having any kind of enforcing body. In our case, penalties are accrued by violating policies, and our mechanisms have built-in functionality to penalise peers. Our proposed solution establishes a barrier for entry, in which peers must pay to participate in "cycles", that is, a fixed unit of time within the network. We impose penalties as "penalty cycles" where, for the duration of that cycle, a peer's ability to participate in the network will be limited. The peer will respond to incoming messages, but will not perform any beneficial actions, such as sending data requests. This is not a penalty that can be bypassed without leaving the network, as it is built into the mechanisms through which the peer participates in the network. If a peer does leave the network, and manages to spoof their identity, they will have successfully avoided the penalty. They will, however, potentially have lost access to data they could previously access, as the policies which permitted them access will not necessarily apply to their new identity.

3   Policy Language

We have proposed an information model and associated formal syntax for a policy language designed to regulate data exchange. We will give a short overview of some of the necessary concepts for this language here, before looking more in depth at the structure of a policy.

Policies make use of predicates to describe the conditions in which they apply, and the actions which they regulate. These predicates have been designed to describe our data exchange scenarios, and provide a convenient way to capture concepts of data exchange, and support the back-end mechanisms of our framework. These predicates can be conveniently changed and adapted to fit other domains, so long as appropriate supporting mechanisms are available.

We use the following three atoms within our predicates: *identity* which refers to the identity of a specific peer (*pId*), or the identity of a group of peers (*gId*); *data* which identifies a specific type of data (d_i), for instance, temperature records or GPS data; and *time* which uses cycles (the time taken for a peer to perform a fixed set of operations) to document the relative passing of time.

The primary interactions our peers have with each other are through transactions, that is, a record of predicates establishing an exchange between two peers regulated by policies. Peers hold a collection of predicates that represents their knowledge of the world. This collection is their knowledge base ($\hat{\mathbb{P}}$), and is subdivided into "states" ($\mathbb{P}_i$), where each state is a collection of predicates associated with a specific time cycle i.

With these concepts in place, we can now discuss our policies in more detail. Policies are defined by peers to describe how their data may be accessed by other peers. These policies may express regulatory statements such as "no more than 10 records can be accessed by any peer", "temperature records can only be accessed by members of my family", or "GPS data may be accessed, but cannot be sent on by the recipient". A policy, π, in our formalism is a tuple of the form $\langle \mathbb{C}_A, \mathbb{C}_D, m_{tgt}^{src} \mathbb{A}, u_r, u_p \rangle$, where [24]:

- $\mathbb{C}_A$ and $\mathbb{C}_D$ refer to the non-empty set of activation and deactivation conditions, respectively. Activation conditions are the predicates (and constraints) which must hold for the policy to become "active". The policy will remain active until all of the deactivation conditions hold.
- m is the deontic modality of the policy, either P, F, or O for Permission, Prohibition, and Obligation. These are the standard deontic modalities representing, respectively, what can, must not, or must be performed.
- *src* is the chain of assignment for the policy, i.e. the identities of all those who have held and passed on the policy starting with the peer who enforces it, of the form $\{pId_1, pId_2, \ldots, pId_n\}$. This set shows not just everyone who has held this policy, but the order in which they held it (i.e., pId_1 passed it to pId_2, who passed it to pId_3).
- *tgt* is the identity of the group targeted by this policy.
- $\mathbb{A}$ is the non-empty set of actions which this policy permits, prohibits, or obliges. These actions are predicates that can, for instance, allow access to data, require a peer to adopt a policy, or prohibit a peer from sending data to anyone. $\mathbb{A}$ is of the form $\{a_0, a_1, \ldots, a_n\}$. This set of actions is joined by implicit conjunctions, for permissions all actions must occur together, for prohibitions all actions must not occur together, and for obligations all actions

must occur before a deadline. Disjunctions can be modelled by having alternative policies for each of the disjuncts.

- u_r and u_p are real numbers ($u_r, u_p \in \mathbb{R}$) representing the reward/penalty accrued by compliance or violation of this policy. We will discuss compliance/violation in the next section.

This definition of policies draws together a number of proposals. The notion of activation/deactivation conditions has been well studied [23,24]. The notion of deontic modality and an associated set of actions are a standard feature of regulatory norms [22,44]. Having specific roles targeted by policies is used in many scenarios, specifically we take this from traditional role-based access control [36]. The chain of assignment is a concept taken from blockchain, used to create a so-called "audit trail" for policies. Rewards and penalties are a game theoretic concept that we adapt to allow for utility calculations, and to provide incentives to comply with our policies. For a full version of the formalism associated with our language we refer readers to the following technical document [8].

Let us take the three example policies we gave above and represent them in our formalism. Some of the representations below have been simplified for presentation, we will note in the text below each example any simplifications which have been made.

Example 1. "No more than 10 records can be accessed by each peer"

$$\pi_1 = \begin{pmatrix} recordsAccessed(g_{any}, d_{any}, -\infty, +\infty, n), \ n < 10, \\ recordsAccessed(g_{any}, d_{any}, -\infty, +\infty, n), \ n \geq 10, \\ \mathsf{P}^{\{pId_1, pId_2\}}_{gId_{any}} \ access(d_{any}, gId_{any}, 10), \\ 5, 10 \end{pmatrix}$$

This policy allows any peer to access 10 records of any data. This policy is active when fewer than 10 records of any data have been accessed (for all time, between $-\infty$ and $+\infty$). This policy deactivates when 10 or more records of any data have been accessed (for all time). We have simplified this policy slightly for presentation, as the *access* action would need to refer to 10, minus the number of records accessed so far. This would be achieved in our formalism through variables and constraints.

Example 2. "Temperature records can only be accessed by members of my family"

$$\pi_2 = \begin{pmatrix} \top, \\ \bot, \\ \mathsf{P}^{\{pId_4\}}_{gId_1} \ access(d_1, gId_1, \infty), \\ 2, 0 \end{pmatrix}$$

This policy allows members of a family (represented by group gId_1) to access as many temperature records (represented by data type d_1) as they like. The policy is always active (vacuously true $\top$), and never deactivates (vacuously false $\bot$).

3.1   Policy Compliance/Violation

With a definition of a policy (and related concepts) in place, we can now discuss the notion of policy compliance and violation. That is, how do we determine whether a peer is complying with, or violating, a given policy? In all cases, a policy must be active when a transaction takes place for a peer to be in compliance/violation with it. A policy π is active in state $\mathbb{P}_i$ if there exists a state $\mathbb{P}_j$ prior to $\mathbb{P}_i$ where the activation conditions held, and there is no state between $\mathbb{P}_j$ and $\mathbb{P}_i$ where the activation or deactivation conditions hold. If there is a more recent state where the activation conditions hold, this should be used as $\mathbb{P}_j$ instead – if we consider situations where a policy has activated, deactivated, and then activated again. We assume there exists a predicate $active(\pi, \widehat{\mathbb{P}}, i)$ which returns whether policy π is active in state $\mathbb{P}_i$ (from a sequence of states $\widehat{\mathbb{P}}$). The full specification of active() and its auxiliary functions are detailed in the following technical document [8].

We define two predicates which determine, respectively, whether a policy π was complied/violated in state $\mathbb{P}_i$ (from a sequence of states $\widehat{\mathbb{P}}$), $complied^X(\pi, \widehat{\mathbb{P}}, i)$ and $violated^X(\pi, \widehat{\mathbb{P}}, i)$, where X stands for one of the deontic modalities $\mathsf{P}, \mathsf{F}, \mathsf{O}$. We show pseudocode for permission only as we handle these differently from existing approaches as we explain next. Our definition for prohibitions are not too different to that of permission. We will provide a short informal description of obligation compliance/violation.

Compliance and violation of a permission are where our approach differs from the standard approaches in the literature [3,15,24]. The two traditional approaches are: (1) everything is prohibited unless permitted, or (2) permissions as exceptions to prohibitions. Most approaches have issues, in particular, with the notion of violating a permission. We provide a clear definition of permission violation specifically relating to our intended scenario of a data sharing environment. A permission, in our approach, is used to provide access to data by other participants. Peers will adopt policies due to their bootstrapping (by the peers designer) or as a result of interaction with other peers. In both cases, this permission becomes an obligation to provide data *when requested* that a peer is permitted to access [20,26]. So a permission is complied with when data, on request by a permitted peer, is provided by the holder of the permission. A permission is violated when the data, on request by a permitted peer, is not provided by the holder of the permission. It may appear then that a permission is really just a recast obligation, but it is closer to being a combination of the two: a permission for a peer to access data, and an obligation on the data holder to provide that data. Note that, in both scenarios, the permission is complied/violated by the *holder* of that permission. This definition of permissions is a more natural way of capturing commonly occurring phenomena of data exchange.

To more clearly illustrate this, we provide the pseudocode for $complied^{\mathsf{P}}()$ in Algorithm 1. Given the proof in Theorem 1 below, we show that we can compute $violated^{\mathsf{P}}()$ as $\neg complied^{\mathsf{P}}()$.

Algorithm 1. Permission Compliance

Require: A policy $\pi = \langle \mathbb{C}_A, \mathbb{C}_D, \mathsf{m}_{tgt}^{src} \mathbb{A}, u_r, u_p \rangle$, a sequence of states $\widehat{\mathbb{P}} = \langle \mathbb{P}_0, \ldots, \mathbb{P}_i, \ldots, \mathbb{P}_n \rangle$, a cycle index i

Ensure: *Complied*, a Boolean variable indicating that π was complied with

```
 1: procedure COMPLIED^P()
 2:     Complied ← ⊥
 3:     if active(π, P̂, i) ∧ there is a request for an action a ∈ A in Pᵢ then    ▷ Without a request,
        the policy is neither complied with nor violated.
 4:         Complied ← ⊤
 5:         for all a' ∈ A do
 6:             if a' did not happen in state Pᵢ then
 7:                 Complied ← ⊥
 8:                 break
 9:             end if
10:         end for
11:     end if
12: end procedure
```

We establish below an important result, namely, that according to our definitions, compliance and violation of permissions are dual concepts, that is, if a permission is complied with then it cannot be violated, and vice-versa.

Theorem 1 (Permission Compliance/Violation Relation). *Given a policy π with modality P, a sequence of states $\widehat{\mathbb{P}}$, and a cycle to check compliance for i, compliance is equivalent to not violating. That is, $complied^P(\pi, \widehat{\mathbb{P}}, i) \equiv \neg violated^P(\pi, \widehat{\mathbb{P}}, i)$.*

Proof. Our proof assumes that there has been a request for at least one of the actions in $\mathbb{A}$. ($\Rightarrow$) The actions associated with a policy π are the set of actions $\mathbb{A}$. Compliance of a permission can only occur when all actions in $\mathbb{A}$ occur in state $\mathbb{P}_i$. Violation of a permission can only occur when there exists at least one action in $\mathbb{A}$ that does not occur in state $\mathbb{P}_i$. If a permission is complied with in state $\mathbb{P}_i$ then all actions in $\mathbb{A}$ occur in that state, and there can be no action in $\mathbb{A}$ that does not occur. Therefore, if a permission is complied with in a state, it cannot possibly be violated in that state, so $complied^P(\pi, \widehat{\mathbb{P}}, i) \Rightarrow \neg violated^P(\pi, \widehat{\mathbb{P}}, i)$. ($\Leftarrow$) To prove the opposite, if a permission is not violated in state $\mathbb{P}_i$ then there no action in $\mathbb{A}$ that does not occur in that state, and all actions in $\mathbb{A}$ have occurred. Therefore, if a permission is not violated in a state, it must always be complied with in that state, so $complied^P(\pi, \widehat{\mathbb{P}}, i) \Leftarrow \neg violated^P(\pi, \widehat{\mathbb{P}}, i)$.

As stated previously, we do not consider that our definitions of compliance/violation of prohibitions contain any details of interest. Instead, we will briefly summarise the definitions for obligations.

We establish that an obligation has been complied with by a peer pId in state i if, and only if, the policy π was active in that state $(active(\pi, \widehat{\mathbb{P}}, i))$, a transaction with pId has occurred in that state, and all of the actions ($a \in \mathbb{A}$) associated with the policy have been logged as performed by pId in one of the states i to $i + deadline(a)$ (where $deadline(a)$ returns the number of cycles that the obliged action a must be completed within). Violation is similar, except it occurs when at leasts one of the actions ($a \in \mathbb{A}$) associated with the policy has reached its deadline ($i + deadline(\mathrm{a})$) and does not have a corresponding entry from pId in any of the states i to $i + deadline(\mathrm{a})$.

4   Decision Mechanisms

Within our approach peers, once provided with policies, function autonomously. Due to this, they must be equipped with appropriate mechanisms to allow them to make decisions relating to transactions. These decisions broadly fall into two categories, depending on the peer's role in the transaction. If the peer is the one providing data (the policy holder), we call that peer the provider. If the peer is the one requesting data (from the provider), we call that peer the requestor.

4.1   Decisions by the Provider

During the course of a transaction, the provider sends a selection of their policies to the requestor. These policies are those which are relevant to the transaction in question, and represent the conditions for accessing (or not accessing) the requested data. The provider must make decisions regarding what policies to provide to the requestor during a transaction. Often this decision will be straightforward, as the provider can just provide all policies relevant to the current transaction. However, when there are conflicting policies in this set, the provider must choose which policies to send. In this case, the provider will come up with one or more conflict-free *permission* policy sets to send to the requestor. These sets can be thought of as "offers" for interactions in which the requestor can access data from the provider. Policies in these sets need not be currently active, but it must be possible for the requestor to take actions to activate them; if they are not active the requestor can suspend the transaction, complete the necessary actions, then return to complete it. For instance, a policy that can only be accessed at a certain time would be acceptable, but not one that requires the requestor to have a different identity. For each of these sets, the provider can calculate a utility value. This utility value is trivial to calculate for permissions and prohibitions, but slightly more complex for obligations. We sketch this in Definition 1, as $Profit_{Allow}(\Pi)$, which calculates the profit of a set of policies (representing an offer).

Definition 1 (Policy Profit (Provider)). *For a set of policies $\Pi = \{\pi^1, \pi^2, \ldots, \pi^n\}$, where $\pi^i = \langle \mathbb{C}_A^i, \mathbb{C}_D^i, m_{tgt^i}^{i\,src^i} \mathbb{A}^i, u_r^i, u_p^i \rangle$, with three subsets, one for each modality, $\Pi^P = \{\pi^i \in \Pi | m^i = P\}$, $\Pi^F = \{\pi^i \in \Pi | m^i = F\}$, $\Pi^O = \{\pi^i \in \Pi | m^i = O\}$, we define two profit functions, $Profit_{Allow} : \Pi \to n \in \mathbb{R}$ and $Profit_{Deny} : \Pi \to n \in \mathbb{R}$ as follows:*

$$Profit_{Allow}(\Pi) = \sum_{\pi^i \in \Pi^P} u_r^i - \sum_{\pi^j \in \Pi^F} u_p^j + \sum_{\pi^k \in \Pi^O} profitObl(\pi^k)$$

$$Profit_{Deny}(\Pi) = \sum_{\pi^i \in \Pi^F} u_r^i - \sum_{\pi^j \in \Pi^P} u_p^j$$

As noted above, the profit of obligations is less trivial to calculate, but below we outline a mechanism, $profitObl(\pi)$, which quantifies the profit of a given obligation. This calculation performs two operations, for each action associated with an obligation. First, it calculates the direct reward to the provider if the requestor completes the action. This varies depending on the type of action, for instance, an action that obliges data to be sent to the provider has a profit equal to the value of that data (a value set by each peer for each type of data). The second operation relates to the passing of obligations. Within our solution, peers are able to pass obligations between each other. When passing on an obligation, the provider forfeits any rewards or penalties that would be accrued by compliance or violation of this obligation. To calculate the utility of passing an obligation, the provider considers the likelihood of completion using its knowledge about the state of the peer-to-peer network, and weights the reward/penalty of the obligation with this value. The probability of completion is by no means exhaustive and is at best an estimate using current (potentially inaccurate) knowledge.

The provider may also come up with a single *prohibition* policy set, that is, the set of policies that will trigger if the requestor's data request is refused (prohibitions that will be complied with, and permission that will be violated). This prohibition set is only used if it is the most profitable set, calculated by $Profit_{Deny}(\Pi)$ in Definition 1.

4.2   Decisions by the Requestor

The decisions made by the requestor are the counterpart to those made by the provider. They relate to deciding whether to accept an offer for access to data via a set of policies. When there are multiple potential policy sets sent by the provider, then the requestor also must determine which, if any, to accept. This again involves determining the utility of each of the policy sets. When the requestor has received policy sets, it does not have to worry too much about fairness to the provider, as the provider will already have eliminated any policies it deems disadvantageous (for example those that have no incentive for the provider). The requestor does however have to select the fairest policy set, for both parties, from those that were provided.

We will start by detailing how the requestor can calculate the utility of a policy set, before discussing how the fairest set can then be chosen. The utility calculation varies depending on the modality of the policy:

- The utility of a permission considers the value of data that can be accessed, and the cost of any actions required to activate the associated policy. It also considers the penalty of any policies the requestor holds to *not* access that data, and the reward of any policies the requestor holds that require access to that data.
- The utility of a prohibition considers the value of data that can no longer be accessed, *or* the cost of any actions required to *deactivate* the associated policy. It also considers the penalty of any policies the requestor holds that *requires* access to that data, and the reward of any policies the requestor holds to *not* access that data.

– The utility of an obligation considers either the cost to complete the obliged actions, or the penalty of violating the obliged actions.

The utility of a policy set is the sum of the utility of the policies within that set, weighted by the likelihood of finding another (potentially better) offer. This weighting is determined by knowledge of other peers and what data they hold; most often this weighting will have a value close to one, having little effect, as a peer may have no knowledge of other potential data sources.

Each of the three modalities makes reference to the cost to complete an action. To discuss this calculation we must first discuss the main actions catered for in our formalism. These come in two broad forms: data related actions, and policy related actions. Data related actions involve obtaining, deleting, or providing data. Policy related actions involve the adoption or revocation of policies. Adoption of policies is how our peers are able to pass obligations and access rights between each other as currency. Considering these two types of actions give shape to how we can calculate the cost to complete a given action.

Data related actions consider the average length of a transaction (in cycles), and the value of the data (and quantity) involved. Policy related actions are more complex, as the requestor must consider currently held policies which are blocked by adopting a new policy, especially when that policy is obliged by another participant. In the case of policy revocation, they must also consider any penalties associated with not holding that policy if it has been obliged by another participant. In addition to this, all actions add the reward/penalty of the policy weighted by the probability of completing/not completing that action before its deadline. This considers knowledge of the peer-to-peer network, the average time to complete transactions, and current obligations.

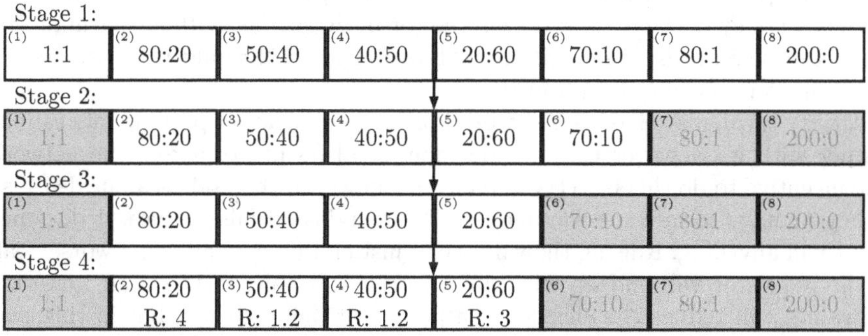

Fig. 1. An example of how the requestor chooses a policy set

As to how the requestor then chooses the fairest policy set, we use a four stage process, carried out by the requestor in the transaction. We use pareto optimality as an initial selection mechanism, and then choose the pair from those remaining with the best profit ratio. The stages are detailed below, and illustrated with an example in Fig. 1:

Stage 1. Provider and requestor compute their personal utility for each policy set. Each cell in Fig. 1 represents a policy set and associated utilities (Provider Utility : Requestor Utility).

Stage 2. The requestor removes those sets which have a value below the minimum profit of either party (less than 10 in this example).

Stage 3. The requestor selects the sets that have the highest utilities for both parties, i.e. the pareto frontier, the sets where neither utility could be improved without lowering the other, that is, there exists no other set with a higher utility for *both* parties.

Stage 4. The requestor then calculates the *normalised* ratio between the utilities (highest value divided by lowest value, to ensure proportional ratios). The requestor then chooses the fairest (closest to 1) set from these utilities, choosing the highest requestor utility if a tie occurs.

This operation is run by the requestor which may appear to give them an advantage, but it is performed as part of our blackbox mechanism without the influence of the participant, so it can be considered tamperproof. This operation ensures that profit is spread as evenly as possible between both parties, and prioritises fairness over total profit. We assume that for any given policy we can accurately compute the utility to ourselves.

The primary criticism of pareto optimality is that it gives no consideration to equitable distribution. This is why we only use it to identify the pareto frontier, and then go on to select the fairest of these options. Selecting the ratio that is closest to a 1:1 distribution is always the fairest, if not necessarily the best (consider two sets, 100:19 and 20:20), of the pareto frontier. While it is possible for a sub-optimal outcome to have a better ratio, it would only be removed if there is a policy set that is better for one (or both) parties without harming the other. In other words, it may filter out fairer ratios (1:2 would be subsumed by 2:5), but no party is worse off in the remaining sets.

Utility is calculated as part of a black-box mechanism, so participants cannot tamper with it. However the provider does send its utility across the network (the incentive to do this is to try and ensure they earn themselves a fair deal), so if they manage to in some way interrupt this and send false values, it does not gain them anything. Raising the values can just end up getting you a worse deal, as the requestor will end up with more to try and balance the deal. Lowering the values will reduce the chances of a policy set being picked, but in this case the provider could (and should) change their policies to have the same effect. The requestor does not send utilities and so has no chance to alter them.

5   Related Work

In our peer-to-peer system it is important for peers to have control over who, when, and how their data is shared. We achieve this through the use of policies/norms [33,35,44]. Norms are a formal representation of expected behaviours of software agents, such as prohibitions, and duties. An integral part of norms concerns deontic logic [22,42], considering permissions, prohibitions, and obligations. Norms and agents are often associated, using norms to control behaviour in societies of self-interested components [12].

Our work draws upon the concept of combining policies with data reported in [24], however our work focuses on a distributed environment and provides supporting mechanisms. The problem of unifying data and policies has, in the past, been addressed only in a centralised context [30,43]. We extend and adapt the policy language and mechanisms from our earlier work in [6] and [7].

We consider normative conflict detection [13,31] and resolution [10,29,38,39]. Conflict detection in our approach is performed when determining whether to accepted a policy related obliged action. That is, when an obligation will cause you to either adopt a new or revoke an old policy, we perform some simple conflict detection to determine how this will conflict with current goals and obligations. We do not attempt to make the policy set of each participant conflict free, only to balance the risk of potential conflict. If conflict does occur, the participant will resolve it by attempting to choose the solution with the highest utility (see Sect. 4).

Role Based Access Control (RBAC) shares some similarities with our work, though with a stronger focus on a controlled environment. Research has been carried out to address RBAC in a distributed environment [9,21,28], but many issues, such as a reliance on the ability to observe and control principals, have not yet been satisfactorily resolved. [9] uses user-to-user relationships to form a "path" of authorisation, but does not consider user-to-resource relationships which limits its usefulness. [21] focuses on transactions passing between two secure environments, rather than between two (potentially) insecure parties. [28] discusses automating compliance within a single secure environment, but does not discuss implementing this in a fully distributed environment.

An important concept within our solution is that of social welfare [27,32]. We use this to refer to the notion of fairness in peer transactions. A number of our mechanisms to promote social welfare are based on concepts from game theory [41]. Through our profit evaluation functions, we equate policy sets within transactions as moves in a game with associated pay-outs.

The distributed portions of our work are based on established peer-to-peer (P2P) technologies and operations [4,34]. P2P refers to networks in which "peers" communicate directly with each other, with minimal reliance on a centralised server. P2P networks can have a variety of different topologies but broadly they are either structured, where peers must organise themselves according to a set of conditions, or unstructured, where peers have a set of unrelated "neighbours" with which they communicate. Peer-to-peer simulations are based on a "network" of agents, lightweight independent processes which each act according to their own agenda, while still following a prescribed protocol [19]. Agents can be cast as a community of interconnected components, as in the Internet of Things [2,17].

6   Conclusions, Discussions, and Future Work

In this paper we proposed a solution which enables users to control how their data is used and traded within a fully distributed environment. This is achieved through the use of fine-grained, user-specified access policies. Our solution comprises a policy formalism, associated semantics, and an outline of the supporting mechanisms. These mechanisms make allowances to maximise the utility to all parties involved in transactions, and include provisions for security without a centralised authority.

We present the most recent version of our language and mechanisms that we have been developing for some time now. Currently we are extending our mechanism (and their implementation) to accommodate recent extension to the language. We have preliminary versions of a prototype where we can simulate large-scale scenarios, however these do not reflect the latest version of our language and mechanisms This prototype will then be used to run a series of experiments to measure the performance and suitability of our language and mechanisms.

We are currently planning an evaluation to determine how participants understand and interact with policies, conducted as three experiments. Experiment 1 examines if participants understand how policy activation ($\mathbb{C}^A$) and deactivation ($\mathbb{C}^D$) conditions work by having them determine what policies are active in a specific context. Experiment 2 tests if participants can understand how a set of policies will affect the actions involved in a specific task by having them consider how a set of active policies will hinder completing a task. Experiment 3 is a variant of experiment 2 that asks participants to consider how policies affect the performance of members of a team that they are in charge of.

In terms of the mechanisms themselves, there are a number of extensions we could make to them to expand their usefulness. For instance, our framework allows for policies to dynamically change over time. At the moment these changes would have to be driven by the user. However, with all the information that our peers gather, we could enable them to make informed changes to their policy set in response to events. These policy changes could occur at any time, and could be in response to interactions, goal changes, and new knowledge about other peers and data.

Another area we could improve is to outfit our peers with more complex reasoning mechanisms to provide some limited ability to predict outcomes based on past experience. We have some provisions for this at the moment, relating to predicting potential sources for data, but we could build upon this. Our peers have the ability to request not just data, but specific pieces of knowledge about other peers in the network, so combining this with better prediction would allow our peers to form more strategic plans. Importantly, these decisions are operating on incomplete information, so our mechanisms must allow peers to take this into account.

As an extra evaluation with the extended prototype incorporating the latest version of the language, we plan to conduct a game theoretic evaluation. We have made initial explorations into standard game theoretic properties (nash equilbiria, pareto optimality, etc.), but would like to carry out a more extensive evaluation of these properties.

References

1. Artikis, A., Kamara, L., Pitt, J., Sergot, M.: A protocol for resource sharing in norm-governed ad hoc networks. In: Leite, J., Omicini, A., Torroni, P., Yolum, I. (eds.) DALT 2004. LNCS (LNAI), vol. 3476, pp. 221–238. Springer, Heidelberg (2005). https://doi.org/10.1007/11493402_13

2. Atzori, L., Iera, A., Morabito, G.: The internet of things: a survey. Comput. Netw. **54**(15), 2787–2805 (2010)

3. Boella, G., van der Torre, L.: Permissions and obligations in hierarchical normative systems. In: Proceedings of the 9th International Conference on AI and Law, pp. 109–118. ACM (2003)

4. Buford, J., Yu, H., Lua, E.K.: P2P Networking and Applications. Morgan Kaufmann, San Francisco (2009)

5. Caragliu, A., Bo, C., Nijkamp, P.: Smart cities in Europe. J. Urban Technol. **18**(2), 65–82 (2011)

6. Cauvin, S.R., Kollingbaum, M.J., Sleeman, D., Vasconcelos, W.W.: Towards a distributed data-sharing economy. In: Cranefield, S., Mahmoud, S., Padget, J., Rocha, A.P. (eds.) COIN -2016. LNCS (LNAI), vol. 10315, pp. 3–21. Springer, Cham (2017). https://doi.org/10.1007/978-3-319-66595-5_1

7. Cauvin, S.R., Kollingbaum, M.J., Vasconcelos, W.W.: A peer-to-peer alternative to blockchain for managing distributed data transactions. In: SmartLaw@ICAIL (2017)

8. Cauvin, S.R., Vasconcelos, W.W.: A policy formalism to facilitate distributed data exchange - technical note (2018). https://www.dropbox.com/s/i2jbc8m1uxzprp3/policy-formalism-technical.pdf

9. Cheng, Y., Park, J., Sandhu, R.: A user-to-user relationship-based access control model for online social networks. In: Cuppens-Boulahia, N., Cuppens, F., Garcia-Alfaro, J. (eds.) DBSec 2012. LNCS, vol. 7371, pp. 8–24. Springer, Heidelberg (2012). https://doi.org/10.1007/978-3-642-31540-4_2

10. Cholvy, L., Cuppens, F.: Solving normative conflicts by merging roles. In: Proceedings of the 5th International Conference on A. I. and Law, pp. 201–209. ACM (1995)

11. Cranefield, S.: A rule language for modelling and monitoring social expectations in multi-agent systems. In: Boissier, O., et al. (eds.) AAMAS 2005. LNCS (LNAI), vol. 3913, pp. 246–258. Springer, Heidelberg (2006). https://doi.org/10.1007/11775331_17

12. Dignum, F.: Autonomous agents with norms. A.I. Law **7**(1), 69–79 (1999)

13. Elhag, A.A.O., Breuker, J.A.P.J., Brouwer, P.W.: On the formal analysis of normative conflicts. Inf. Commun. Technol. Law **9**(3), 207–217 (2000)

14. García-Camino, A., Rodríguez-Aguilar, J.A., Sierra, C., Vasconcelos, W.: A distributed architecture for norm-aware agent societies. In: Baldoni, M., Endriss, U., Omicini, A., Torroni, P. (eds.) DALT 2005. LNCS (LNAI), vol. 3904, pp. 89–105. Springer, Heidelberg (2006). https://doi.org/10.1007/11691792_6

15. Governatori, G., Olivieri, F., Rotolo, A., Scannapieco, S.: Computing strong and weak permissions in defeasible logic. J. Phil. Logic **42**(6), 799–829 (2013)

16. Grigorik, I.: Minimum Viable Block Chain (2014). https://www.igvita.com/2014/05/05/minimum-viable-block-chain/

17. Gubbi, J., Buyya, R., Marusic, S., Palaniswami, M.: Internet of Things (IoT): a vision, architectural elements, and future directions. Future Gener. Comput. Syst. **29**(7), 1645–1660 (2013)

18. Harper, R.: Inside the Smart Home. Springer, London (2006)
19. Hayes, C.C.: Agents in a nutshell-a very brief introduction. IEEE Trans. Knowl. Data Eng. **11**(1), 127–132 (1999)
20. Kanger, S.: Law and logic. Theoria **38**(3), 105–132 (1972)
21. Karjoth, G., Schunter, M., Waidner, M.: Platform for enterprise privacy practices: privacy-enabled management of customer data. In: Dingledine, R., Syverson, P. (eds.) PET 2002. LNCS, vol. 2482, pp. 69–84. Springer, Heidelberg (2003). https://doi.org/10.1007/3-540-36467-6_6
22. Meyer, J.J.C., Wieringa, R.J.: Deontic Logic in Computer Science Normative System Specification. In: International Workshop on Deontic Logic in Computer Science (1993)
23. Oren, N., Panagiotidi, S., Vázquez-Salceda, J., Modgil, S., Luck, M., Miles, S.: Towards a formalisation of electronic contracting environments. In: Hübner, J.F., Matson, E., Boissier, O., Dignum, V. (eds.) COIN 2008. LNCS (LNAI), vol. 5428, pp. 156–171. Springer, Heidelberg (2009). https://doi.org/10.1007/978-3-642-00443-8_11
24. Padget, J.A., Vasconcelos, W.W.: Fine-grained access control via policy-carrying data. ACM Trans. Internet Technol. **18**(3), 1–24 (2018)
25. Postscapes: Blockchains and the Internet of Things, March 2016. http://postscapes.com/blockchains-and-the-internet-of-things
26. Pörn, I.: The Logic of Power. Barnes & Noble, New York (1970)
27. Rabin, M.: Incorporating fairness into game theory and economics. Am. Econ. Rev. 1281–1302 (1993)
28. Sackmann, S., Kahmer, M.: ExPDT: a policy-based approach for automating compliance. Wirtschaftsinformatik **50**(5), 366 (2008)
29. Santos, J.S., Zahn, J.O., Silvestre, E.A., Silva, V.T., Vasconcelos, W.W.: Detection and resolution of normative conflicts in multi-agent systems: a literature survey. Auton. Agent. Multi-Agent Syst. **31**(6), 1236–1282 (2017)
30. Saroiu, S., Wolman, A., Agarwal, S.: Policy-carrying data: a privacy abstraction for attaching terms of service to mobile data. In: Proceedings of the 16th International Workshop on Mobile Computing Systems and Applications, pp. 129–134. ACM (2015)
31. Sartor, G.: Normative conflicts in legal reasoning. AI & Law **1**(2–3), 209–235 (1992)
32. Sen, A.: Collective Choice and Social Welfare, Expanded edn. Penguin, London (2017)
33. Sergot, M.: A computational theory of normative positions. ACM Trans. Comput. Logic **2**(4), 581–622 (2001)
34. Shen, X.S., Yu, H., Buford, J., Akon, M.: Handbook of peer-to-peer networking, vol. 34. Springer, Boston (2010). https://doi.org/10.1007/978-0-387-09751-0
35. Shoham, Y., Tennenholtz, M.: On social laws for artificial agent societies: off-line design. Artif. Intell. **73**(1), 231–252 (1995)
36. Suhendra, V.: A survey on access control deployment. In: Kim, T., Adeli, H., Fang, W., Villalba, J.G., Arnett, K.P., Khan, M.K. (eds.) SecTech 2011. CCIS, vol. 259, pp. 11–20. Springer, Heidelberg (2011). https://doi.org/10.1007/978-3-642-27189-2_2
37. Vasconcelos, W.W., García-Camino, A., Gaertner, D., Rodríguez-Aguilar, J.A., Noriega, P.: Distributed norm management for multi-agent systems. Expert Syst. Appl. **39**(5), 5990–5999 (2012)

38. Vasconcelos, W.W., Kollingbaum, M.J., Norman, T.J.: Resolving conflict and inconsistency in norm-regulated virtual organizations. In: Proceedings of the 6th International Joint Conference on Autonomous Agents and Multiagent Systems, p. 91. ACM (2007)
39. Vasconcelos, W.W., Kollingbaum, M.J., Norman, T.J.: Normative conflict resolution in multi-agent systems. AAMAS **19**(2), 124–152 (2009)
40. Viganò, F., Fornara, N., Colombetti, M.: An event driven approach to norms in artificial institutions. In: Boissier, O., et al. (eds.) AAMAS 2005. LNCS (LNAI), vol. 3913, pp. 142–154. Springer, Heidelberg (2006). https://doi.org/10.1007/11775331_10
41. Von Neumann, J., Morgenstern, O.: Theory of Games and Economic Behavior (commemorative edition). Princeton University Press, Princeton (2007)
42. Von Wright, G.H.: Deontic logic. Mind **60**(237), 1–15 (1951)
43. Wang, X., Yong, Q., Dai, Y.H., Ren, J., Hang, Z.: Protecting outsourced data privacy with lifelong policy carrying. In: IEEE International Conference on High Performance Computing and Communications and Embedded and Ubiquitous Computing (HPCC-EUC), pp. 896–905, November 2013. https://doi.org/10.1109/HPCC.and.EUC.2013.128
44. von Wright, G.H.: Norm and Action: A Logical Enquiry. Routledge and Kegan Paul, New York (1963)
45. Zheng, Y., Capra, L., Wolfson, O., Yang, H.: Urban computing: concepts, methodologies, and applications. ACM Trans. Intell. Syst. Technol. **5**(3), 38:1–38:55 (2014)

Developing a Method for Quantifying Degree of Discussion Progress Towards Automatic Facilitation of Web-Based Discussion

Ko Kitagawa[✉], Shun Shiramatsu, and Akira Kamiya

Nagoya Institute of Technology,
Gokiso-cho, Showa-ku, Nagoya 466–8555, Japan
{kitagawa,siramatu,a.kamiya.208}@srmtlab.org

Abstract. Online discussion has major potential for large-scale consensus building. However, existing SNSs, microblogs, and chat systems lack facilitation functions for avoiding stagnation and flaming of discussion. To develop a function for detecting the stagnation of discussion, we need to quantify the degree of discussion progress, as just the amount of content is not enough to accurately gauge the discussion progress. Our definition of the degree of discussion progress is based on the Issue-Based Information System (IBIS). Specifically, it is defined as a sum of weights representing the importance of IBIS node types extracted from online discussion. In this paper, we determine the optimal weights of the IBIS node types to maximize the correlation coefficient between calculated progress and the subjective progress of human participants. The optimal weights are determined using a genetic algorithm. Experimental results showed that the maximized correlation coefficient was +0.54. Although the current definition of the discussion progress is simple summation, we plan to further refine it with the hierarchical structure of IBIS in future work.

Keywords: Autonomous facilitator agent · Online discussion ·
Discussion progress · Consensus building · Genetic algorithm

1 Introduction

In recent years, with the widespread use of SNS and the like, large-scale discussions are increasingly being conducted on the Web. One reason for this is that a wide range of stakeholders are engaged in collaborative discussions to deal with social problems. For example, social systems for public collaboration such as GoalShare [1] and MissonForest [2] require online consensus building for better collaboration.

We developed autonomous facilitator agents for online discussion in an earlier work [3]. To automatically generate facilitator utterances[1], we first analyzed the utterances of human facilitators and found that the questions they asked are important [4, 5]. However, the suitable timing of facilitator utterances is not yet known because

---

[1] In this paper, an utterance refers to a post on a Web-based discussion forum.

© Springer Nature Switzerland AG 2019
M. Lujak (Ed.): AT 2018, LNAI 11327, pp. 162–169, 2019.
https://doi.org/10.1007/978-3-030-17294-7_12

we do not have a sophisticated method to detect stagnation of discussion. When discussing something on the Web, stagnation of discussion is likely to occur at some point. In this research, we want to detect that stagnation as soon as it starts. Our aim is to implement facilitator agents that are equipped with this function. In order to detect the stagnation, it is necessary to quantify how far the discussion has currently progressed. The criterion for judging this is different depending on the state of discussion. The state of discussion is classified into two phases: divergence and convergence. In this paper, we examine the quantification of the discussion progress during the divergence phase.

There are a few related works in this vein. Dringus and Ellis tried to evaluate discussion progress with several metrics related to participant activities [6]; however, they did not integrate these metrics for representing the discussion progress. Klein developed a method for identifying the useful part of a discussion for each participant by using attention-mediation metrics [7], and although their metrics have potential to be used for our purpose, they are also not integrated. We need an integrated metric that can be applied to autonomous facilitator agents. To this end, we propose a novel metric for representing the discussion progress.

2 Proposed Method: A Metric for Discussion Progress

One method for recording a human decision making process is the Issue-Based Information System (IBIS) [8]. This is a structured representation of tasks, ideas, etc. as nodes (Fig. 1). In this research, we use IBIS to quantify the degree of discussion progress. IBIS nodes handle 13 kinds of issues, ideas, etc. First, the IBIS structure is extracted from the discussion up to a certain time t. A weight is assigned according to the type of each node and the relationship between the nodes, and the sum of the weights of all the nodes is set as the discussion progress degree $P(t)$ at t. We prepared a set $U_t = \{u_1, u_2, \cdots, u_n\}$ of the discussion up to time t and a set $E(u_i) = \{e_1, e_2, \ldots, e_i\}$ of the IBIS nodes of the utterance u_i. The type determined by IBIS node e and its relation r is represented as $type(e, r)$, and the weight is expressed as $w(type(e, r))$. Using these, we formulate it as

$$w(u_k) = \sum_{e \in E(u_k)} w(type(e, r))$$

$$P(t) = \sum_{k=1}^{n} w(u_k)$$

The slope $\frac{\Delta P(t)}{\Delta t}$ represents the degree of progress of the discussion due to the change in the weight (contribution).

We prepared a set S of $type(e, r)$ and collected data on the degree of progress experienced by human participants in order to determine the optimal weights $w(type(e, r))$ for all $type(e, r) \in$ S. Concretely, the optimal weights are determined by maximizing the correlation between the sum of the weights $w(type(e, r))$ of the nodes included in one utterance and the subjective importance of the utterance felt by the participants. However, the number of $type(e, r)$, 13, is too many for a brute-force search. Therefore, we use a genetic algorithm with the weight of each node as one gene in order to optimize $w(type(e, r))$. This approach enables us to quantify the weight of one utterance perceived by humans.

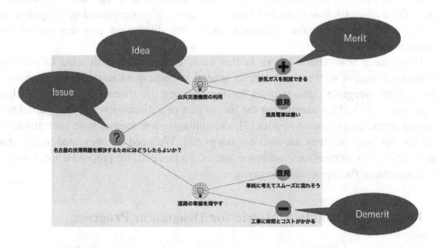

Fig. 1. Example of Issue-Based Information System (IBIS).

3 Data Collection

In order to determine the weight of each node, experiments were carried out using a discussion that was done in the past (Fig. 2). Specifically, as data for discussion, we utilized data of a large-scale social experiment (1) performed in November 2013 using the online discussion system COLLAGREE [9]. The purpose of the divergence phase is to have the discussion participants come up with as many possible solutions to a problem as possible. For that reason, we asked participants to evaluate each utterance in the discussion on a 6-point Likert scale (from 0 to 5) in terms of whether the utterance had a new and important perspective or not. In other words, participants evaluated the importance of each utterance while browsing a visualization of the cumulative sum of his/her subjective importance, which is shown in Fig. 2. The cumulative sum of the importance can be regarded as the progress of discussion. These subjective weights are regarded as reference data for optimizing the node weights. Statistics are listed in Table 1. This data was used as reference data for optimizing the parameters $w(type(e, r))$ with the genetic algorithm.

For each of 17 discussions with more than 10 and less than 21 utterances, the above experiment was conducted for 13 people, each of whom was asked to experiment with about four discussions, collecting 51 samples.

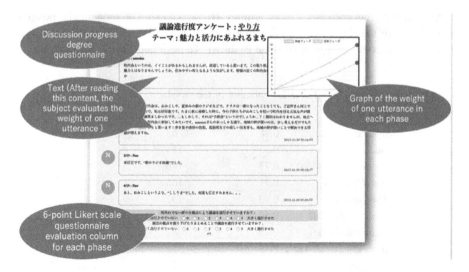

Fig. 2. Questionnaire form for collecting subjective importance of each utterance with visualizing cumulative sum of the importance.

Table 1. Statistics of questionnaire elements and number of samples.

Questionnaire elements	Number of samples
Number of threads	17
Number of utterances	260
Number of subjects	13
Average number of threads assigned to each subject	3.92
Sum of sample data	51

4 Experiment Contents

The questionnaire results revealed how important each statement was in the discussion progress. We regard this as the degree of progress of each utterance perceived by humans. Also, by setting the weight with a random number between 0 and 1 in the IBIS nodes, the degree of progress of each utterance was determined by the weight of the node. By optimizing the weight of each IBIS node by the genetic algorithm, we tried to optimize the progress of discussion by IBIS so as to maximize the correlation between the above two degrees of progress. In this process of the genetic algorithm, the gene length was 13, the number of node types, and each gene stored a random number set for each node. Python's random function was used for generating random numbers with its default seed because we did not set the seed. The number of individuals was 130. BLX-α was used as the crossing method. Roulette selection and elite selection were used as the selection methods. We optimized the node weights by maximizing the correlation between the summation of node weights in each utterance and reference data obtained by the questionnaire, i.e., subjective weights of each utterance.

As a result, the correlation was around +0.54, showing a moderately positive correlation with the degree of progress that humans feel. The variation of the weight and correlation coefficient of each node is shown Table 2 and Fig. 3, respectively.

Table 2. Variation of the weight.

Type	Importance (weight)	Amount of samples
Argument (Example)	0.98	63
Issue	0.85	151
Argument (Opinion)	0.73	146
Idea (Opinion)	0.7	105
Idea (Solution)	0.63	132
Argument (Merit)	0.52	40
Argument (None)	0.43	82
Argument (Reason)	0.39	36
Question	0.36	122
Argument (Answer)	0.3	95
Argument (Demerit)	0.14	23
Idea (None)	0.03	94
Idea (Answer)	**−0.47**	6

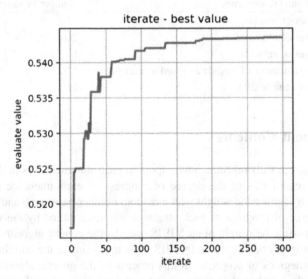

Fig. 3. Correlation coefficient of each node.

5   Discussion

The results showed a moderate positive correlation: +0.54. Although this correlation is not enough for actual use, it shows potential to be applied to autonomous facilitator agents. In the future, we should be able to improve the correlation by considering a hierarchical structure. For example, assume a particular sub tree of IBIS has shifted topics. In such a case, the weight of that sub tree should be less. The weights of sub trees can be calculated as the similarity between the sub tree and the main topic. We need to verify this hypothesis in a future experiment.

It seems that the reason the weight of the node concerning the task and the idea got larger is that the participant evaluated a new viewpoint as having been shown. In addition, the weight of the exemplified idea became the highest because there were many participants who felt that the idea was detailed and that understanding was promoted by giving an example opinion.

We believe that if we can estimate the weight more accurately, we will be able to detect not only the stagnation of a discussion but also flaming. Violent words do not include elements that advance the discussion, so if the degree of discussion progress does not rise even though the number of utterances rises, this can be considered flaming.

6   Future Prospects

Discussion is considered to be hierarchical in structure in that some parts are deeply related to the theme and others are not (Fig. 4). Therefore, it is insufficient to regard the sum of the weights of the nodes alone as the progress degree. It is necessary to adjust the magnification of the weight so as to also consider hierarchy.

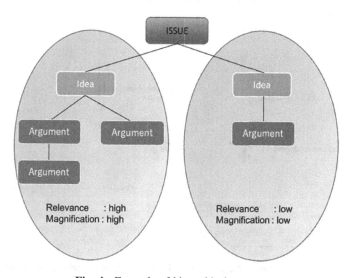

Fig. 4. Example of hierarchical structure.

Number of utterances
within a certain period

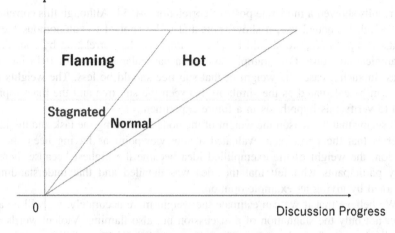

Fig. 5. Four states in the discussion.

Our degree of discussion progress can applied to the development of autonomous facilitator agents. For example, facilitator agents need to recognize the state of discussion to judge whether they should perform some action or not. We define four states of the discussion on the basis of our degree of discussion progress: (1) normal, (2) flaming, (3) stagnation, and (4) hot, as shown in Fig. 5. The discussion states can be defined on the basis of the relationship between the amount of speech in the recent time unit and the amount of increase in the degree of progress. If we can appropriately determine the thresholds to divide the discussion states, facilitator agents can estimate the current discussion state using calculated degree of discussion progress and select an utterance suitable for facilitating current discussion.

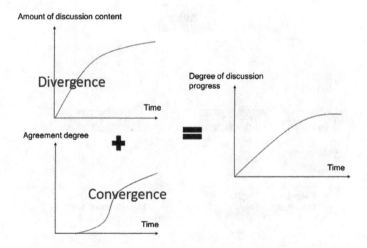

Fig. 6. The relationship between the amount of discussion content and the degree of discussion agreement.

Although we only considered the divergence phase in this paper, the convergence phase is also important. The relationship between the amount of discussion content and the discussion agreement degree is considered to be as depicted in Fig. 6. By considering this relation, we believe that the relationship between time and progress degree in the whole discussion can be more accurately judged.

For these reasons, our future work will involve improving the accuracy considering the state of discussion and the hierarchical structure of discussion.

Acknowledgements. This work was partially supported by JST CREST (JPMJCR15E1) and JSPS KAKENHI (17K00461).

References

1. Tossavainen, T., Shiramatsu, S., Ozono, T., Shintani, S.: A linked open data based system utilizing structured open innovation process for addressing collaboratively public concerns in regional societies. Appl. Intell. Int. J. Artif. Intell. Neural Netw. Complex Probl. Solving Technol. **44**(1), 196–207 (2016)
2. Watanabe, M., Shiramatsu, S., Goto, Y.: Tag-based approaches to sharing background information regarding social problems towards facilitating public collaboration. In: eGose 2017 Proceedings of the International Conference on Electronic Governance and Open Society: Challenges in Eurasia, pp. 113–118 (2017)
3. Ikeda, Y., Shiramatsu, S.: Generating questions asked by facilitator agents using preceding context in web-based discussion. In: Proceedings of the 2nd IEEE International Conference on Agents, pp. 127–132 (2017)
4. Shiramatsu, S., Nishida, T., Ito, T., Fujita, K.: Feature expression extraction from discussion facilitators' utterances in web-based forum system towards autonomous facilitator agents. In: Proceedings of the 2016 5th IIAI International Congress on Advanced Applied Informatics, pp. 687–691 (2016)
5. Shiramatsu, S., Ikeda, Y.: An approach to discussion facilitators' action selection based on expected utility calculated with random forest regression. In: Proceedings of the 2016 International Conference on Crowd Science and Engineering (ICCSE 2016), pp. 1–6 (2016)
6. Dringus, L.P., Ellis, T.: Using data mining as a strategy for assessing asynchronous discussion forums. Comput. Educ. **45**(1), 141–160 (2005)
7. Klein, M.: Enabling large-scale deliberation using attention-mediation metrics. Comput. Support. Coop. Work (CSCW) **21**(4–5), 449–473 (2012)
8. Noble, D., Rittel, H.W.J.: Issue-based information systems for design (1988)
9. Ito, T., Imi, T., Ito, T., Hideshima, E.: COLLAGREE: a facilitator-mediated large-scale consensus support system. In: Collective Intelligence 2014 (2014)

Coordination in Open Distributed Systems with Applications

Monotonicity, Duplication Monotonicity, and Pareto Optimality in the Scoring-Based Allocation of Indivisible Goods

Benno Kuckuck[1] and Jörg Rothe[2(✉)]

[1] Mathematisches Institut, Heinrich-Heine-Universität Düsseldorf,
Düsseldorf, Germany
`kuckuck@uni-duesseldorf.de`
[2] Institut für Informatik, Heinrich-Heine-Universität Düsseldorf,
Düsseldorf, Germany
`rothe@cs.uni-duesseldorf.de`

Abstract. We study the properties of scoring allocation correspondences and rules, due to Baumeister et al. [7], that are based on a scoring vector (e.g., Borda or lexicographic scoring) and an aggregation function (e.g., utilitarian or egalitarian social welfare) and can be used to allocate indivisible goods to agents. Extending their previous results considerably and solving some of their open questions, we show that while *necessary* duplication monotonicity (a notion inspired by the twin paradox [21] and false-name manipulation [1]) fails for most choices of scoring vector when using leximin social welfare, *possible* duplication monotonicity holds for a very wide range of scoring allocation rules. We also show that a very large family of scoring allocation rules is monotonic. Finally, we show that a large class of scoring allocation correspondences satisfies possible Pareto-optimality, which extends a result of Brams et al. [12].

Keywords: Computational social choice · Fair division ·
Scoring allocation rule · Duplication monotonicity

1 Introduction

The allocation of indivisible goods to a number of agents is an important problem that has been studied intensively both in economics and computer science; for an overview we refer to the book by Moulin [22], the book chapters by Bouveret et al. [11] and Lang and Rothe [20], and the survey by Nguyen et al. [24]. In a setting where agents specify their preferences in a cardinal form, i.e., by ascribing a utility to each good, so-called *max-min allocations* have received particular attention in the literature: Here it is assumed that a bundle of goods is worth the sum of the goods' individual utilities to each agent, and an allocation is considered optimal if it maximizes egalitarian social welfare, i.e., the minimum

© Springer Nature Switzerland AG 2019
M. Lujak (Ed.): AT 2018, LNAI 11327, pp. 173–189, 2019.
https://doi.org/10.1007/978-3-030-17294-7_13

of the agents' individual utilities. The problem of finding such an allocation is known as the Santa Claus problem [4] and the complexity of this problem as well as the properties of *max-min allocations* have been extensively studied. However, as is well-known from the theory of voting, eliciting cardinal preferences can be tricky, and in fact we consider it likely that most of the wishlists Santa receives each year will consist not of numerical utilities but rather of ranked lists of items, i.e., *ordinal preferences*.

Building on the work by Brams et al. [12,13], Baumeister et al. [7] recently introduced and studied the families of *scoring allocation correspondences* and *rules*: Taking a cue from voting theory, ordinal preferences submitted by the agents are turned into cardinal preferences by means of a *scoring vector*, assigning a fixed utility to each rank in the agents' preferences (e.g., the Borda scoring vector assigns one point to each agent's least favorite good, two points to her second-to-last favorite good, etc.). In this way, one obtains a vector of individual utilities for each allocation and (as in the Santa Claus problem) an allocation is considered optimal if it maximizes social welfare. There is no reason, a priori, to limit oneself to egalitarian social welfare, and so a scoring allocation correspondence in the sense of Baumeister et al. [7] is parametrized by both a scoring vector and a social welfare aggregation function.

Of course, we have certain expectations about how a reasonable fair division procedure should behave. For example, intuitively, (i) an agent ranking an item higher should not decrease her chances of receiving this item (all else being equal); (ii) two agents with identical preferences should together receive a share at least as good as what a single agent with that preference would receive; and (iii) the procedure should not consider an allocation optimal if another allocation provides a better share to some agent without making anyone else worse off. These three intuitions can be formalized as the notions of *monotonicity*, *duplication monotonicity*, and *Pareto optimality*. The first two have been studied by Baumeister et al. [7], for all scoring allocation rules using utilitarian or egalitarian social welfare. Monotonicity was shown to hold in those cases, but for duplication monotonicity the picture remained rather incomplete. Pareto optimality was studied by Brams et al. [12], but again only for a few particular combinations of scoring vector and social welfare function. But since the family of scoring allocation rules derives much of its power from the flexibility in varying the scoring vector and social welfare function, it is highly desirable to have results that apply not only to particular choices of parameters but to formulate general conditions on the parameters that ensure the property in question. That is the goal of this paper.

Our main contributions are the following: (1) We extend one of the results of Baumeister et al. [7, Theorem 1] by showing monotonicity for a very large family of scoring allocation rules (Theorem 1). Solving most of the questions left open by Baumeister et al. [7, Section 4.3], (2) we give examples showing that *necessary* duplication monotonicity fails for most choices of scoring vector when using leximin social welfare, and (3) our main result (Theorem 2 and its Corollaries 1 and 3) shows that *possible* duplication monotonicity holds for a very wide range of scoring allocation rules.[1] (4) We generalize a result of Brams et al. [12, Theorem 4.9] by proving possible Pareto optimality for a large class of scoring allocation correspondences (Theorem 3). While it turns out to be quite simple to find the correct conditions ensuring monotonicity or Pareto optimality, our analysis of duplication monotonicity is much more technically involved – in particular necessitating the introduction of a novel condition on social welfare aggregation functions, which we call *split-coherence*, enjoyed by a large family of such functions.

Duplication monotonicity is of particular interest due to its connections to other well-studied phenomena that have received considerable attention in computational social choice [14] and in cooperative game theory (see, e.g., [17]): The failure of necessary duplication monotonicity in fair division is akin to the *twin paradox* [21] in voting. An alternative interpretation of the question duplication monotonicity intends to answer is whether agents can (always or sometimes) profit from "cheating" by posing as two agents, submitting their preferences to the allocation rule twice. This latter interpretation is inspired by *false-name manipulation* in weighted voting games [1,25] as well as, to a lesser extent, by *control by adding voters* [6] (cf. also the more remotely related notion of *cloning in voting* [16,28]).

Organization of the Paper. In Sect. 2 we introduce scoring allocation correspondences as defined by Baumeister et al. [7] as our underlying model of resource allocation with ordinal preferences. In Sect. 3 we briefly treat monotonicity, showing that weak monotonicity of the employed social welfare ordering ensures monotonicity of scoring allocation correspondences. In Sect. 4 we recall the notion of (necessary and possible) duplication monotonicity and provide examples which show that necessary duplication monotonicity mostly does not hold for scoring allocation correspondences. We then propose a new property of social welfare orderings, split-coherence, and show that this property (analogous to weak monotonicity in Sect. 3) guarantees possible duplication monotonicity for scoring allocation correspondences. We then show that split-coherence is satisfied for a large family of social welfare functions. Finally, we briefly consider Pareto-optimality in Sect. 5, showing that monotonicity of social welfare functions ensures possible Pareto-optimality for associated scoring allocation rules and that necessary Pareto-optimality can fail quite badly.

2   Preliminaries

Let $N = \{1, \ldots, n\}$ denote a set of *agents* and G a finite set of *goods* or *items*. The allocation procedures we want to consider take as their input a *preference profile* $(>_1, \ldots, >_n)$ consisting of strict total orders on G. Their results are allocations

---

[1] Possible and necessary duplication monotonicity are inspired by the notions of possible and necessary winner in voting [9,10,18,29] that have been used not only in fair division [3,7] but were also applied, e.g., to strategy-proofness in judgment aggregation [8] and to stability concepts in hedonic games [19,26].

of G to N, i.e., tuples $(\pi_1, \ldots, \pi_n)$ with $G = \bigcup_{i=1}^{n} \pi_i$ and $\pi_i \cap \pi_j = \emptyset$ for $i \neq j$. A function that produces a single such allocation for every preference profile, we will call an *allocation rule*. More generally, an *allocation correspondence* returns a nonempty subset of allocations. Denoting the set of preferences over G by $\mathscr{P}(G)$ and the set of allocations of G to N by $\Pi(G, N)$ an allocation rule can thus formally be defined as a map $\mathscr{P}(G)^n \rightarrow \Pi(G, N)$, while an allocation correspondence is a map $\mathscr{P}(G)^n \rightarrow 2^{\Pi(G,N)} \setminus \{\emptyset\}$.

Scoring allocation correspondences were first defined by Baumeister et al. [7] and Nguyen et al. [23], but special cases were previously used by Brams et al. [12,13]. These correspondences choose an allocation maximizing social welfare, which is computed by means of two parameters: First, a *scoring vector* $s = (s_1, \ldots, s_{|G|})$ consists of rational numbers $s_1 \geq s_2 \geq \cdots \geq s_{|G|} \geq 0$ with $s_1 > 0$. It is used to assign a score to each rank in the agents' preferences and thus allows us to compute the individual utility of each agent's share to that agent. Second, a *social welfare ordering* (SWO) is a weak order (i.e., a transitive, reflexive, and complete relation) on $\mathbb{Q}_{\geq 0}^n$, that specifies which vectors of individual utilities are socially preferable. It often comes in the form of an *aggregation* or *social welfare function* (SWF) $W \colon \mathbb{Q}_{\geq 0}^n \rightarrow \mathbb{R}$ that computes a collective utility from the individual utilities, thus inducing an SWO on $\mathbb{Q}_{\geq 0}^n$:
$$a \succsim_W b \iff W(a) \geq W(b).$$

Definition 1. *Let s be a scoring vector and $\succsim$ a social welfare ordering. For a preference $>$ on G and a subset $B \subset G$, define the individual utility of B with respect to $>$ and s as $u_{>,s} = \sum_{g \in B} s_{\mathrm{rank}(g,>)}$, where $\mathrm{rank}(g, >) = |\{g' \in G \mid g' \geq g\}|$ is the rank of g in the linear order $>$. For a preference profile $P = (>_1, \ldots, >_n)$ and an allocation π of G to N, denote by $u_{P,s}(\pi) = (u_{>_1,s}(\pi_1), \ldots, u_{>_n,s}(\pi_n))$ the vector of individual utilities of each agent's share. The scoring allocation correspondence $F_{s,\succsim}$ is the function which picks the allocation(s) with maximal utility vector according to $\succsim$, so $F_{s,\succsim}(P) = \arg\max_{\pi \in \Pi(G,N)}^{\succsim} u_{P,s}(\pi)$.*

If $\succsim = \succsim_W$ is induced by an aggregation function $W \colon \mathbb{Q}_{\geq 0}^n \rightarrow \mathbb{R}$, we write $F_{s,W}$ in place of $F_{s,\succsim_W}$, so $F_{s,W}(P) = \arg\max_{\pi \in \Pi(G,N)} W(u_{P,s}(\pi))$.

As there might be more than one allocation maximizing social welfare, the scoring allocation correspondences typically return a (nonempty) set of winning allocations, not just a single one. A tie-breaking scheme is a function $T \colon 2^{\Pi(G,n)} \setminus \{\emptyset\} \rightarrow \Pi(G, n)$ with $T(S) \in S$ for all nonempty sets $S \subseteq \Pi(G, n)$. We write $F_{s,\star}^T = T \circ F_{s,\star}$ for the allocation *rule* that picks a set of winning allocations according to $F_{s,\star}$ and then breaks ties using T. We will always consider tie-breaking schemes of the form $T(S) = \max^{>^T}(S)$ for some total order $>^T$ over all allocations from G to N.

Choosing the Parameters. The freedom in choosing the scoring vector and social welfare function affords a high degree of flexibility and leads to a rather large and varied family of allocation procedures.

Example 1. Let $G = \{a, b, c, d, e, f, g, h, i, j\}$ and consider the following preference profile $P = (>_1, >_2, >_3)$ over G:

$$g >_1 i >_1 e >_1 f >_1 c >_1 h >_1 b >_1 d >_1 a >_1 j$$
$$a >_2 d >_2 i >_2 g >_2 j >_2 c >_2 f >_2 e >_2 b >_2 h$$
$$g >_3 f >_3 j >_3 d >_3 b >_3 e >_3 a >_3 i >_3 c >_3 h$$

which we will shorten to $P = (giefchbdaj, adigjcfebh, gfjdbeaich)$.

For any $k, m \geq 1$ and $M > m^2$, we define the following commonly used scoring vectors: the *Borda scoring vector* borda $= (m, m-1, \ldots, 2, 1)$, the *lexicographic scoring vector* lex $= (2^{m-1}, 2^{m-2}, \ldots, 2^1, 2^0)$, and the *Borda-based quasi-indifference scoring vector* borda-qi $= (1 + \frac{m}{M}, 1 + \frac{m-1}{M}, \ldots, 1 + \frac{1}{M})$. Using the lex scoring vector corresponds to the assumption that agents always value getting *good* items over getting *many* items, whereas using borda-qi corresponds to the opposite assumption; borda is a compromise.

Commonly used SWFs include the *utilitarian SWF* $(u_1, \ldots, u_n) \mapsto \sum_{i=1}^{n} u_i$ (which we will denote for short by $+$) and the *egalitarian SWF* $(u_1, \ldots, u_n) \mapsto \min_{1 \leq i \leq n} u_i$ (denoted by min). The latter is often refined to the leximin SWO, first introduced by Sen [27, Section 9.2]: For $u, v \in \mathbb{Q}^n$, define $u \succsim^{\text{lm}} v \iff u^* \geq^{\text{lex}} v^*$, where u^* denotes the vector resulting from u by sorting the components in ascending order, and $\geq^{\text{lex}}$ denotes the lexicographic ordering on $\mathbb{Q}^n$.

It is easy to observe that every scoring allocation correspondence $F_{s,+}$ based on utilitarian social welfare with a strictly decreasing scoring vector s assigns every item to an agent who ranks it highest, hence (using, e.g., $(bdeg, ch, afij)$ as a shorthand for the allocation $(\{b, d, e, g\}, \{c, h\}, \{a, f, i, j\})$): $F_{\text{borda},+}(P) = F_{\text{lex},+} = F_{\text{borda-qi},+} = \{(bdeg, ch, afij), (beg, ch, adfij)\}$.

By way of contrast, using leximin social welfare the winning allocations for borda, lex, and borda-qi are all distinct: $F_{\text{borda,leximin}}(P) = \{(cehi, adj, bfg)\}$, $F_{\text{lex,leximin}}(P) = \{(bcdefhij, a, g)\}$, $F_{\text{borda-qi,leximin}}(P) = \{(bceh, adi, fgj)\}$.

These examples exhibit some typical features: In combination with leximin social welfare, e.g., borda-qi scoring will always produce even-shares allocations – fairly balancing all agents' desires to have as many items as possible. Characteristically, using utilitarian social welfare means that no such balancing is attempted in favor of simply getting goods to those who favor them most.

Often, it might be desirable to interpolate between these two extremes: This can be achieved, e.g., by using a member of the following prominent family of aggregation functions (see, e.g., [22, Section 3.2]), of which utilitarian and leximin social welfare are the extreme cases $p = 1$ and $p \to -\infty$:

Definition 2. *For $p \leq 1$, define $W_p \colon \mathbb{Q}^n_{>0} \to \mathbb{Q}$ by*

$$W_p(u) = \begin{cases} u_1^p + \cdots + u_n^p & \text{if } p > 0, \\ \log(u_1) + \cdots + \log(u_n) & \text{if } p = 0, \\ -u_1^p - \cdots - u_n^p & \text{if } p < 0. \end{cases}$$

Comparing Sets of Items. As we saw in the example, choosing a scoring vector corresponds to making some assumptions on what kinds of shares the agents favor: For a preference list $abcdefgh$, the share $\{a, d, e, g\}$ will never receive a worse score than $\{b, d, h\}$ (we will say that the former is *necessarily* better) but it may or may not receive a worse score than $\{a, b\}$ (we will say they are both *possibly* better than the other). Ultimately, we cannot know which of the shares the agent really favors.[2] This can be formalized in the following (standard) definitions and well-known lemma:[3]

Definition 3. *Let G be a finite set of goods and $>$ a preference over G (i.e., a strict total order). The* universal responsive set extension $\succeq^{\text{nec}}$ *in 2^G is defined by $B \succeq^{\text{nec}} A \Leftrightarrow$ there exists an injection $f \colon A \hookrightarrow B$ with $f(a) \geq a$ for all $a \in A$. This is a partial order on 2^G.*

A utility function compatible with $>$ *is a map $v \colon G \to \mathbb{R}_{\geq 0}$ such that $v(a) \geq v(b) \Leftrightarrow a \geq b$. Such a function induces an* additively representable *[5] or* additively separable *[2] set extension $\succsim_v$ defined by $A \succsim_v B \Leftrightarrow \sum_{a \in A} v(a) \geq \sum_{b \in B} v(b)$.*

Lemma 1. *Let $>$ be a preference on G and $\succeq^{\text{nec}}$ its universal responsive set extension. For $A, B \in 2^G$, we have $A \succeq^{\text{nec}} B$ if and only if $A \succsim_v B$ for every additively representable set extension $\succsim_v$ of $>$.*

This lemma is well known and widely used in the literature. Baumeister et al. [7] also use the notation[4] $A \succeq^{\text{pos}} B$ ("A is possibly as good as B") if $B \succ^{\text{nec}} A$ does *not* hold, meaning that there is some additively separable extension $\succsim$ of $>$ for which $A \succsim B$.

3   Monotonicity

Baumeister et al. [7] consider the following property:

Definition 4. *Let $N = \{1, \ldots, n\}$ be a finite set of agents and G a set of goods. An* allocation rule $F \colon \mathcal{P}(G)^n \to \Pi(G, n)$ *is called* monotonic *if it has the following property: For every preference profile $P \in \mathcal{P}(G)^n$, if $F(P)$ gives good g to agent i, then for every modified preference profile P', resulting from P by ranking g higher in agent i's preference and keeping all else fixed, the allocation $F(P')$ also gives good g to agent i.*

Baumeister et al. [7] show that monotonicity holds for scoring allocation rules $F_{s,\star}^T$ with s an arbitrary scoring vector, $\star \in \{+, \min, \text{leximin}\}$, and an arbitrary

---

[2] This is the price we pay for the simplicity of eliciting only *ordinal* preferences on *single* items (as opposed to ordinal, or even cardinal, preferences on all shares).

[3] Responsive set extensions are the most suitable in our context as they precisely capture the uncertainty in choosing the "right" scoring vector.

[4] Note that while $\succeq^{\text{nec}}$ is a partial order, $\succeq^{\text{pos}}$ is neither transitive nor antisymmetric in general.

tie-breaking scheme induced by a tie-breaking relation $>^T$. This result is easily generalized as Theorem 1 below, showing that monotonicity of $F_{s,\star}^T$ holds when $\star$ is an arbitrary SWO satisfying just one very mild assumption:

Definition 5. *We call an SWO $\succsim$ on $\mathbb{Q}_{\geq 0}^n$ weakly monotonic if for all $u, v \in \mathbb{Q}_{\geq 0}^n$ such that $u_i \leq v_i$ for all i, we have $u \precsim v$. We call an SWF $W : \mathbb{Q}_{\geq 0}^n \to \mathbb{R}$ weakly monotonic if for all $u, v \in \mathbb{Q}_{\geq 0}^n$ such that $u_i \leq v_i$ for all i, we have $W(u) \leq W(v)$.*

If W is a weakly monotonic SWF, then $\succsim_W$ is a weakly monotonic SWO. All of the SWFs W_p from Definition 2 are easily seen to be monotonic, as is the function min (which fails to be monotonic in the classic sense, see Moulin [22]) and the leximin ordering. In fact, weak monotonicity is such a mild assumption that it is hard to think of a sensible SWO that does not satisfy it. We omit the proof of Theorem 1 due to space limitations.

Theorem 1. *For any scoring vector $s \in \mathbb{Q}_{\geq 0}$, any weakly monotonic SWO $\succsim$, and any tie-breaking relation T, the scoring allocation rule $F_{s,\succsim}^T$ is monotonic.*

4   Duplication Monotonicity

Another regularity property studied by Baumeister et al. [7] is *duplication monotonicity*, demanding that two agents with identical preferences should always receive a better share (in total) than a single agent with that preference would. From another perspective, it tells us whether an agent who cheats by posing as two agents (with identical preferences) gets a better share than she would have without cheating.[5] In light of the discussion at the end of Sect. 2, we actually need to define two properties, *possible* and *necessary* duplication monotonicity:

Definition 6. *Let G be a finite set of goods and let $P = (>_1, \ldots, >_n) \in \mathscr{P}(G)^n$ be a preference profile. Denote, for each i, by $\succeq_i^{\mathrm{nec}}$ and $\succeq_i^{\mathrm{pos}}$ the necessary and possible preference relations on 2^G associated to $>_i$, as defined above. Now, with $P^{\mathrm{dup}} = (>_1, \ldots, >_n, >_n)$, an extended version of P with the final preference doubled, an allocation rule F satisfies possible (resp., necessary) duplication monotonicity if $F(P^{\mathrm{dup}})_n \cup F(P^{\mathrm{dup}})_{n+1} \succeq_n^{\mathrm{pos}} F(P)_n$ (resp., $F(P^{\mathrm{dup}})_n \cup F(P^{\mathrm{dup}})_{n+1} \succeq_n^{\mathrm{nec}} F(P)_n$) for every choice of preference profile P.*

---

[5] While enabling such cheating might not seem like a desirable property, this really is a common tradeoff: Procedures that behave predictably and naturally with respect to changing inputs will always be easier to manipulate than ones that behave chaotically. We believe that one should rather err on the side of regularity. Compare the situation to voting: Under most reasonable voting rules, cheaters who manage to improperly submit multiple ballots actually increase the chances of their favored candidates being selected. But that should not be held against the voting rule: It almost necessarily comes with trying to give equal weight to all votes, which is a principle that should not be carelessly abandoned in the name of deterring cheaters.

Since this notion is defined for allocation *rules* only, we need to break ties and this tie-breaking scheme needs to be suitably chosen: A tie-breaking relation[6] $>^T$ is *duplication-compatible*[7] if for any two allocations $\pi, \pi' \in \Pi(G, n+1)$ satisfying that $\pi >^T \pi'$, either $(\pi_1, \ldots, \pi_{n-1}, \pi_n \cup \pi_{n+1}) = (\pi'_1, \ldots, \pi'_{n-1}, \pi'_n \cup \pi'_{n+1})$ or $(\pi_1, \ldots, \pi_{n-1}, \pi_n \cup \pi_{n+1}) >^T (\pi'_1, \ldots, \pi'_{n-1}, \pi'_n \cup \pi'_{n+1})$.

Necessary Duplication Monotonicity. As we saw in Example 1, any scoring allocation correspondence using a strictly decreasing scoring vector and utilitarian social welfare simply gives each good to an agent who ranks it highest, essentially ignoring the scoring vector. It is then easy to see that such a rule satisfies necessary duplication monotonicity. Baumeister et al. [7] leave open the question: *Does necessary duplication monotonicity hold for any scoring allocation rule using* min *or* leximin *as their social welfare ordering?*

In the following examples we show that the answer is "no" for many common choices of scoring vectors. In each case we exploit the possibility of a mismatch of the agents' "real" preferences over sets and the "proxy" preferences induced by the scoring vector, which the allocation rule actually uses to make its decision. This can mean that the allocation rule tries hard to give *good* items to an agent and her clone, whereas in fact the agent might prefer getting *many* items. This makes necessary duplication monotonicity quite hard to satisfy.

Example 2. Consider the following preference profiles over 8 resp. 9 goods:

$$P_1 = (fdcbaehg, agfehdcb, abcdefgh), \quad P_2 = (abecdgfh, dbhfecag, abcdefgh),$$
$$P_3 = (bfceiahgd, hcibfdeag, abcdefghi).$$

We then have

$$F^T_{\text{lex,leximin}}(P_1) = F^T_{\text{lex,min}}(P_1) = \{(f, a, bcdegh)\},$$
$$F^T_{\text{lex,leximin}}(P_1^{\text{dup}}) = F^T_{\text{lex,min}}(P_1^{\text{dup}}) = \{(f, degh, a, bc), (f, degh, bc, a)\},$$
$$F^T_{\text{borda,leximin}}(P_2) = \{(beg, dfh, ac)\},$$

---

[6] more precisely, a family of tie-breaking relations $>^T_n$ on $\Pi(G, n)$ for all $n \geq 1$ (note that this property is really about how the orders $>^T_n$ and $>^T_{n+1}$ interact)

[7] Note that this condition, which is taken from Baumeister et al. [7], is more a technical device than a substantive suggestion for how to choose tie-breaking mechanisms. In the definition of duplication monotonicity the *last* agent gets duplicated. This choice is arbitrary, but this is justified by the fact that scoring allocation correspondences are anonymous, so the choice does not matter for our results, as long as no tied winning allocations occur. However, after applying a tie-breaking mechanism, the resulting allocation rule will no longer be anonymous, by necessity—non-trivial anonymous allocation *rules* do not exist. The definition here is carefully chosen to match the particular choice of duplicating the last agent, so we can give succinct statements of our main theorems that hold even in cases of tied winners. In those (and only those) cases, the results do depend on the arbitrary choices here, so are not entirely natural.

$$F^T_{\text{borda,leximin}}(P^{\text{dup}}_2) = \{(ag, fh, be, cd), (ag, fh, cd, be)\},$$

$$F^T_{\text{borda-qi,leximin}}(P_3) = F^T_{\text{borda-qi,min}}(P_3) = \{(cef, dhi, abg)\},$$

$$F^T_{\text{borda-qi,leximin}}(P^{\text{dup}}_3) = F^T_{\text{borda-qi,min}}(P^{\text{dup}}_3) = \{(bf, hi, ac, deg), (bf, hi, deg, ac)\}.$$

The first two lines show that $F^T_{\text{lex,leximin}}$ and $F^T_{\text{lex,min}}$ cannot satisfy necessary duplication monotonicity for any tie-breaking scheme T. For no matter which of the two winning allocations for P^{dup}_1 the tie-breaker T picks, agent 3 and her clone will receive a, b, and c, which is not necessarily better than receiving $\{b, c, d, e, g, h\}$ as agent 3 did on her own. Similarly, the other two examples show that neither the scoring allocation rule with Borda scoring and leximin social welfare nor the one with qi scoring and min or leximin social welfare (and arbitrary tie-breaking schemes) satisfy necessary duplication monotonicity.

Possible duplication monotonicity, potentially, is much easier to satisfy than the necessary variant, because it is at least possible that agent n's true preferences over sets agree exactly with the "proxy" utilities that the scoring allocation tries to maximize. More precisely, let s be a strictly decreasing scoring vector, $\succsim$ an SWO, and P a preference profile and let $\pi = F^T_{s,\succsim}(P)$ and $\pi' = F^T_{s,\succsim}(P^{\text{dup}})$. (with a duplication-compatible tie-breaking relation $>^T$). For possible duplication monotonicity we need to show that $\pi'_n \cup \pi'_{n+1} \succsim^{\text{pos}}_n \pi_n$. By Lemma 1, this is equivalent to $v(\pi'_n \cup \pi'_{n+1}) \geq v(\pi_n)$ holding true for some additive utility function $v \colon 2^G \to \mathbb{R}_{\geq 0}$ compatible with the ranking $>_n$. But one such utility function is $u_{>_n,s}$, used in the definition of the scoring allocation rule. So it is in fact enough to show that $u_{>_n,s}(\pi'_n) + u_{>_n,s}(\pi'_{n+1}) \geq u_{>_n,s}(\pi_n)$. The utilities appearing here are exactly what the scoring allocation correspondence $F_{s,\succsim}$ is trying to maximize. Essentially then, what remains to be proved is that the social welfare maximizing allocation rule for additive *cardinal preferences* satisfies duplication monotonicity. This is far from apparent, even for the case where $\succsim$ is the leximin ordering. Baumeister et al. [7] only show that $F^T_{\text{lex,leximin}}$ and $F^T_{\text{borda-qi,leximin}}$ satisfy possible duplication monotonicity.[8]

We will show in Theorem 2 that those are just two very particular cases of a vastly more general fact: $F^T_{s,\succsim}$ satisfies possible duplication monotonicity for any strictly decreasing s and any *split-coherent* $\succsim$ (see below), which includes leximin and utilitiarian social welfare and also all the SWFs W_p from Definition 2.

Definition 7. *Let $\succsim$ be a family of SWOs (formally, $\succsim = (\succsim^{(n)})_{n \geq 1}$, where $\succsim^{(n)}$ is a total preorder on $\mathbb{Q}^n_{\geq 0}$ for each n, though we will write all the $\succsim^{(n)}$ as $\succsim$). Then $\succsim$ is called* split-coherent *if the following holds: For all $u, v \in \mathbb{Q}^n_{\geq 0}$ such that $u \succsim v$ and all rational numbers $x \geq y \geq 0$ and $x' \geq y' \geq 0$ with $x + x' = u_n$ and $y + y' = v_n$, we have $(u_1, \ldots, u_{n-1}, x, x') \succsim (v_1, \ldots, v_{n-1}, y, y')$. We require this relation to be strict whenever $u \succsim v$ is strict.*

---

[8] The proof for lexicographic scoring also supposes that a winning allocation for $F_{\text{lex,leximin}}$ can give more than one item only to agents whose individual utility is minimal among all agents. That assumption is not correct, as Example 2 illustrates.

While the utilitarian SWO is easily seen to be split-coherent, the proof of split-coherence for the leximin ordering is technical and fairly involved, requiring in particular a proof that a relation $u \succsim^{\mathrm{lm}} v$ for $u, v \in \mathbb{Q}_{\geq 0}^n$ is preserved when we replace some u_i by a smaller number $a < u_i$, as long as we also replace one of the components v_j of v by some b, which is smaller than both v_j and a.

Lemma 2. *The utilitarian and the leximin SWO are split-coherent.*

Proof. The easy proof of split-coherence for the utilitarian SWO is omitted due to space limitations. The technically rather involved proof that the leximin SWO is split-coherent rests on the following two lemmas the first of which establishes a fairly simple property that also holds for all the social welfare orderings $\succsim_{W_p}$ from Definition 2 (excluding some bad cases when $p \leq 0$).

Lemma 3. *For $u, v \in \mathbb{Q}_{\geq 0}^n$ two vectors and a $\in \mathbb{Q}_{\geq 0}$, $u \succsim^{\mathrm{lm}} v \iff (u_1, \ldots, u_n, a) \succsim^{\mathrm{lm}} (v_1, \ldots, v_n, a)$; if either relation is strict, then so is the other.*

Proof. First note that u is a permutation of v if and only if the vector $(u_1, \ldots, u_n, a)$ is a permutation of the vector $(v_1, \ldots, v_n, a)$, so $u \sim^{\mathrm{lm}} v$ if and only if $(u_1, \ldots, u_n, a) \sim^{\mathrm{lm}} (v_1, \ldots, v_n, a)$ (we refer to this as the "permutation property"). In other words: Either relation *fails* to be strict if the other fails to be strict. Therefore, the claim about strictness in the statement follows from the main claim.

We now show the main claim by induction on n. First, let $n = 1$. Then $u = (u_1)$ and $v = (v_1)$. If $u \succsim^{\mathrm{lm}} v$, i.e., $u_1 \geq v_1$, then weak monotonicity of the leximin ordering (which can be easily observed) shows that $(u_1, a) \geq (v_1, a)$. Conversely, assume that $(u_1, a) \succsim^{\mathrm{lm}} (v_1, a)$. Four cases may occur:

  i. $a \leq u_1, v_1$. Then (recalling that $\geq^{\mathrm{lex}}$ denotes the lexicographic order on $\mathbb{Q}^n$) we have $(a, u_1) = (u_1, a)^* \geq^{\mathrm{lex}} (v_1, a)^* = (a, v_1)$. By the definition of the lexicographic order, this holds if and only if $u_1 \geq v_1$.
  ii. $v_1 \leq a \leq u_1$. Then we can immediately conclude $u_1 \geq v_1$.
  iii. $u_1 \leq a \leq v_1$. Then $(u_1, a) = (u_1, a)^* \geq^{\mathrm{lex}} (v_1, a)^* = (a, v_1)$. By the definition of the lexicographic order, we must have $u_1 \geq a$, so $u_1 = a$. But then, looking to the second component, we must have $a \geq v_1$, so $a = v_1$. Thus we have $u_1 = v_1$.
  iv. $u_1, v_1 \leq a$. Then $(u_1, a) = (u_1, a)^* \geq^{\mathrm{lex}} (v_1, a)^* = (v_1, a)$, and the definition of the lexicographic order gives us $u_1 \geq v_1$.

Now assume the statement is true for some $n \geq 1$. Let $u \in \mathbb{Q}_{\geq 0}^{n+1}$ and $v \in \mathbb{Q}_{\geq 0}^{n+1}$ and set $\overline{u} = (u_1, \ldots, u_{n+1}, a)$ and $\overline{v} = (v_1, \ldots, v_{n+1}, a)$. First assume $u \succsim^{\mathrm{lm}} v$. Consider the following cases:

  i. $\min(\overline{u}) = a$. Now either $\min(\overline{v}) < a$, in which case $\overline{u} \succsim^{\mathrm{lm}} \overline{v}$ and we are done, or $\min(\overline{v}) = a$. In that case, by the definition of the leximin order, $\overline{u} \succsim^{\mathrm{lm}} \overline{v} \iff \overline{u}_{-(n+2)} \succsim^{\mathrm{lm}} \overline{u}_{-(n+2)} \iff u \succsim^{\mathrm{lm}} v$, and we are also done.
  ii. $\min(\overline{u}) \neq a$ and $\min(\overline{v}) = a$. In this case, $u_i < a$ for some $i \in \{1, \ldots, n+1\}$, whereas $v_j \geq a$ for all $j \in \{1 \ldots, n+1\}$. Hence $\min(u) \leq u_i < a \leq \min(v)$, in contradiction to $u \succsim^{\mathrm{lm}} v$. So this case cannot actually occur.

iii. $\min(\overline{u}) \neq a$ and $\min(\overline{v}) \neq a$. In this case $\min(\overline{u}) = u_i$ and $\min(\overline{v}) = v_j$ for suitably chosen $i, j \in \{1, \ldots, n+1\}$. Then we also have $\min(u) = u_i$ and $\min(v) = v_j$. Since $u \succsim^{\mathrm{lm}} v$, we either have $v_j < u_i$, in which case $\overline{u} \succsim^{\mathrm{lm}} \overline{v}$, or we have $v_j = u_i$ and $u_{-i} \succsim^{\mathrm{lm}} v_{-j}$. Now $u_{-i}, v_{-j} \in \mathbb{Q}_{\geq 0}^n$, so by the induction hypothesis $(u_1, \ldots, u_{i-1}, u_{i+1}, \ldots, u_n, a) \succsim^{\mathrm{lm}} (v_1, \ldots, v_{j-1}, v_{j+1}, \ldots, v_n, a)$, and so $\overline{u}_{-i} \succsim^{\mathrm{lm}} \overline{v}_{-j}$. Hence $\overline{u} \succsim^{\mathrm{lm}} \overline{v}$.

Conversely, assume $\overline{u} \succsim^{\mathrm{lm}} \overline{v}$. We go through three cases again:

i. $\min(\overline{v}) = a$. In this case, $a = \min(\overline{v}) \leq \min(\overline{u}) \leq u_i$ for all $i \in \{1, \ldots, n+1\}$. Therefore, $\min(\overline{u}) = a = \min(\overline{v})$, showing that $u = \overline{u}_{-(n+2)} \succsim^{\mathrm{lm}} \overline{v}_{-(n+2)} = v$.

ii. $\min(\overline{v}) \neq a$ and $\min(\overline{u}) = a$. In this case there is some $j \in \{1, \ldots, n+1\}$ with $v_j = \min(\overline{v}) < a$ while $a \leq u_i$ for all $i \in \{1, \ldots, n+1\}$. Then $\min(v) = v_j < a \leq \min(u)$ and thus $u \succsim^{\mathrm{lm}} v$.

iii. $\min(\overline{v}) \neq a$ and $\min(\overline{u}) \neq a$. In this case $\min(\overline{v}) = v_j < a$ and $\min(\overline{u}) = u_i < a$ for certain $i, j \in \{1, \ldots, n+1\}$. In particular then, $u_i = \min(u)$ and $v_j = \min(v)$. Since $\overline{u} \succsim^{\mathrm{lm}} \overline{v}$ we either have $u_i > v_j$, in which case $u \succsim^{\mathrm{lm}} v$, or $u_i = v_j$ and $\overline{u}_{-i} \succsim^{\mathrm{lm}} \overline{v}_{-j}$. But then $(u_1, \ldots, u_{i-1}, u_{i+1}, \ldots, u_n, a) \succsim^{\mathrm{lm}} (v_1, \ldots, v_{j-1}, v_{j+1}, \ldots, v_n, a)$, and we obtain $u_{-i} = (u_1, \ldots, u_{i-1}, u_{i+1}, \ldots, u_n) \succsim^{\mathrm{lm}} (v_1, \ldots, v_{j-1}, v_{j+1}, \ldots, v_n) = v_{-j}$ by the induction hypothesis, thus $u \succsim^{\mathrm{lm}} v$.

This completes the proof. $\square$

The second lemma, however, seems to be rather peculiar to the leximin ordering.

Lemma 4. *Let $u, v \in \mathbb{Q}_{\geq 0}^n$ with $u \succsim^{\mathrm{lm}} v$. Now let $a, b \in \mathbb{Q}_{\geq 0}$ with $a > b$ and $b < v_n$ and set $u' = (u_1, \ldots, u_{n-1}, a)$ and $v' = (v_1, \ldots, v_{n-1}, b)$. Then $u' \succsim^{\mathrm{lm}} v'$. If u and v even satisfy $u \succ^{\mathrm{lm}} v$, then also $u' \succ^{\mathrm{lm}} v'$.*

Proof. We prove the claim by induction over n. For $n = 1$ we always have $u' = (a) \succ^{\mathrm{lm}} (b) = v'$, since $a > b$. So assume the claim is true for some $n \geq 1$. Let $u, v \in \mathbb{Q}_{\geq 0}^{n+1}$ with $u \succsim^{\mathrm{lm}} v$ and $a, b \in \mathbb{Q}_{\geq 0}$ with $a > b$ and $b < v_{n+1}$. Set $u' = (u_1, \ldots, u_n, a)$ and $v' = (v_1, \ldots, v_n, b)$. We distinguish three cases:

i. $\min(u') = a$. In this case, $\min(v') \leq b < a = \min(u')$, so $u' \succ^{\mathrm{lm}} v'$.

ii. $\min(u') \neq a$ and $\min(v) = v_{n+1}$. In this case $\min(u') = u_i < a$ for some $i \in \{1, \ldots, n\}$ and $b < v_{n+1} = \min(v) \leq v_j$ for all $j \in \{1, \ldots, n\}$. Hence, $b = \min(v')$. But now $\min(u') = u_i \geq \min(u) \geq \min(v) = v_{n+1} > b = \min(v')$, and hence $u' \succ^{\mathrm{lm}} v'$.

iii. $\min(u') \neq a$ and $\min(v) \neq v_{n+1}$. In this case $\min(u') = u_i < a$ for some $i \in \{1, \ldots, n\}$ and $\min(v) = v_j < v_{n+1}$ for some $j \in \{1, \ldots, n\}$. If $b < v_j$, then $\min(v') = b < v_j = \min(v) \leq \min(u) \leq u_i = \min(u')$, so, again, $u' \succ^{\mathrm{lm}} v'$ and we are done. Otherwise $v_j = \min(v')$. Then we have $\min(v') = v_j = \min(v) \leq \min(u) \leq u_i = \min(u')$. If $\min(v') < \min(u')$, we have $u' \succ^{\mathrm{lm}} v'$ and we are done. Otherwise, $\min(v') = \min(u')$ and we need to show that $u'_{-i} \succsim^{\mathrm{lm}} v'_{-j}$. In this case, equality holds everywhere in the above inequalities and in particular we have $\min(u) = \min(v)$ and $\min(u) = u_i$. So since $u \succsim^{\mathrm{lm}} v$, we need to have $u_{-i} \succsim^{\mathrm{lm}} v_{-j}$. We then have $u'_{-i} = (u_1, \ldots, u_{i-1}, u_{i+1}, \ldots, u_n, a) \succsim^{\mathrm{lm}} (v_1, \ldots, v_{j-1}, v_{j+1}, \ldots, v_n, b) = v'_{-j}$ by the induction hypothesis, and therefore $u' \succsim^{\mathrm{lm}} v'$.

If $u \succ^{\mathrm{lm}} v$, then we even have $u_{-i} \succ^{\mathrm{lm}} v_{-j}$, and again the induction hypothesis gives $u'_{-i} \succ^{\mathrm{lm}} v'_{-j}$ and hence $u' \succ^{\mathrm{lm}} v'$.

This completes the proof. $\square$

Now, using Lemmas 3 and 4, we are ready to complete the proof that the leximin ordering $\succsim^{\mathrm{lm}}$ is split-coherent. We are given $u, v \in \mathbb{Q}_{\geq 0}^n$ such that $u \succsim^{\mathrm{lm}} v$ and rational numbers $x \geq y \geq 0$ and $x' \geq y' \geq 0$ with $x + x' = u_n$ and $y + y' = v_n$.

First, we need to get some trivial cases out of the way. Consider the case that at least one of x, x' is zero (hence the other is u_n) and at least one of y, y' is zero (hence the other is v_n). Then using the "permutation property" (which is defined in the first paragraph in the proof of Lemma 3) and Lemma 3 gives $(u_1, \ldots, u_{n-1}, x, x') \sim^{\mathrm{lm}} (u_1, \ldots, u_{n-1}, u_n, 0) \succsim^{\mathrm{lm}} (v_1, \ldots, v_{n-1}, v_n, 0) \sim^{\mathrm{lm}} (v_1, \ldots, v_{n-1}, y, y')$, with strictness whenever $u \succ^{\mathrm{lm}} v$.

Next, consider the case that one of y and y' is zero (hence the other is v_n), but $x, x' > 0$. For any $r \geq 1$ and any $w \in \mathbb{Q}_{\geq 0}^r$, denote by $Z(w) = \{i \in \{1, \ldots, r\} \mid w_i = 0\}$ the number of zero components in w. Since $u \succsim^{\mathrm{lm}} v$, we have $Z(u) \leq Z(v)$. Furthermore,

$$Z((v_1, \ldots, v_{n-1}, y, y')) = Z((v_1, \ldots, v_{n-1}, v_n, 0)) = Z(v) + 1.$$

Meanwhile,

$$Z((u_1, \ldots, u_{n-1}, x, x')) = Z((u_1, \ldots, u_{n-1})) = Z(u) \leq Z(v).$$

This implies $(u_1, \ldots, u_{n-1}, x, x') \succ^{\mathrm{lm}} (v_1, \ldots, v_{n-1}, y, y')$.

Having covered all the cases where one of y, y' is zero, we may now assume, for the rest of the proof, that both $y, y' \neq 0$. We distinguish three more cases:

i. $x > y$. Note that $y < y + y' = v_n$. Then, by Lemma 4, we have

$$(u_1, \ldots, u_{n-1}, x) \succsim^{\mathrm{lm}} (v_1, \ldots, v_{n-1}, y),$$

with strictness if $u \succ v$. By monotonicity of the leximin ordering and Lemma 3 we obtain

$$(u_1, \ldots, u_{n-1}, x, x') \succsim^{\mathrm{lm}} (u_1, \ldots, u_{n-1}, x, y') \succsim^{\mathrm{lm}} (v_1, \ldots, v_{n-1}, y, y'),$$

with strictness if the former relation was strict.

ii. $x' > y'$. With the same argument as in the first case and using the permutation property, we obtain $(u_1, \ldots, u_{n-1}, x, x') \sim (u_1, \ldots, u_{n-1}, x', x) \succsim^{\mathrm{lm}} (v_1, \ldots, v_{n-1}, y', y) \sim (u_1, \ldots, u_{n-1}, y, y')$, with strictness if $u \succ v$.

iii. $x = x'$ and $y = y'$. Then $u_n = v_n$. Using Lemma 3 three times, we obtain

$$
\begin{aligned}
u \succsim v \implies & (u_1, \ldots, u_{n-1}) \succsim (v_1, \ldots, v_{n-1}) \\
\implies & (u_1, \ldots, u_{n-1}, x) \succsim (v_1, \ldots, v_{n-1}, y) \\
\implies & (u_1, \ldots, u_{n-1}, x, x') \succsim (v_1, \ldots, v_{n-1}, y, y'),
\end{aligned}
$$

and all these implications preserve strictness.

This shows that the leximin SWO is split-coherent, completing the proof of Lemma 2. □

Now we show our main result.

Theorem 2. *Let G be a finite set of m goods, $s \in \mathbb{Q}_{\geq 0}^m$ a strictly decreasing scoring vector, $\succsim$ a split-coherent SWO, and $>^T$ a duplication-compatible tie-breaking relation. Then $F_{s,\succsim}^T$ satisfies possible duplication monotonicity.*

Proof. Let $P = (>_1, \ldots, >_n)$ be a preference profile and denote the extended profile $P^{\text{dup}} = (>_1, \ldots, >_n, >_{n+1})$ with $>_{n+1} = >_n$. Let $\pi = (\pi_1, \ldots, \pi_n) = F_{s,\succsim}^T(P)$ and $\rho' = (\rho_1', \ldots, \rho_n', \rho_{n+1}') = F_{s,\succsim}^T(P^{\text{dup}})$. Define $\rho = (\rho_1', \ldots, \rho_{n-1}', \rho_n' \cup \rho_{n+1}') \in \Pi(G, n)$. Suppose for a contradiction that $\rho_n' \cup \rho_{n+1}' \succsim_n^{\text{pos}} \pi_n$ does *not* hold. Then $\pi_n \succ_n^{\text{nec}} \rho_n' \cup \rho_{n+1}' = \rho_n$. By Lemma 1, there is then an injection $f \colon \rho_n \hookrightarrow \pi_n$ with $f(a) \geq_n a$ for all $a \in \rho_n$. Let $\pi_n' = f(\rho_n')$ and $\pi_{n+1}' = \pi_n \setminus \pi_n' = f(\rho_{n+1}') \cup (\pi_n \setminus f(\rho_n))$. Since the restrictions of f to ρ_n' and ρ_{n+1}' are still injections to π_n' and π_{n+1}', respectively, with $f(a) \geq a$ for all a in the domain, we have $\pi_n' \succsim^{\text{nec}} \rho_n'$ and $\pi_{n+1}' \succsim^{\text{nec}} \rho_{n+1}'$.

Consider the vectors $v = u_{P,s}(\pi)$ and $w = u_{P,s}(\rho)$. Since $\pi \in F_{s,\succsim}(P)$, we must have $v \succsim w$. We also have $v_n = u_{>_n,s}(\pi_n) = u_{>_n,s}(\pi_n' \cup \pi_{n+1}') = u_{>_n,s}(\pi_n') + u_{>_n,s}(\pi_{n+1}')$ and $w_n = u_{>_n,s}(\rho_n) = u_{>_n,s}(\rho_n' \cup \rho_{n+1}') = u_{>_n,s}(\rho_n') + u_{>_n,s}(\rho_{n+1}')$. Note that $u_{>_n,s} \colon 2^G \to \mathbb{R}_{\geq 0}$ is an additive utility function, which is compatible with $>_n$ since s is strictly decreasing. Let $x = u_{>_n,s}(\pi_n')$, $x' = u_{>_n,s}(\pi_{n+1}')$, $y = u_{>_n,s}(\rho_n')$, and $y' = u_{>_n,s}(\rho_{n+1}')$. By Lemma 1, it follows that $x \geq y$ and $x' \geq y'$. Since $\succsim$ is split-coherent, we have

$$
\begin{aligned}
u_{P^{\text{dup}},s}(\pi') &= (u_{>_1,s}(\pi_1), \ldots, u_{>_{n-1},s}(\pi_{n-1}), u_{>_n,s}(\pi_n'), u_{>_n,s}(\pi_{n+1}')) \\
&= (v_1, \ldots, v_{n-1}, x, x') \succsim (w_1, \ldots, w_{n-1}, y, y') \\
&= (u_{>_1,s}(\rho_1), \ldots, u_{>_{n-1},s}(\rho_{n-1}), u_{>_n,s}(\rho_n'), u_{>_n,s}(\rho_{n+1}')) = u_{P',s}(\rho').
\end{aligned}
$$

If the relation $v = u_{P,s}(\pi) \succsim u_{P,s}(\rho) = w$ were strict, we would even get $u_{P^{\text{dup}},s}(\pi') \succ u_{P^{\text{dup}},s}(\rho')$, again by the definition of split-coherence. But this cannot be true, since $\rho' \in F_{s,\succsim}(P^{\text{dup}})$ implies that $u_{P^{\text{dup}},s}(\rho') \succsim u_{P^{\text{dup}},s}(\pi')$. Hence we must have $u_{P,s}(\pi) \sim u_{P,s}(\rho)$ and $u_{P^{\text{dup}},s}(\rho') \sim u_{P^{\text{dup}},s}(\pi')$. But since $\pi = F_{s,\succsim}^T(P)$ and $\rho' = F_{s,\succsim}^T(P^{\text{dup}})$, the tie-breaking relation $>^T$ must satisfy $\pi >^T \rho$ and $\rho' >^T \pi'$. This is a contradiction to the duplication-compatibility of $>^T$. □

Corollary 1. *For s a strictly decreasing scoring vector, $\star \in \{+, \text{leximin}\}$, and $>^T$ a duplication-compatible tie-breaking relation, $F_{s,\star}^T$ satisfies possible duplication monotonicity.*

Proof. This follows from Lemma 2 and Theorem 2.   □

Theorem 2 applies to many more SWOs than just these two. The proof of Lemma 5 is omitted due to space limitations; it essentially follows from the fundamental theorem of calculus.

Lemma 5. *Let* $W \colon \mathbb{Q}_{\geq 0}^n \to \mathbb{R}$ *be an SWF, defined by* $W(u_1,\dots,u_n) = \sum_{i=1}^n f(u_i)$, *for some* $f \colon \mathbb{R}_{\geq 0} \to \mathbb{R}$. *If* f *satisfies* $f(x+a)-f(x) \leq f(y+a)-f(y)$ *for all* $x \geq y \geq 0$ *and* $a \geq 0$, *then* $\succsim_W$ *is split-coherent. This holds, in particular, whenever* f *is differentiable and concave.*

Corollary 2. *For each* p, $0 < p < 1$, *the social welfare orderings* $\succsim_{W_p}$ *induced by* $W_p \colon \mathbb{Q}_{\geq 0}^n \to \mathbb{R}$, $u \mapsto \sum_{i=1}^n u_i^p$, *are split-coherent.*

Corollary 3. *For* s *a strictly decreasing scoring vector,* $0 < p \leq 1$, *and* $>^T$ *a duplication-compatible tie-breaking relation,* F_{s,W_p}^T *satisfies possible duplication monotonicity.*

Proof. This is now immediate from Lemma 5, Corollary 2, and Theorem 2.   □

This central result still essentially holds for the W_p with $p \leq 0$, though the statements in this case have to be slightly modified, in order to deal with the complications presented by utility vectors with zero entries.

5   Pareto Optimality

Brams et al. [12] study the question of Pareto optimality of $F_{s,\star}(P)$ with $\star \in \{+, \min, \mathrm{leximin}\}$.[9] Informally, an allocation π is called *Pareto-optimal* (with respect to some preference profile) if there is no other allocation which makes all agents at least as well off as π and some agent better off. As in the previous section we actually obtain two variants of this notion. Definition 8 is due to Brams et al. [12].

Definition 8. *Let* G *be a finite set of goods. For a preference* $> \in \mathscr{P}(G)$ *over* G, *denote by* $\mathscr{E}_{\mathrm{add}}(>)$ *the set of all additively representable set extensions of* $>$ *to* 2^G. *For a preference profile* $P = (>_1,\dots,>_n) \in \mathscr{P}(G)^n$, $\mathscr{E}_{\mathrm{add}}(P) = \mathscr{E}_{\mathrm{add}}(>_1) \times \cdots \times \mathscr{E}_{\mathrm{add}}(>_n)$. *Let* $\pi, \rho \in \Pi(G,n)$. *For* $\widehat{P} = (\succeq_1,\dots,\succeq_n) \in \mathscr{E}_{\mathrm{add}}(P)$, *we say that* ρ *Pareto-dominates* π *with respect to* $\widehat{P}$ *if* $\rho_i \succeq_i \pi_i$ *for all* $i \in \{1,\dots,n\}$ *and* $\rho_j \succ_j \pi_j$ *for some* $j \in \{1,\dots,n\}$. *We say that* π *is Pareto-optimal for* $\widehat{P}$ *if no* $\rho \in \Pi(G,n)$ *Pareto-dominates* π *with respect to* $\widehat{P}$. *We say that* π *is possibly (respectively, necessarily) Pareto-optimal for* P *if* π *is Pareto-optimal for some (respectively, for all)* $\widehat{P} \in \mathscr{E}_{\mathrm{add}}(P)$.

The following is a generalization of a result of Brams et al. [12, Theorem 4.9] (which treats only the special case of Borda scoring and the utilitarian or leximin ordering). The proof of Theorem 3 is omitted due to space limitations.

---

[9] In their terminology, *maxsum divisions*, *maxmin divisions*, and *equimax divisions*.

Theorem 3. *Let G be a set of m goods, $s \in \mathbb{Q}_{\geq 0}^m$ a scoring vector, and $\succsim$ a monotonic social welfare ordering (e.g., the leximin ordering or any of the orderings induced by the W_p from Definition 2). For all preference profiles $P \in \mathscr{P}(G)^n$, every $\pi \in F_{s,\succsim}(P)$ is possibly Pareto-optimal for P.*

Necessary Pareto optimality is much harder to satisfy. Such divisions always exist, but the trivial examples tend to violate intuitive notions of fairness and are not usually of the kind returned by scoring allocation correspondences.

Brams et al. [12] give an example of a preference profile of two agents over five goods, namely, $P = (abcde, cadeb)$, such that $F_{\text{borda},+}(P)$ as well as $F_{\text{borda,leximin}}(P)$ consist of a unique allocation, $\pi = (ab, cde)$, which yet fails to be necessarily Pareto-optimal for P. The following example shows that even if all the scoring allocation correspondences $F_{s,\text{leximin}}(P)$ return the same unique allocation for all strictly decreasing scoring vectors $s \in \mathbb{Q}_{>0}^m$, this allocation can still fail to be necessarily Pareto-optimal for P.

Example 3. Consider the profile $P = (abcde, daebc)$. We can show that $\pi = (ab, cde)$ is the unique allocation in $F_{s,\text{leximin}}(P)$ for every strictly decreasing scoring vector $s \in \mathbb{Q}_{>0}^5$. Still, π is not necessarily Pareto-optimal for P, since the allocation $\rho = (bce, ad)$ might be preferred over π by both agents.

6   Conclusions and Outlook

Following Baumeister et al. [7], we have studied the family of scoring allocation correspondences. We have further extended and improved upon their results regarding the properties of monotonicity and duplication monotonicity. We also generalized results of Brams et al. [12] regarding Pareto optimality. Note that our results on monotonicity, duplication monotonicity, and Pareto optimality are very exhaustive, as they cover not just arbitrary strictly decreasing scoring vectors but also utilitarian and leximin social welfare as well as the entire family of social welfare functions W_p.

In future work, it would be interesting to study the computational aspects of the related problems in the spirit of Baumeister et al. [7] and Darmann and Schauer [15].

Acknowledgments. This work was supported in part by DFG grant RO 1202/14-2.

References

1. Aziz, H., Bachrach, Y., Elkind, E., Paterson, M.: False-name manipulations in weighted voting games. J. Artif. Intell. Res. **40**, 57–93 (2011)
2. Aziz, H., Brandt, F., Seedig, H.: Computing desirable partitions in additively separable hedonic games. Artif. Intell. **195**, 316–334 (2013)
3. Aziz, H., Walsh, T., Xia, L.: Possible and necessary allocations via sequential mechanisms. In: Proceedings of IJCAI 2015, pp. 468–474 (2015)

4. Bansal, N., Sviridenko, M.: The Santa Claus problem. In: Proceedings of STOC 2006, pp. 31–40 (2006)
5. Barberà, S., Bossert, W., Pattanaik, P.: Ranking sets of objects. In: Barberà, S., Hammond, P., Seidl, C. (eds.) Handbook of Utility Theory, vol. 2: Extensions, pp. 893–977. Kluwer Academic Publisher (2004)
6. Bartholdi III, J., Tovey, C., Trick, M.: How hard is it to control an election? Math. Comput. Model. **16**(8/9), 27–40 (1992)
7. Baumeister, D., et al.: Positional scoring-based allocation of indivisible goods. J. Auton. Agents Multi Agent Syst. **31**(3), 628–655 (2017)
8. Baumeister, D., Erdélyi, G., Erdélyi, O., Rothe, J.: Complexity of manipulation and bribery in judgment aggregation for uniform premise-based quota rules. Math. Soc. Sci. **76**, 19–30 (2015)
9. Baumeister, D., Rothe, J.: Taking the final step to a full dichotomy of the possible winner problem in pure scoring rules. Inf. Process. Lett. **112**(5), 186–190 (2012)
10. Betzler, N., Dorn, B.: Towards a dichotomy for the possible winner problem in elections based on scoring rules. J. Comput. Syst. Sci. **76**(8), 812–836 (2010)
11. Bouveret, S., Chevaleyre, Y., Maudet, N.: Fair allocation of indivisible goods. In: Brandt, F., Conitzer, V., Endriss, U., Lang, J., Procaccia, A. (eds.) Handbook of Computational Social Choice, pp. 284–310. Cambridge University Press (2016)
12. Brams, S., Edelman, P., Fishburn, P.: Fair division of indivisible items. Theory Decis. **55**(2), 147–180 (2003)
13. Brams, S., King, D.: Efficient fair division: help the worst off or avoid envy? Rat. Soc. **17**(4), 387–421 (2005)
14. Brandt, F., Conitzer, V., Endriss, U., Lang, J., Procaccia, A. (eds.): Handbook of Computational Social Choice. Cambridge University Press, New York (2016)
15. Darmann, A., Schauer, J.: Maximizing Nash product social welfare in allocating indivisible goods. Eur. J. Oper. Res. **247**(2), 548–559 (2015)
16. Elkind, E., Faliszewski, P., Slinko, A.: Cloning in elections: finding the possible winners. J. Artif. Intell. Res. **42**, 529–573 (2011)
17. Elkind, E., Rothe, J.: Cooperative game theory. In: Rothe, J. (ed.) Economics and Computation, pp. 135–193. Springer, Heidelberg (2015). https://doi.org/10.1007/978-3-662-47904-9
18. Konczak, K., Lang, J.: Voting procedures with incomplete preferences. In: Proceedings of the Multidisciplinary IJCAI-05 Workshop on Advances in Preference Handling, pp. 124–129, July/August 2005
19. Lang, J., Rey, A., Rothe, J., Schadrack, H., Schend, L.: Representing and solving hedonic games with ordinal preferences and thresholds. In: Proceedings of AAMAS 2015, pp. 1229–1237 (2015)
20. Lang, J., Rothe, J.: Fair division of indivisible goods. In: Rothe, J. (ed.) Economics and Computation, pp. 493–550. Springer, Heidelberg (2015). https://doi.org/10.1007/978-3-662-47904-9_8
21. Moulin, H.: Condorcet's principle implies the no show paradox. J. Econ. Theory **45**(1), 53–64 (1988)
22. Moulin, H.: Fair Division and Collective Welfare. MIT Press, London (2004)
23. Nguyen, N., Baumeister, D., Rothe, J.: Strategy-proofness of scoring allocation correspondences for indivisible goods. Soc. Choice Welf. **50**(1), 101–122 (2018)
24. Nguyen, T., Roos, M., Rothe, J.: A survey of approximability and inapproximability results for social welfare optimization in multiagent resource allocation. Ann. Math. Artif. Intell. **68**(1–3), 65–90 (2013)
25. Rey, A., Rothe, J.: False-name manipulation in weighted voting games is hard for probabilistic polynomial time. J. Artif. Intell. Res. **50**, 573–601 (2014)

26. Rothe, J., Schadrack, H., Schend, L.: Borda-induced hedonic games with friends, enemies, and neutral players. Math. Soc. Sci. **96**, 21–36 (2018)
27. Sen, A.: Collective Choice and Social Welfare. Holden Day, San Francisco (1970)
28. Tideman, N.: Independence of clones as a criterion for voting rules. Soc. Choice Welf. **4**(3), 185–206 (1987)
29. Xia, L., Conitzer, V.: Determining possible and necessary winners given partial orders. J. Artif. Intell. Res. **41**, 25–67 (2011)

Dynamic Delivery Plan Adaptation in Open Systems

Miguel Ángel Rodríguez-García◉, Alberto Fernández(✉)◉,
and Holger Billhardt◉

Universidad Rey Juan Carlos, Madrid, Spain
{miguel.rodriguez,alberto.fernandez,
holger.billhardt}@urjc.es

Abstract. Open fleets offer a dynamic environment where the fleet is continually rebuilt ad-hoc since vehicles can enter or leave the fleet anytime, and the only immutable entity is the item to be delivered. Therefore, we need to be able to define a changeable delivery plan capable of adapting to such a dynamic environment. Hence, we propose Open Fleet Management, a Self-Management platform capable of optimizing plan delivery dynamically. The platform utilizes information about location, routes, delivery in transit and delivery costs to change the shipment plan according to the available carrier. Therefore, if two carriers are doing a shipment service to the same place, the platform will be able to discover such a situation and put them in contact to optimize the efficiency of the shipment.

Keywords: Multi-agent systems · Delivery ·
Intelligent transportation systems · Semantic technologies · Open systems

1 Introduction

Nowadays, the transportation sector has become one of the primary components of the global economy [1]. Hence, this sector needs the development of innovative transportation technologies capable of reducing the costs, improving the reliability and helping to motivate the globalization process. Since Gaspard Monge formalized the transportation problem in 1781 as an optimization problem [2], it has been reformulated into different ways to investigate similar obstacles which aim for the same target, to reduce the associated costs. Between different proposed approaches, we can find typical problems that logistics companies are usually facing in the current transportation model such as to diminish the CO_2 emissions [3], build new algorithms to face vehicle routing optimization problems [4, 5], develop new smart systems methods to monitor and improve the coordination of their fleets [6, 7]. Generally, such transportation model is based on closed fleet where the volume of the vehicles does not change dynamically; their capabilities are well-known by the company, the delivery plans are not usually changeable (with rare exceptions unavailable vehicles due to puncture, engine problems and so on).

© Springer Nature Switzerland AG 2019
M. Lujak (Ed.): AT 2018, LNAI 11327, pp. 190–198, 2019.
https://doi.org/10.1007/978-3-030-17294-7_14

With the arrival of The Web 2.0 technologies, this model has been affected by the proliferation of Transportation Network Companies (TNC) that provide a more dynamic and disruptive transport model by which whoever vehicle owner can provide transportation services. This new model offers even more complicated challenges because vehicles can dynamically change their status by joining or leaving the fleet. Moreover, vehicles do not belong to a company but rather private owners. Then, we do not know their vehicles capabilities, technical features which offer even more obstacles to coordinate the vehicles efficiently. Different works have been proposed in the literature to tackle some of these problems, for instance, the vehicle routing problems using optimization algorithms [6], a management system for optimizing the coordination in open fleets [7] and innovative methods to define a match factor for heterogeneous fleets of trucks [8].

In this article, we present a formal description of collaborative dynamic plan delivery adaptation. Plan adaptations involve the cooperation among (usually two) agents to deliver transportation tasks more efficiently. Plan improvements are defined in terms of agents' utility, which may be defined as higher commercial revenues, lower CO_2 emissions, among others.

The remainder of the paper is organized as follows. Next section describes the dynamic transportation planning we tackle in this work. In Sect. 3, we describe in depth the designed architecture examining the primary functions of each module. Section 4 shows an example scenario in which we apply our approach. We end up the article highlighting the conclusions and giving some future research lines.

2 Problem Definition

In our system agents can play two main roles, namely *providers* or *clients*. We focus on service *providers*, which carry out transportation *tasks*, such as parcel delivery or human transportation. Service providers have transportation plans P consisting of a sequence of one or more transportation tasks $[t_1, t_2, ..., t_n]$. In the following, we consider parcel delivery tasks. In our approach plan adaptation is analyzed locally. We exploit close geographical location of provider agents so as to analyze whether agents can exchange or delegate tasks, such that both agents benefit from the potential agreement. For example, provider agents delivering/picking parcels in the same residential area at the same time and having also another similar delivery spot might be interested in only one of them going to that destination with both packages and sharing the benefits.

There are two different types of prices for packet deliveries:

- *Price* to client: is the price that client c pays to agent a to carry out task t (*Price(a, t)*), i.e. delivering a package p. It may depend on characteristics such as package physical features (height, width, weight, ...), constraints (temperature, fragility, ...), distance from origin to destination, etc.
- *Cost* of task t for deliverer a (*Cost(a, t)*): is the cost for the delivery agent, which includes petrol, vehicle maintenance, resources spent, distance travelled, value of time spent, etc.

The utility of agent provider a for carrying out a transportation task t, $U_a(t)$, is the difference between the price paid by the client and the cost of carrying the task:

$$U_a(t) = Price(a, t) - Cost(a, t)$$

In the following, we analyze the economic effect that a plan adaptation proposal would have in the involved agents and the conditions for them to reach an agreement on carrying out the adaptation. Given a set of agents in a close proximity, a re-planning proposal requires that each involved provider agent obtains higher revenue than without applying re-planning, i.e. they should accept the proposal. If needed, incentives have to be assigned to tasks exchanges so as to compensate agents for lower revenues.

Given a set of agents A in a vicinity, each of them having a set of tasks to be carried out. Let T be the set of all such tasks. The initial assignment of tasks to delivery agents, $As_0 = \{<t_i, a_j> \mid t_i \in T, a_j \in A\}$, where $<t_i, a_j>$ represents that task t_i is assigned to agent a_j.

The goal of a plan adaptation method is to propose some modifications M of assignments $<t, a_j>$ to $<t, a_k>$ such that a_j and a_k both agree with M, i.e. $U'_{aj} > U_{aj}$ and $U'_{ak} > U_{ak}$, where U'_{aj} and U'_{ak} are the new utilities of a_j and a_k, respectively, after applying M. That is possible if:

$$U'_{aj} = U_{aj} + Cost(a_j, t) - \Delta_{tjk} - \sigma_j(t, a_k)$$

$$U'_{ak} = U_{ak} - Cost(a_k, t) + \Delta_{tjk} - \sigma_k(t, a_j)$$

Where Δ_{tjk} is a compensation that a_j has to pay to a_k for delegating t to a_k, so both agents agree with the deal, and $\sigma_j(t, a_k)$ is a coordination cost for a_j (e.g. time spent for synchronization with a_k, impact on other tasks, etc.). Thus:

$$Cost(a_k, t) + \sigma_k(t, a_j) < \Delta_{tjk} < Cost(a_j, t) - \sigma_j(t, a_k)$$

Note that $Cost(a_k, t)$ takes into account that a_k had already scheduled to go to that destination anyway, so it should be rather low. Thus, the same type of task may have different cost depending on the rest of the plan. The range in which Δ can take values represents the joint benefits resulted from the cooperation.

3 Architecture

The architecture of the platform that we present in this work comprises three modules: (i) the *Repository*, which is one of the primary modules in the platform. It represents the primary data deposit where data related to customers, shipments, vehicles, delivery plans and others is stored. That material is extremely relevant since is used by other modules to carry out their functions; (ii) the *Semantic Descriptor*, which aims at translating data into semantic instances; (iii) the *Semantic Matching* responsible for finding proper vehicles to ship delivery items and finally (iv) the *Plan Manager* implements the functions necessaries to optimize the coordination of vehicles in the fleet. Figure 1 depicts the entire platform architecture highlighting each decomposed module, its tasks, and how it interacts with others.

The working of the platform is as follows: we are assuming a transport scenario where there is a user who needs to utilize a delivery service to transport an item to other location, and different providers who are working in an open fleet. Hence, firstly, the user needs to describe in natural language the items to be delivered. Consequently, he/she has to provide features such as size, fragility or conditions like temperature, refrigeration, etc. Then, the Semantic Descriptor module will transform systematically it into semantic instances representing them using the language RDF. The instances will be stored in the repository together with semantic descriptions about vehicles, providers and users. Next, the semantic matching module is in charge of finding a list of delivery vehicle which fulfill the user's item requirements. For instance, when a user requires a transportation service to a box whose size is 20×20, it requires refrigeration, and it contains fragile objects. Then, the module will recommend to user a set of providers whose vehicles satisfy all the requirements. Once the user selects the driver, the Plan Manager module will assign a new task to the delivery plan of the provider. During the shipping process, the Plan Manager module analyzes continuously other plans to try to coordinate in a better way the fleet. Therefore, a delivery plan can suddenly suffer changes that are suggested to the provider. For instance, given two providers P1 and P2 who have as a task to ship an item approximately in the same place, the Plan Manager will suggest P1 give such item to P2 such that only one driver goes to such location.

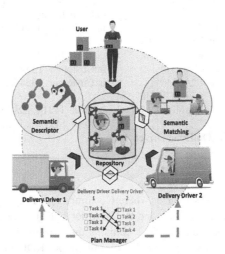

Fig. 1. Architecture of the platform organized in modules

In the following sections, we analyze each module in detail. Hence, we will decompose each one to study their functions and relations to others.

3.1   Semantic Descriptor Module

Due to the way that the database management system structures the data, we have had to develop a module capable of changing the representation of the data into RDF triples. The *Semantic Descriptor* integrates a set of algorithms that aims for translating structured data into triples of the type subject-predicate-object. In the following sections, we detail the procedure that we have developed to describe entities like vehicles, shipment items, delivery tasks, etc. using such structure based on three main elements.

Describing and Matching Delivery Tasks. When an agreement between customer and provider is mutually accepted, the plan manager has to build and assign a new delivery task to the providers' plan. To avoid duplicate data in the repository, we have used the predicate element to relate the duet item-customer, which will represent a delivery task. Then, the *Plan Manager* will relate this duet to the provider in charge of shipping by using a different predicate. Thereby, we make the delivery tasks easy interchangeable among providers. For instance, whether the *Plan Manager* estimates that a concrete task has to be moved from one provider's delivery map to other. Then, it only implies to re-assign the delivery task to the new driver.

Table 1. Data model to represent a delivery task in RDF Turtle format.

Costumer	Task
@prefix rdf: <http://www.w3.org/ 1999/02/22-rdf-syntax-ns#> .	@prefix rdf: <http://www.w3.org/ 1999/02/22-rdf-syntax-ns#> .
@prefix ia: <http://www.ia.urjc.es/ onto/openfleet"> .	@prefix ia: <http://www.ia.urjc.es/ onto/openfleet"> .
ia:Driver_14 ia:driver_id "14".	ia:Task_14214 delivery_task_id "14214".
ia:Driver_14 ia:drives ia:Vehicle_30978.	
ia:Vehicle_30978 ia:vehicle_id "30978".	ia:Task_14214 ia:*assignedTo*
ia:Vehicle_30978 ia:brand "Audi".	ia:Customer_1354.
ia:Vehicle_30978 ia:model "A6".	ia:Customer_1354 ia:customer_id "1354".
ia:Vehicle_30978 ia:max_weight "2430".	...
ia:Vehicle_30978 ia:fuel "Gasoline".	ia:Task_14214 ia:*deliver* Item_14314.
...	ia:Item_14314 ia:item_id "14314".
Task_14214 ia:isCarriedOutBy ia:Driver_14.	...
...	

Let's assume a normal scenario, where Costumer 1 (C1) query service to transport an Item 1 (I1) to a specific location and the Provider 1 (P1) represents the driver who is going to carry out the service. Table 1 contains the data model designed to represent the entities Tasks and Providers. Firstly, it contains an RDF Turtle representation of this scenario, it describes the Provider instance, which is related to other two instances: Vehicle_30978, which stands for the vehicle that belongs the Provider, and Task_14214 that represents the task to deliver by the Provider. Secondly, we define a delivery task that includes the instances Task_14214 and Costumer_1354.

Describing Transportation Capabilities (Vehicle). In this domain vehicles play an extremely relevant role in the dialogue between customer and driver due to their technical features establish whether or not the vehicle could be selected to carry out the service. Therefore, we need to represent a vehicle taking into account physical features such as size, capacity, weights, heights, refrigeration system, etc. to fit properly into the features of the items. In this work, we have used the conceptual model developed in [9]. In this approach, we conducted an intensive literature review to analyze cutting-edge approaches that utilize semantic technologies to represent knowledge associated to the car world.

Describing Delivery Items. Delivery items represent even the most relevant entity to the open fleets domain. Its optimized shipment concerning analyzed variables such as reducing CO_2, finding the shortest path, avoiding waste resources, among others. Those variables represent the primary target that we try to achieve by developing this platform. Thereby, we need to take extremely carefully into account their physical characteristics because the success of the delivery plan is highly dependent on them. To represent a delivery item, we have built a new ontology model which contains the following features: shape (box), height (cm), width (cm), weight (kg), fragility (yes/no), priority (yes/no), temperature-sensitive (yes/no).

3.2   Semantic Matching Module

We utilize SPARQL language to query for all vehicles that match with the given semantic item description. Then, the retrieved vehicles will be sorted by taking into account the space available in their trailer for that date. For instance, we assume that we want to transport a fragile box of 20 × 20 dimension to Murcia on 20th October. Once the *Semantic Descriptor* module translates these details to an RDF representation, then the *Semantic Matching* module will utilize this semantic representation to retrieve from repository all vehicles that match with this description. Thereby, a SPARQL query is systematically built to query the repository. Next, a list of instances is retrieved and sorted taking into account the available space of the vehicle to this date, the requirements given and also the date.

3.3   Plan Manager

The *Plan Manager* has a main function for the good performance of the platform presented in this work. Its aim is building and managing the delivery plan according that we discussed in the Sect. 2. Therefore, when there is an agreement between user and driver, we need to build a delivery plan that includes all the shipment for a concrete date. Generally, in a closed fleet, the fleet manager system generates a fixed plan which the provider has to carry out. However, in open fleets, the plan can be suddenly modified to enhance its performance providing a new plan capable of reducing the CO_2 emissions, orchestrating better or providing a more optimized transportation service.

4 Use Case (Plan Adaptation)

In this section, we introduce a real scenario where we will define the main relevant issues known in collaborative transportation domain. We focus on plan adaptation. In the scenario we assume that there are three delivery agents D_1, D_2, D_3 in close locations at a given time with the plans shown in Fig. 2.

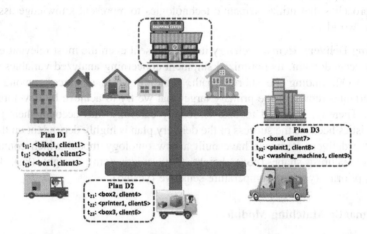

Fig. 2. Scenario configured to perform the use case.

Items *book1* and *printer1* have the following descriptions:

- "book1": [*ia:height: 30 cm, ia:width: 20 cm, ia:weight: 1.8 kg, ia:fragility: no, ia: destination: {shop12, shopping mall central, zip code:12345}]*
- "printer1": [*ia:height: 40 cm, ia:width: 60 cm, ia:weight: 5 kg, ia:fragility: no, ia: destination: {travel agency TA, shopping mall central, zip code:12345}]*

In the current delivery plans, tasks t12 and t22 have the following prices: $Price(D_1, t_{12}) = 3.99 €$, $Cost(D_1, t_{12}) = 2 €$, $Price(D_2, t_{22}) = 6.99 €$, $Cost(D_2, t_{22}) = 3.5 €$.

The system realizes that there is a potential improvement of plans of D_1 and D_2. They both have to go to the "central shopping mall" at some point to deliver a book and a printer, respectively. The system put them in contact. There are two possible improvements: (i) t_{12} is assigned from D_1 to D_2, or (ii) t_{22} is assigned from D_2 to D_1.

Let's assume that for both carriers the cost of taking a small object to a planned destination is 0.50€, and that coordination costs in both cases is $\sigma_{D1} = \sigma_{D2} = 0.20€$.

Now, we can analyze the two possibilities:

(A) t_{12} is assigned from D_1 to D_2. In this case, $Cost(D_2, t_{12}) = 0.50€$
   $Cost(D_2, t_{12}) + \sigma_{D2}(t_{12}, D_1) < \Delta < Cost(D_1, t_{12}) - \sigma_{D1}(t_{12}, D_2)$
   $0.50 + 0.20 < \Delta < 2 - 0.20$
   $0.70 < \Delta < 1.80$
   They could reach an agreement in which D_1 pays an amount between 0.70€ and 1.80€, for example, the mid quantity 1.25€.

(B) t_{22} is assigned from D_2 to D_1. In this case, $Cost(D_1, t_{22}) = 0.50€$

$Cost(D_1, t_{22}) + \sigma_{D1}(t_{22}, D_1) < \Delta < Cost(D_2, t_{22}) - \sigma_{D2}(t_{22}, D_1)$

$0.50 + 0.20 < \Delta < 3.5 - 0.20$

$0.70 < \Delta < 3.3$

In this case, the agreement would be reached if D_2 pays between 0.70€ and 3.3€ to D_1, for example 2€.

From the previous analysis, the best option is (B) since the savings are bigger, and the benefits for both agents are higher.

5   Conclusions

In this work, we have formalized the delivery problem in open fleets, where transportation tasks appear dynamically and deliverer agents may join and leave the fleet at their will. We have seen how the decomposition of a delivery plan in a set of tasks can directly affect the performance of the fleet. We have explored the conditions to dynamically carry out task re-assignment among deliverer agents. Finally, we have also proposed an architecture that is responsible for implementing this model.

Despite of generating a mathematical model capable of solving the analyzed problems, there are still several issues related to dynamic fleet management and coordination that need to be considered. Therefore, we consider them as a research future lines to extend this work. In addition, although we use a centralized infrastructure, we believe that a centralized platform cannot provide the performance that is necessary to coordinate such large open fleets. Therefore, we believe that changing the model into a decentralized approach, it will help us to have a better control of the vehicles' behavior. Moreover, this disruptive model implies new challenges such as to orchestrate and coordinate the new decentralized infrastructure, to provide mechanisms that enable those nodes to share information and control the dynamic fleet. Hence, those are some of the research lines to conduct as future work.

Acknowledgments. Work partially supported by the Autonomous Region of Madrid (grants "MOSI-AGIL-CM" (S2013/ICE-3019) co-funded by EU Structural Funds FSE and FEDER and Talent Attraction Program ("2017-T2/TIC-5664")), project "SURF" (TIN2015-65515-C4-4-R (MINECO/FEDER)) funded by the Spanish Ministry of Economy and Competitiveness, and through the Excellence Research Group GES2ME (Ref. 30VCPIGI05) co-funded by URJC-Santander Bank.

References

1. Rodrigue, J.P., Comtois, C., Slack, B.: The Geography of Transport Systems. Routledge, New York (2009)
2. Monge, G.: Mémoire sur la théorie des déblais et des remblais. Histoire de l'Académie Royale des Sciences de Paris (1781)
3. Wang, W.W., Zhang, M., Zhou, M.: Using LMDI method to analyze transport sector CO2 emissions in China. Energy **36**(10), 5909–5915 (2011)

4. Liu, Y., Wei, L.: The optimal routes and modes selection in multimodal transportation networks based on improved A* algorithm. In: 2018 5th International Conference on Industrial Engineering and Applications (ICIEA), pp. 236–240. IEEE, April 2018
5. Andreica, M.I., Briciu, S., Andreica, M.E.: Algorithmic solutions to some transportation optimization problems with applications in the metallurgical industry. arXiv preprint arXiv: 0903.3622 (2009)
6. Herrero, R., Villalobos, A.R., Cáceres-Cruz, J., Juan, A.A.: Solving vehicle routing problems with asymmetric costs and heterogeneous fleets. Int. J. Adv. Oper. Manage. 6(1), 58–80 (2014)
7. Billhardt, H., et al.: Coordinating open fleets. A taxi assignment example. AI Commun. 30(1), 37–52 (2017)
8. Burt, C.N., Caccetta, L.: Match factor for heterogeneous truck and loader fleets. Int. J. Min. Reclam. Environ. 21(4), 262–270 (2007)
9. Rodríguez-García, M.Á., Fernández, A., Billhardt, H.: Provider recommendation in heterogeneous transportation fleets. In: Bajo, J. (ed.) PAAMS 2018. CCIS, vol. 887, pp. 416–427. Springer, Cham (2018). https://doi.org/10.1007/978-3-319-94779-2_36

Autonomous Vehicles Coordination Through Voting-Based Decision-Making

Miguel Teixeira[1,2](✉) ⓘ, Pedro M. d'Orey[1,2](✉) ⓘ, and Zafeiris Kokkinogenis[1] ⓘ

[1] Universidade do Porto, Porto, Portugal
{up201607941,kokkinogenis}@fe.up.pt, pedro.dorey@dcc.fc.up.pt
[2] Instituto de Telecomunicações, Porto, Portugal

Abstract. This paper proposes the application of computational social choice mechanisms to establish cooperative behavior within traffic scenarios involving autonomous vehicles. The main aim is to understand the suitability of commonly used voting rules as a potential mechanism for collective decision making in platoon applications considering unreliable communications. To realistically assess the system performance, we designed an integrated simulation platform composed of an agent-based platform, a microscopic traffic and a vehicular network models. Results show the viability of these simple voting mechanism to maintain high satisfaction among platoon members, which that can lead to stable formations and consequently better traffic conditions. However, additional mechanisms might need to be considered for larger platoon formations to timely guarantee consensus between voters.

Keywords: Platooning · Voting mechanisms ·
Computational social choice · Connected Automated Vehicle ·
Collective decision-making

1 Introduction

Autonomous driving has gained momentum in recent years due to impressive technological advances put forward by both academic and industrial researchers [24]. The current main focus of automotive manufacturers is to design, build and test vehicles that navigate autonomously in complex (urban) scenarios without explicit cooperation with human drivers or users, i.e. the concept of collective decision-making is considered mainly from an automation point of view. In parallel, advances in vehicular communication networks have enabled cooperation

This work is a result of grant UID/EEA/50008/2013 and the project MobiWise (POCI-01-0145/FEDER-016426), funded by the European Regional Development Fund (FEDER), through the Competitiveness and Internationalization Operational Programme (COMPETE 2020) of the Portugal 2020 framework, and by national funds, through Fundação para a Ciência e Tecnologia (FCT) and by FCT/MEC through national funds.

© Springer Nature Switzerland AG 2019
M. Lujak (Ed.): AT 2018, LNAI 11327, pp. 199–207, 2019.
https://doi.org/10.1007/978-3-030-17294-7_15

between vehicles (V2V, vehicle-to-vehicle communications), and between vehicles and infrastructure (V2I, vehicle-to-infrastructure communications) in an explicit way. In this context, cooperation stems from the periodic or event-driven exchange of static and dynamic data e.g. through the broadcast of Cooperative Awareness Messages (CAM) [6]. Only more recently the concept of Connected Automated Vehicles (CAVs) has gained momentum [18].

Multi-Agent Systems (MAS) research has devised various collective decision-making mechanisms (e.g. auctions, voting) to reach consensus over the agents' aggregated preferences for tactical and strategic decision-making levels[1]. Nevertheless, previous research on vehicle coordination has not studied extensively the application of these approaches in certain domains or the evaluation was mostly done under unrealistic conditions. For instance, MAS research on vehicle coordination has not considered an unreliable communication channel.

In this paper, we study - under realistic conditions - the viability of voting schemes for the coordination of CAVs. We argue that the evaluation of collective decision making should take into account realistic (communication) constraints. Specifically, we argue that collective decision making can be impacted by an unreliable communication channel and bound to the performance of the underlying communication system. As a vehicular coordination use case, we consider a platoon speed negotiation scenario to study the behavior of different voting mechanisms and the impact of the vehicular communication network. Platooning is seen as a promising approach to reduce road congestion and improve safety [13]. To realistically evaluate vehicle coordination mechanisms, we have designed a hybrid simulation framework that encompasses an agent-oriented platform (LightJason [3]), a traffic simulation model (SUMO [16]), and a vehicular communication network simulator (OMNET++ [23]).

The main contributions of this paper are: (1) a multi-resolution and multi-domain simulator for the development and evaluation of agent-based ITS applications considering realistic communication and vehicle constraints, and (2) a preliminary study on the viability of social consensus (specifically, voting schemes) for autonomous vehicles coordination (e.g. platoon cruising speed setting).

The remainder of this paper is organized as follows. In Sect. 2, we outline the application of social choice mechanisms for vehicle coordination. Section 3 details the application of these mechanism in a vehicle platooning use case. The realistic evaluation of voting rules for vehicular coordination is given in Sect. 4. In Sect. 5, we review the relevant work on social consensus mechanisms for vehicle coordination. The main conclusions are provided in Sect. 6.

2   Social Choice in Vehicle Coordination

Social choice theory provides tools for aggregating the preferences/plans of multiple agents, and reaching consensus on any subject matter. We hypothesize that the use of *voting mechanisms* can promote fair cooperative interactions among

---

[1] Hollnagel et al. [12] classified vehicular decision-making levels into strategic (e.g. route), tactical (e.g. maneuvering) and operational (e.g. vehicle control).

a group of agents (i.e. vehicles). In a standard voting procedure, the preferences of all voting members across a set of candidates is aggregated, and based upon their collective preference, a winner or a set of winners is determined.

Model: Let $N = [n]$ be the set of *voters* participating in coordination tasks, A be the set of m *alternatives*, $\{a_1, ..., a_m\}$, and V be the list of votes over A, $\{v_1, ..., v_n\}$. A tuple (A, V) is the election ε. Each voter i has an utility function u_i for alternative a, which is translated into a vote. Each voter is represented by the vote that specifies its preferences over the alternatives in A.

Voting Rule: Within every election, all members must agree upon a voting rule that determines how members cast their votes and how winners are determined. Formally, a voting mechanism is a rule that given a profile ε determines the winner, which can be represented by a social choice correspondence function:

$$F : \{\varepsilon = (A, V) | V \text{ is a preference profile}\} \rightarrow P(A)$$

where $P(A)$ is the power set of A. For any election ε, $F(\varepsilon) \subseteq A$, corresponds to the set of the election winners. In case of multiple winners, a tie-breaking rule is applied. In this paper we consider four common voting rules [2] for single candidate elections, namely:

- *Plurality*: A voter states its preferred candidate, and the winner is the candidate who scores the highest among its competitors.
- *Approval*: Each voter selects a set of favourite candidates. The winner is the candidate with the highest number of approvals.
- *Borda*: Each voter ranks each candidate according to their preferences and attributes a score to each one. For a candidate set of size m, voters give $m - n$ points to the nth ranked candidate (e.g. $m - 1$ to their first choice, $m - 2$ to their second, ... , 0 to their least approved). The winner is the candidate with the most points.
- *Copeland*: Uses a round-robin style election, where each voter casts their preference on every possible pairwise candidate set. The winner is the candidate with the most pairwise wins.

We consider an iterative voting process that is triggered by defined events. Also, we assume the existence of a chair that is responsible for the election process. When an election is initiated, the chair provides the context and candidate set to all voters in N. Next, all members communicate their votes to the chair, which applies the voting rule to determine the score of each candidate. At the end of each iteration, the chair creates a new set of candidates composed of the top-50% highest scored candidates. This subset is sent again to the voters and a new voting iteration begins. When only three or less candidates remain, the candidate with the highest scoring is declared the winner. All voters are notified once the winner has been determined. The exchange of information between voters and chair is performed preferably through (encrypted) V2V communications.

Tie-Breaking Mechanisms: There exists several mechanisms to identify a single winner. In case of a tie, we consider that the chair casts its preferential vote based on their preference as proposed in [7].

3   Case Study

To study the viability of voting mechanisms for cooperative traffic applications, we consider a platooning scenario where vehicles need to reach consensus on the formation's cruising speed. We assume that there already exists a platoon formation, and that there exists a mechanism to assign a vehicle as chair. Each agent has its own desired speed chosen randomly in a given range (e.g. [85, 120] km/h). Each agent casts its vote based upon their perceived utility on each candidate's speed and the given voting rule. We resort to the utility function defined in [15], where the utility of agent i being in the platoon C_j is:

$$U(i, C_j) = 1 - \frac{|D_i - S_{ij}|}{D_i} - \lambda(j)\frac{|P_i - S_{ij}|}{P_i} \tag{1}$$

where D_i is agent's i desired speed, P_i its current speed, and S_{ij} the candidate speed offered by platoon j to agent i. The cost factor for joining the platoon, $\lambda(j)\frac{|P_i-S_{ij}|}{P_i}$, is zero for all elements in the platoon. Each agent calculates the utility of each candidate speed and converts the sequence of utility into a vote according to the voting rule. Despite its simplicity, this use case allows us to present initial findings on the following two relevant research questions:

– Q_1: Do different voting rules applied to vehicular platooning express significant differences in driver satisfaction?
– Q_2: How an imperfect vehicular communications affects the viability and/or performance of different voting mechanism for vehicular coordination?

Question Q_1 is evaluated by measuring the average platoon utility and comparing the results among the different voting rules defined in Sect. 2. Question Q_2 is assessed by analyzing the time needed to reach a consensus on cruising speed. We consider the following baseline scenarios as benchmark:

– Q_1: cruising speed is decided by the platoon leader unilaterally (*totalitarian*);
– Q_2: V2V communications are perfect (e.g. no packet loss, zero delay).

4   Framework Evaluation

4.1   Simulation Framework

In order to simulate real-world constraints of a vehicular network, the decision-making agents should interact in an environment that imposes both constraints to wireless communication and on mobility. To achieve this goal, a hybrid simulation framework (Fig. 1) integrating the following components was developed:

– **agent-oriented platform (LightJason** [3]) that defines the agent behaviours and is responsible for high-level decision making (i.e. voting).
– **microscopic traffic simulator (SUMO** [16]) that replicates the vehicular traffic dynamics (e.g. vehicle kinematics or vehicle interactions).

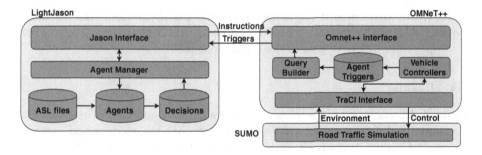

Fig. 1. Simulation framework.

- **network simulator (OMNeT++** [23]) that simulates the protocols of the communication stack.

The framework follows a client-server design, with the LightJason application acting as the server and the OMNeT++ side as the client. Vehicle applications continuously send information to the server (i.e. *Triggers*), and periodically request the server for any decisions made by the agents (i.e. *Instructions*). The interaction between the microscopic traffic simulator SUMO and the network simulator OMNET++ follows the concept presented in [23].

Message transmission occurs via broadcast using dedicated messages for negotiation similar to the protocols developed in [22] and [21]. A key difference is that we resort to dedicated broadcast messages, instead of piggybacking acknowledgments in the CAMs. Potential alternative could also be receiver-based approaches [11]. The assessment of the most efficient method for reliable message exchange out of scope of this work.

4.2 Metrics

We consider the following evaluation metrics:

- **Average (normalized) platoon utility** (U_p): average utility of all platoon members used for evaluating the utilitarian social welfare of the platoon. This metric is normalized with respect to the platoon size for comparison reasons.
- **Time to consensus (TtC):** time interval between the start t_s and conclusion t_e of an election including all iterations needed to reach consensus;

4.3 Scenario and Parameter Settings

- **Use Case Scenario:** We consider platoons with 4 to 8 elements. For statistical significance reasons, we run 30 simulation runs for each platoon size and voting rule.
- **Microscopic traffic simulation:** The scenario consists of a 1 km stretch of highway with three lanes where the platoon and other injected traffic at a density of 90 vehicles/km co-exist.

– **Network simulation:** The transmission power is 15 dBm. All vehicles transmit CAMs with a frequency of 10 Hz and with 200 Bytes in size. The two-ray propagation model is used in the simulations [23].

4.4 Results

Figure 2 depicts the average platoon utilities U_p as a function of the platoon size and for different voting rules. We observe that the median and average values of U_p vary around 0.9, which demonstrates the viability of the voting mechanism to maintain high satisfaction levels. Note also that, on average, all rules obtain higher utility scores than the baseline scenario (i.e. cruising speed decided unilaterally by platoon leader). These results indicate that voting may be beneficial as a negotiation mechanism for AVs.

For a given platoon size, we also apply the Kolmogorov–Smirnov (K-S) to determine if two given voting rules follow the same distribution (with significance level of 5%). The K-S test shows that - for a given platoon size - in general we cannot reject the null hypothesis H_0 that two given U_p distributions are equal. However, the test confirms the difference between the baseline and voting rules U_p distributions (H_0 rejected) for all platoon sizes.

Figure 3 depicts the Time to Consensus (TtC) metric. The results show that for smaller platoons ($<= 8$) this metric is - on average - within typical time-horizons for tactical level decision-making (<2 s) and, as expected, the TtC

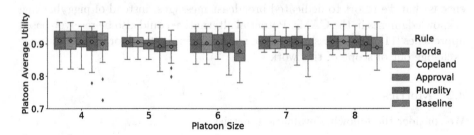

Fig. 2. Average platoon utility as a function of the platoon size and voting rule (mean values represented by the red diamond).

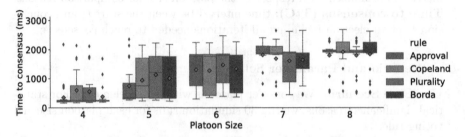

Fig. 3. Time To Consensus (TtC) as a function of the platoon size and voting rule (mean values represented by the red diamond).

increases for larger platoon sizes. Thus, the communication system adds a non-negligible delay to the decision making process since several nodes contend for channel access within a very small time interval. For larger sizes, the latency induced to create social consensus is large enough that vehicles may not be able to achieve complete consensus in a reasonable time interval. From a communication perspective, the iterative voting mechanism appears viable for reliable use in vehicular networks at small platoon sizes. For larger platoons, a smaller number of voting iterations or other voting mechanisms might be needed to maintain short negotiation times. Longer negotiation times could impair a number of phenomena (e.g. traffic flow) if no additional actions are taken (e.g. queue at end of platoon).

5 Related Work

Tactical (Platoon) Coordination: Several computational social choice approaches have been applied to vehicular coordination at a tactical level. Dennisen et al. [8] proposed an agent-based voting architecture for traffic applications and theorized possible applications for taxi-sharing and platooning scenarios. In [9] iterative committee elections are considered for reaching consensus in ride-sharing applications. Sanderson and Pitt [19] propose an institutionalized consensus approach in platoon applications using self-organizing electronic institutions. Voting mechanisms for leader elections have been used in vehicle coordination in intersection management scenarios as in Ferreira et al. [10]. In [4] vehicular coordination is achieved using consensus for the vehicle leader election.

Operational Platoon Coordination: Santini et al. [20] present a longitudinal controller based on distributed consensus approach as potential solution, where communication delays and topology of the vehicles' network are taken into consideration. Jia and Ngoduy [14] consider a leader-follower consensus-based controller for multi-platoon cooperative driving. Their results show that the leader's information is crucial for the platoon stability and the leader-follower communication scheme is more suitable for vehicle platooning.

Alternative to computational social choice methods are the market-based approaches. Although auctions have been extensively used in road intersection management, [17] is one of the few works to consider auctions for driving plans negotiation in platoon applications.

Simulation: Similar approaches to the proposed simulation frameworks in this paper have been conducted by various authors as in [5] a traffic arterial management solution is discussed, although without consideration for a communications network simulator. Evaluation of platooning maneuvers when communication failure occurs is done in [1], using an OMNeT++ and SUMO integration, however without the MAS component.

To summarize, the novel contribution of this paper is the analysis of various voting rules in an agent-based platoon scenario in the presence of unreliable communications settings for *tactical* decision-making (e.g. platoon speed).

6   Conclusion and Discussion

We studied the viability of four commonly used voting mechanisms (Plurality, Borda, Copeland and Approval) to enable coordination in a platooning scenario considering an unreliable communication channel. The results indicate that these social consensus mechanisms show good results in maintaining high satisfaction and that voting may be an appropriate negotiation mechanism for autonomous vehicles. We can also conclude that voting mechanisms have an acceptable response time for low platoon sizes (i.e. <9), but larger platoons might need additional methods to timely achieve consensus.

Future research will look into the voting rules and market-based mechanisms in more complex scenarios, including platoon formation where computational social choice mechanisms are associated to a cost, as well to intra-platoon interactions at intersections.

References

1. Amoozadeh, M., Deng, H., Chuah, C.N., Zhang, H.M., Ghosal, D.: Platoon management with cooperative adaptive cruise control enabled by vanet. Veh. Commun. **2**(2), 110–123 (2015)
2. Arrow, K., Sen, A., Suzumura, K.: Handbook of Social Choice and Welfare, vol. 1. Elsevier, Amsterdam (2002)
3. Aschermann, M., Kraus, P., Müller, J.P.: LightJason: a BDI framework inspired by Jason. In: Criado Pacheco, N., Carrascosa, C., Osman, N., Julián Inglada, V. (eds.) EUMAS/AT -2016. LNCS (LNAI), vol. 10207, pp. 58–66. Springer, Cham (2017). https://doi.org/10.1007/978-3-319-59294-7_6
4. Asplund, M., Lövhall, J., Villani, E.: Specification, implementation and verification of dynamic group membership for vehicle coordination. In: IEEE Pacific Rim International Symposium on Dependable Computing, pp. 321–328. IEEE (2017)
5. Batista, A., Coutinho, L.R.: A multiagent system for combining green wave and adaptive control in a dynamic way. In: IEEE Conference on Intelligent Transportation Systems, pp. 2439–2444. IEEE (2013)
6. Boban, M., d'Orey, P.M.: Exploring the practical limits of cooperative awareness in vehicular communications. IEEE Trans. Veh. Technol. **65**(6), 3904–3916 (2016)
7. Brandt, F., Saile, C., Stricker, C.: Voting with ties: strong impossibilities via sat solving. In: International Conference on Autonomous Agents and Multiagent Systems (2018)
8. Dennisen, S.L., Müller, J.P.: Agent-based voting architecture for traffic applications. In: Müller, J.P., Ketter, W., Kaminka, G., Wagner, G., Bulling, N. (eds.) MATES 2015. LNCS (LNAI), vol. 9433, pp. 200–217. Springer, Cham (2015). https://doi.org/10.1007/978-3-319-27343-3_11
9. Dennisen, S.L., Müller, J.P.: Iterative committee elections for collective decision-making in a ride-sharing application. In: International Workshop on Agents in Traffic and Transportation (ATT) (2016)
10. Ferreira, M., d'Orey, P.: On the impact of virtual traffic lights on carbon emissions mitigation. IEEE Trans. Intell. Transp. Syst. **13**, 284–295 (2012)
11. Gholibeigi, M., Heijenk, G., Moltchanov, D., Koucheryavy, Y.: Analysis of a receiver-based reliable broadcast approach for vehicular networks. Ad Hoc Netw. **37**, 63–75 (2016)

12. Hollnagel, E., Nåbo, A., Lau, I.V.: A systemic model for driver-in-control. In: International Driving Symposium on Human Factors in Driver Assessment, Training and Vehicle Design, pp. 86–91 (2004)
13. Jia, D., Lu, K., Wang, J., Zhang, X., Shen, X.: A survey on platoon-based vehicular cyber-physical systems. IEEE Commun. Surv. Tutor. **18**(1), 263–284 (2016)
14. Jia, D., Ngoduy, D.: Platoon based cooperative driving model with consideration of realistic inter-vehicle communication. Transp. Res. Part C Emerg. Technol. **68**, 245–264 (2016)
15. Khan, M.A., Boloni, L.: Convoy driving through ad-hoc coalition formation. In: IEEE Real Time and Embedded Technology and Applications Symposium, pp. 98–105. IEEE (2005)
16. Krajzewicz, D., Erdmann, J., Behrisch, M., Bieker, L.: Recent development and applications of SUMO - Simulation of Urban MObility. Int. J. Adv. Syst. Meas. **5**, 128–138 (2012)
17. Rewald, H., Stursberg, O.: Cooperation of autonomous vehicles using a hierarchy of auction-based and model-predictive control. In: 2016 IEEE Intelligent Vehicles Symposium (IV), pp. 1078–1084. IEEE (2016)
18. Rios-Torres, J., Malikopoulos, A.A.: A survey on the coordination of connected and automated vehicles at intersections and merging at highway on-ramps. IEEE Trans. Intell. Transp. Syst. **18**(5), 1066–1077 (2017)
19. Sanderson, D., Pitt, J.: Institutionalised consensus in vehicular networks: executable specification and empirical validation. In: IEEE International Conference on Self-Adaptive and Self-Organizing Systems Workshops, pp. 71–76. IEEE (2012)
20. Santini, S., Salvi, A., Valente, A.S., Pescapé, A., Segata, M., Cigno, R.L.: A consensus-based approach for platooning with intervehicular communications and its validation in realistic scenarios. IEEE Trans. Veh. Technol. **66**(3), 1985–1999 (2017)
21. Segata, M., Bloessl, B., Joerer, S., Dressler, F., Cigno, R.L.: Supporting platooning maneuvers through IVC: an initial protocol analysis for the join maneuver. In: Annual Conference on Wireless On-demand Network Systems and Services (WONS), pp. 130–137. IEEE (2014)
22. Segata, M., Dressler, F., Cigno, R.L.: Jerk beaconing: a dynamic approach to platooning. In: IEEE Vehicular Networking Conference, pp. 135–142 (2015)
23. Sommer, C., German, R., Dressler, F.: Bidirectionally coupled network and road traffic simulation for improved IVC analysis. IEEE Trans. Mob. Comput. **10**(1), 3–15 (2011)
24. Ziegler, J., Bender, P., Schreiber, M., et al.: Making bertha drive–an autonomous journey on a historic route. IEEE Intell. Transp. Syst. Mag. **6**(2), 8–20 (2014)

Balancing Strategies for Bike Sharing Systems

Alberto Fernández[✉] [iD], Holger Billhardt[iD], Sandra Timón,
Carlos Ruiz, Óscar Sánchez, and Iván Bernabé

CETINIA, University Rey Juan Carlos, Madrid, Spain
{alberto.fernandez,holger.billhardt,sandra.timon,
carlos.ruiz,oscar.sanchezsa,ivan.bernabe}@urjc.es

Abstract. The increase of population in big cities has produced several problems related to mobility of humans in the city, such as congestions, CO_2 emissions, etc. Lately, governments are trying to mitigate this situation by promoting the use of greener means of transportation such as electrical vehicles or bikes. In this paper, we focus on station-based bike sharing systems (BSS). This type of infrastructure (bikes and parking docks) is shared by many users. However, there are some inefficiencies in their management to imbalanced situations in which some stations fail to provide the service (bike hires or returns) because they are empty or full. We tackle this problem by suggesting users to take (or return) bikes from stations with the goal of keeping the system as balanced as possible. We evaluate our proposal with Bike3S, a bike sharing system simulator developed for testing these types of strategies.

Keywords: Bike sharing · Smart transportation · Smart mobility ·
Multi-agent systems

1 Introduction

Currently, the management of urban mobility is a topic of growing interest in our society because it affects our lives, particularly in large cities. Citizens not only need to move around the city in a comfortable and fast way, but they also want to be eco-friendly. However, this does not happen regularly and citizens do not only have to deal with traffic congestion problems, parking problems and delays in public transport every day. But they (or at least the governments) also have to think about the sustainable future and try to reduce pollution and to avoid future health problems.

In recent years, to alleviate this situation, some proposals have appeared that try to reduce the number of displacements promoting habits related to teleworking and others so as to improve urban mobility. The use of bike sharing systems (BSS) is an effective way to deal with these problems. BSS allow users to take a bicycle and facilitates the movement around the city.

These systems can be managed by different business models but, basically, users register in the system for an economic price and users are free to take a bicycle, move around the city and return the bike in another different location. Regardless of the business model, bike-sharing-systems are limited by resources and the main problem is that those resources must be managed efficiently for the proper functioning of the system, i.e. maximize their availability to citizens.

M. Lujak (Ed.): AT 2018, LNAI 11327, pp. 208–222, 2019.
https://doi.org/10.1007/978-3-030-17294-7_16

While in some recent BSS idle bikes are left "floating" anywhere in the city [1, 2], in most systems there are docking stations where bikes have to be left and taken. In this paper we focus on the latter type of BSS.

The main resources of these systems are bike stations distributed geographically around the city and, specifically, the available bikes and empty slots to park them. A system is effective if users arriving at stations to hire bikes find at least one available, likewise they find empty slots to return them.

Sometimes the effectiveness of these systems depends on external services (fleet operator) responsible for keeping the system balanced.

In this paper we deal with balancing station-based bike sharing systems. We consider systems in which short-term demand is not known (e.g. historic data are not available, or they are very variable). We propose individualized incentives to persuade users to take (or leave) bikes from stations with the goal of keeping the system as balanced as possible. Our proposal is scalable to systems with high number of stations.

The rest of the paper is organized as follows. In Sect. 2 we analyze some related works on balancing BSS. Section 3 describes our vision of a BSS infrastructure. We describe several quality metrics for comparing BSS in Sect. 4. Our proposed balancing strategies are described in Sect. 5. We describe the experimental settings and the results obtained in Sect. 6. Finally, we close the paper with some conclusions and future lines.

2 Related Works

Bicycle sharing systems (BSS) are gaining interest due to the benefits they bring to the cities. [3–5] present the benefits that BSS bring socially, to the environment and to business models, mainly in Europe, Asia and America. In particular, [6] presents the evolution, adoption and expansion of these systems.

The operation of a BSS can be improved from several directions. Some works focus on predicting user demand or the stock of stations in future periods [7–11]. Basically, they present prediction mechanisms and can be classified into two categories: solutions based on station demand prediction models or models centered on a set of stations in global. For example, [7] tries to predict bicycles in each station from parameters such as the historical average, previous trends, previous values, etc. [8–10] use time series analysis methods to predict hourly demand for each station. However, these solutions depend on the state of the city at every moment, so if the city is in an abnormal state these solutions may not work efficiently.

[11, 13] present a hierarchical prediction model that predict the number of bicycles that will be rented or returned in each cluster of stations. These solutions balance the number of bikes in a cluster offering a coarse grain balance of the number of available bicycles. In our work, we try to make a fine grain balance at station level.

Many existing systems in cities use trucks to move bikes among stations and try to keep the BSS balanced. In fact, some works have proposed approaches to optimize the routes of trucks during periods of low activity such as at night or off-peaks, e.g. [1, 2].

Other works, such as [12–15], present the problem in a dynamic way where the demand of bikes at each station is forecasted and they try to optimize the distribution of bikes in each station to maximize the number of trips. Using tracks to move bikes among different stations is one option to reduce the unbalance situation, but other works such as [15–17] propose giving incentives to users to collaborate in the distribution of bikes. Chemla et al. [15] uses demand prediction and propose an optimization problem to maximize the average number of users that find a bike per time unit. The problem is NP-hard and they use heuristics to solve it. They also use dynamic pricing that is charged when a user leaves a bike. Pfrommer et al. [17] propose a combination of trucks and incentive for users. Price incentives is the most used approach (and maybe intuitive), but other options might be possible (promotions, points, etc.).

3 Bike Sharing System

The aforementioned solutions improve the general functioning of BSS, however they present scalability problems limiting the use of the system to scenarios with low/medium number of stations and few bikes (small geographical areas). Big cities are increasing the resources devoted to this kind of transport system, for example London and New York have more that 750 stations and about 12000 bikes each. In this work we are interested in scalable balancing strategies.

Figure 1 represents a common scenario in an area of the city. There is a set S of docking stations (squares in the picture). Users are interested in renting (or returning) bikes in nearby stations (within a radius R_u, e.g. 500 m of walking distance). The user shown in Fig. 1 is located at distance d_i from station i. A station i has a number b_i of bikes and e_i of empty slots. They also have information about the stations in their neighborhood N_i, which are the stations located in a range R_s, i.e. $N_i = \{j \in S \mid d_{ij} \leq R_s\}$. Neighborhood of stations represent other stations that are located at a short distance, so they could be considered by users in case there are not available bikes in their current station.

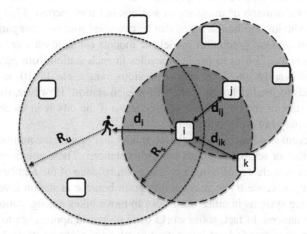

Fig. 1. Bike sharing system. Squares represent stations. Each user and station have a range of action, R_u and R_s respectively, which represent the maximum distance a user is willing to walk.

The general functioning of the system is as follows. A user u wants to hire a bike near her location. She can either walk to the closest station or use an official app to get information and recommendation about which station to go. By recommendation we mean request to go to a station that is good for improving the balanced distribution of bikes through stations.

4 Quality Measures for Bike Sharing Systems

In this section we describe several metrics for evaluating the quality of service provided by bike sharing systems. The goal is to use them to compare different balancing strategies.

4.1 Metrics Considering Absence of Bikes/Slots

The lack of available resources implies that some users might not satisfy their demand (renting or returning a bike). As a consequence of this absence of bikes and/or slots, users cannot make a reservation of any of these two resources. This means they are not receiving a good service from the bike sharing system.

A way of discovering the bad system operation (because of a bad balancing strategy) is analyzing how many failed attempts of renting/returning a bike or making a reservation have occurred. Then, it is possible to calculate more significant quality metrics to evaluate the effectiveness of the system in general.

We use the following metrics (N is the total number of users, i.e. total bike demand), which are calculated from these basic definitions: *Successful hires* (*SH*, total number of bike rentals), *Failed hires* (*FH*, total number of attempts to hire a bike that failed due to unavailability), *Successful returns* (*SR*) and *Failed returns* (*FR*):

- *Demand satisfaction* (*DS*): ratio of users who were able to hire a bike (either at first trial or not), including those who booked a bike in advance.

$$DS = SH / N$$

- *Return satisfaction* (*RS*): ratio of users who were able to return their bikes (either at first trial or not), including those who booked a dock in advance. Note that return demand is SH (those who actually hired a bike). The result should be 1, otherwise there are users who did not find an empty slot.

$$RS = SR / SH$$

- *Hire efficiency* (*HE*): ratio between the number of rentals and the total rental attempts of those users who hired a bike (FH_h).

$$HE = SH / (SH + FH_h)$$

- *Return efficiency (RE)*: ratio between the number of returns and the total return attempts:

$$RE = SR / (SH + FR)$$

4.2   Time with Low Resources

One of the problems with the metrics described in the previous section is that in real settings it is difficult to count the number of failed attempts to rent or return bikes. That is due to several reasons. Firstly, only successful actions are registered in the system. Secondly, users frequently have access to information about resource availability via an app or web page, so they go to the nearest station with available resources (this is more common to rent than to return bikes).

The time a station is empty (of bikes/slots for renting/returning) can be used to alleviate the failed service metrics. An empty station is potentially denying a service. Thus, the longer a station is empty the lower the quality of service it provides. Obviously, not always an empty station is provoking service failures, but it is an indicator that can be combined with others for a better analysis.

We can generalize this approach and consider not only empty states but also availability of resources under a given threshold φ.

Given the total time T equally divided in time units t_i, $T = \{t_1, t_2, ..., t_n\}$, the time with low resources for station i, TES_i, is obtained as:

$TES_i = |\{t \mid b_i(t) \leq \varphi \vee e_i(t) \leq \varphi\}|$, where $b_i(t)$ and $e_i(t)$ are the number of available bikes and empty slots in station i at time t.

4.3   Deviation with Regards to a Reference Balanced Situation

Some strategies aim at keeping the number of available bikes in station i as close as possible to a reference balance situation θ_i (typically half its capacity). If demand estimation is known, this value should be adapted to face the net demand (hires – returns).

Figure 2 shows graphically the idea of this metric. The goal is to calculate the area striped above and under the reference value θ, which is a straight line. Then, the larger this area is, the worse the situation is, because it means the stations are moving further away from the desired state.

Average deviation (D_i) of station i is defined as the mean number of bikes deviation through time, and is obtained by the following equation:

$$D_i = \frac{1}{|T|} \sqrt[\beta]{\sum_{t \in T} |b_i(t) - \theta_i|^\beta}$$

where $b_i(t)$ is the number of available bikes in station i at time t. $\beta \geq 1$ is a constant to give more importance to deviation. For example, four bikes of deviation during one-time unit (e.g. one hour) values the same as one bike deviation in four-time units. The former seems worse balanced that the latter, so $\beta > 1$ can adjust D_i in that sense.

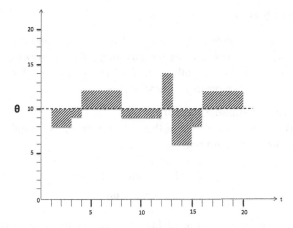

Fig. 2. Example deviation of number of bikes with regards to a reference value θ through time.

4.4 Users' Time in the System

Many users use shared bikes as transportation mean. In those cases, they are interested in finding a bike as close as possible to their origin, and an empty slot as close as possible to their destination. If nearby stations do not have available resources, then they have to walk longer distances so the quality of service decreases. Therefore, users' total time is one of the metrics to estimate service quality. Total time (TT) is the sum of walking time to origin station (T_{os}), cycling travel time to return station (T_{rs}) and walking time to final user destination (T_{fd}):

$$TT = T_{os} + T_{rs} + T_{fd}$$

Note that T_{os} and T_{rs} include walking or cycling (respectively) from station to station in no available resources are found.

5 Our Proposal for Balancing BSS

In this section we describe several strategies that aim at keeping a bike sharing system balanced. We consider a strategy as a method that returns a list of candidate stations (within a maximum distance) sorted by a function f that represents the interest to the global system according to the strategy criterion (the higher f the better).

We start presenting methods that only consider for each station its own availability of resources. Then, we propose how to incorporate the influence that neighbor stations may have on each other. Finally, we present approaches that include incentives so as to influence users to take the actions that are proposed for the interest of the global fleet operation.

5.1   Independent Stations

In this type of strategy, stations are considered independent and only their status is taken into account. This approach has the advantage that it works even though the station gets disconnected from the others. It also serves as a base for designing more sophisticated methods as we present in next sections.

Absolute Number of Available Resources (A)
The most intuitive strategy is to assign the station with higher number of bikes (for hiring) or empty slots (for returning).

$$f_i = b_i \quad \text{(hiring)}$$
$$f_i = e_i \quad \text{(returning)}$$

where b_i and e_i are the number of available bikes and empty slots in station i.

Ratio (R)
If the capacity of the stations is not the same, then strategy A does not work well. Candidate stations are ordered by ratio of available resources/capacity. Thus, if the request is for hiring or returning a bike the list of candidate stations is ordered by:

$$f_i = rh_i = b_i/(b_i + e_i) \quad \text{(hiring)}$$
$$f_i = rr_i = e_i/(b_i + e_i) \quad \text{(returning)}$$

Available Resources/Distance (A/D)
Humans usually decide the target station as close as possible to their location so as to minimize the walking distance. A/D strategy combines the ratio of available resources with the distance from the station to the user. We measure distances in meters. Nevertheless, the unit is not relevant since it only affects as a constant factor to the result, which is only used to rank the candidate stations.

$$f_i = b_i/ d_i \quad \text{(hiring)}$$
$$f_i = e_i/ d_i \quad \text{(returning)}$$

Ratio/Distance (R/D)
This strategy is similar to A/D but using the ratio of available resources instead of the absolute value, i.e. is a combination of strategy R with the distance to the station.

$$f_i = rh_i/ d_i \quad \text{(hiring)}$$
$$f_i = rr_i/ d_i \quad \text{(returning)}$$

5.2   Considering Areas

Balancing strategies described in Sect. 5.1 consider stations independently, i.e. their ranking value only depends on their own status (number of bikes and empty slots).

However, station information in isolation may not correctly reflect the status of an area where the station is located.

However, consider the situation shown in Fig. 3. A user is located to equal distance d of two stations, which have 4 and 5 available resources (e.g. bikes). According to the previous strategies, the one to the right would be preferable by the strategy (let's assume all have the same capacity). However, the one to the left has many more available bikes nearby (17 vs 3). Thus, it may be recommended to take the bike from that one because that zone of the city is still better covered with extra bikes.

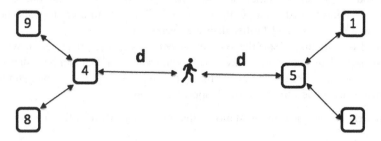

Fig. 3. Example of influence of neighbor stations. Squares represent stations, the number of available resources is shown inside squares.

We model the influence of nearby stations as two "virtual" numbers: available bikes vb and empty slots ve. Virtual values are obtained by combining the actual value with the influence of neighbor stations proportional to their distances, as described by the following equations:

$$vb_i = \sum_{j \in N_i} b_j \cdot w_j$$

$$ve_i = \sum_{j \in N_i} e_j \cdot w_j$$

Where N_i is the neighborhood of station i, i.e. those stations located within the neighborhood radio R_s, including i itself, and weighted factor:

$$w_j = 1 - \frac{d_{ij}}{R_s}$$

This strategy uses vb and ve.

$$f_i = vb_i \quad \text{(hiring)}$$
$$f_i = ve_i \quad \text{(returning)}$$

5.3 Including Incentives

The strategies proposed in previous sections try and balance resource distribution in a fleet of bikes by proposing users where to take or return bikes. However, we did not deal with how to convince users to use the proposed station in case it does not coincide with their preference. This can be done using incentives (e.g. discounts).

Devising an incentive-based strategy requires knowing users' behaviors with regards to those incentives. In general, users have preferences regarding the station they want to use, normally based on the walking distance to their location. Thus, we assume users decide their target station as close as possible to their position. By using incentives, we have to compensate the extra "effort" it takes to users to walk the extra distance to a station located farther than the nearest one.

Instead of adopting a specific type of incentive (money, prizes, etc.), we define incentive *units*. This allows us to have a common framework that can be instantiated in particular cases and even being adaptable to different users (for example, some users prefer discounts while others are more appealed to points).

User model. Users select target station s that maximizes their utility, i.e.:

$$s^* = argmax_s U(s)$$

The utility of station s is modelled as (value of incentive minus extra distance to walk):

$$U(s) = d(inc_s) - (d_s - \min_i d_i)$$

Where d_i is the walking distance from the user location to station i, and $d(x)$ is a function that map incentive x to walking distances (e.g. 1 incentive = 100 m). We adopt linear functions, $d(x) = k \cdot x$.

Incentives Design. Our general approach to balancing strategies consists in two basic elements. Firstly, we calculate a *reward* a user must receive to compensate the effort to go to a farther station. Secondly, if we only provide a compensation all stations would have the same utility for the user, so we need to add some extra value δ, so the user definitely will choose the proposed station. Formally, the incentive given to the user for going to station i is calculated as follows:

$$Inc_i = comp_i + \delta_i$$
$$comp_i = (d_i - d_{min})/k$$

Where d_i is the distance from the user to i, and d_{min} is the distance to the closer station to the user. Note that if the ideal station is the nearest one then compensation is no needed ($comp_i = 0$).

δ values must be chosen such that they keep the order according to f_i, i.e. $\delta_i > \delta_j$ if and only if $f_i > f_j$, which can be obtained as $\delta_i = \alpha \cdot f_i$, with $\alpha > 1$.

In the experiments presented in this paper we assume that the incentives given to users by the strategies are high enough to convince them to accept the recommended station to hire or return bikes.

6 Evaluation

In this section we detail the evaluation carried out. We first describe the simulator used for the experiments. Then we describe the chosen scenario and configuration. Finally, we present the results and analysis.

6.1 Bike3S Simulator

Bike3S [18] is a simulator that allows analyzing the behavior of station-based bike-sharing systems. The ultimate goal of the simulator is to help to evaluate dynamic rebalancing algorithms based on user incentives (e.g. discounts) in different settings. In this sense, different user types (behaviors) can be defined and different balancing strategies can be implemented.

The main characteristics of the simulator include:

- *Event-based engine*: the core of Bike3S follows a discrete or event-based approach, since the state of the system only changes when new events occur (e.g. a new user appears, bike rentals or returns, etc.).
- *User models*: several different types of bike users are predefined. Each user type has a particular behavior. During the simulation, users, depending on their behavior, can use operator's services to make decisions such as which station to take a bike from. The user types catalog can be extended by developers.
- *Configuration*: simulation experiments are configured by providing three types of parameters: (i) infrastructure (location, capacity and initial state of stations), (ii) user generation (e.g. type of user, location, probability distribution, etc.) and (iii) global configuration (simulation time, geographical area, etc.). These configuration parameters are stored in json files but graphical user interfaces are available to facilitate its creation.
- *Results analysis*: several metrics are taken to assess the quality of a balancing strategy based on the success or fail attempts to hire/return bikes, total time of empty/full stations and others.
- *Graphical visualization*: the evolution of the simulation can be shown on a map.

The modular design of Bike3S allows separating the configuration and user generation from the simulation execution, and the latter from the visualization and analysis. Thus, the simulator can generate users or load them from a file. Likewise, the visualization interface or data analysis tool can load previously stored simulation histories.

The simulator can be used with different objectives. On one hand, it can be used to assess a specific bike-sharing system infrastructure (station locations, size, etc.) before deploying it by testing how the proposed infrastructure behaves to a given expected demand. On the other hand, different incentive based strategies can be implemented and evaluated.

6.2 Scenarios

We have carried out several experiments to evaluate our proposals. We used real data from BiciMAD[1], the public bike sharing system of Madrid (Spain), which covers an area of about 5×5 km square of central Madrid. BiciMAD counts on 173 stations and 1702 bikes. Each station has around 20 slots to plug in bikes.

We simulated the operation of one day of BiciMAD with real data of bike trips. In particular we used the data of the 5th of October 2017, the day with the highest usage of the system in 2017. For each trip (14877 in total), data include time of taking a bike, origin station, time of returning, destination station and speed. Origin and returning times are given just in hours (without minutes). In order to simulate the trips in a more legalistic way we randomly[2] generated appearance time in minutes within the specified hour. In addition, we also randomly generated the appearance and destination location of users within a radius of 200 m from the real origin and destination station, respectively. All the stations were initialized with a ratio bikes/empty slots of 0.5 (stations initial state information was not available in the historic data). We set a maximum of three failed attempts to rent or book a bike before leaving the system without using it, and radios $R_u = R_s = 600$ m. Figure 4 shows a snapshot of the chosen scenario in the simulator.

We compared the performance of the system for different recommendation strategies and user types. In particular, we tested two scenarios without strategies and six with different balancing strategies:

(1) *Dummy*. No strategy is used. Users always go to the nearest station.
(2) *Informed Users*. No strategy is used. Users have information about stations and always go to the nearest station with available bikes (when they get the information). It might be possible that upon arrival time there is not any bikes (e.g. the last one was rented while walking to the station).
(3) *Incentive-A*. Applies strategy "Absolute number of resources" with incentives.
(4) *Incentive-R*. Applies strategy "Ratio" with incentives.
(5) *Incentive-A/D*. Applies strategy "Available Resources/Distance" with incentives.
(6) *Incentive-R/D*. Applies strategy "Ratio/Distance" with incentives.
(7) *Incentive A-N*. Applies strategy A combined with stations in the neighborhood, and incentives.
(8) *Incentive A/D-N*. Applies strategy A/D combined with stations in the neighborhood, and incentives.

---

[1] https://www.bicimad.com/.

[2] Uniform probability distribution is used unless stated differently.

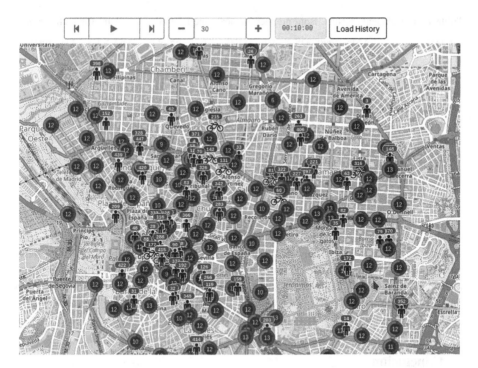

Fig. 4. Snapshot of the simulated scenario. Stations are represented by circles, with the number of available bikes shown in them. The ratio of available bikes and free slots is shown in red and green, respectively. Bike and person symbols represent users riding or walking, respectively. (Color figure online)

6.3 Results and Analysis

In order to evaluate the proposed strategies, we used the quality metrics defined in Sect. 4. We recall that *DS*, *HE* and *RE*, stand for demand satisfaction, hire efficiency and return efficiency, respectively. We did not use return satisfaction (*RS*) because its value is 1 (everyone with a bike eventually returns it). We measured the average time a station is empty (*time with low resources*, with $\varphi = 0$) and the average deviation per station with regards to a reference level θ of 50% of capacity and $\beta = 1$. Finally, we also measured the average total time users that hired bikes are in the system.

Table 1 shows the results of the experiments. Demand satisfaction (*DS*) and efficiency (*HE* and *RE*) are very high in general, specially using incentives. This is normal because the historic data used in the simulation only contain successful hires. Despite this fact, those values are not always 1 since we had to randomly distribute users within each hour and close location as explained in Sect. 6.2, so the data are not exactly the same as the historic records. Scenarios with strategies using incentives outperform those without any strategy in most metrics. In particular, *Dummy* users get the lowest performance in demand satisfaction (*DS*) and efficiency (*HE* and *RE*). That is due to the fact that users go to their nearest station without even checking whether there are bikes available. Strategies *Incentive-A* and *Incentive-R* obtain the best results in average

Table 1. Experiments results. Bold numbers indicate the best obtained result for each metric.

Strategy	Abandoned	DS	HE	RE	Avg. empty time (min)	θ-deviation (avg)	Avg. total time (min)
Dummy	210	0.986	0.934	0.826	92.8	5.6	16.5
Informed	46	0.997	0.981	0.942	90.6	5.6	16.0
Incentive-A	**0**	**1**	0.993	**0.999**	**1.1**	2.1	25.7
Incentive-R	**0**	**1**	0.991	0.997	1.5	**2.0**	25.9
Incentive-A/D	19	0.999	**0.999**	0.956	98.3	5.0	17.7
Incentive-R/D	8	0.999	0.998	0.986	17.1	4.3	**15.7**
Incentive A-N	17	0.999	0.963	0.976	44.1	3.9	26.7
Incentive A/D-N	7	**1**	0.993	0.981	54.0	5.0	15.8

empty time and deviation. The reason is that those metrics analyze station status and both strategies try to keep individual stations as balanced as possible. However, they get worse performance when we analyze the users' perspective, i.e. the time users spend in the system. Results of strategies using "distances" (A/D, R/D and A/D-N) confirm that a tradeoff between distances and available resource results in good efficiency and low total time, since users walk shorter distances.

7 Conclusion

In this paper, we have proposed several balancing strategies for bike sharing systems. Our approach tries to keep the situation of each station balanced using only local information, so it can be computed decentralized providing good scalability. We presented four basic strategies that only used local station information, then complemented them with information of nearby stations. Finally, we presented a method for providing incentives to users so as to try to influence in their behavior to hire or leave a bike in a station that is better for the balancing of the system. We also proposed several quality metrics to evaluate the performance of different BSS, i.e. assess different balancing strategies.

We conducted several experiments using a real scenario obtained from data of Madrid BSS. The results of our experiments showed that using balancing strategies with incentives the quality of service is better. In addition, we confirmed that strategies using information about the distance from origin or destination points to candidate stations outperform the others.

There are quite a few open lines of research that we plan to explore in the near future. The main work we plan to carry out is analyzing the economic effect of using incentives. In particular, how much money is necessary to get a good performance, how it affects to get extra incomes (more users), how many resources can be saved to get the same QoS when using incentives, etc., are some of the questions we want to explore. We also plan to improve and propose new balancing strategies, specially including demand prediction.

Acknowledgments. Work partially supported by the Autonomous Region of Madrid (grants "MOSI-AGIL-CM" (S2013/ICE-3019) co-funded by EU Structural Funds FSE and FEDER, and "PEJD-2017-PRE/TIC-3412" by "Consejería de Educación, Juventud y Deporte" and FSE), project "SURF" (TIN2015-65515-C4-4-R (MINECO/FEDER)) funded by the Spanish Ministry of Economy and Competitiveness, and through the Excellence Research Group GES2ME (Ref. 30VCPIGI05) co-funded by URJC-Santander Bank.

References

1. Pal, A., Zhang, Y.: Free-floating bike sharing: Solving real-life large-scale static rebalancing problems. Trans. Res. Part C: Emerg. Technol. **80**, 92–116 (2017)
2. Reiss, S., Bogenberger, K.: Optimal bike fleet management by smart relocation methods: combining an operator-based with an user-based relocation strategy. In: IEEE 19th International Conference on Intelligent Transportation Systems (ITSC), pp. 2613–2618 (2016)
3. Shaheen, S., Zhang, H., Martin, E., Guzman, S.: China's hangzhou public bicycle: understanding early adoption and behavioral response to bikesharing. Trans. Res. Rec. J. Transp. Res. Board **2247**, 33–41 (2011)
4. Shaheen, S.A., Guzman, S., Zhang, H.: Bikesharing in Europe, the Americas, and Asia. Transp. Res. Rec. J. Transp. Res. Board **2143**, 159–167 (2010)
5. Shaheen, S.A., Cohen, A.P., Martin, E.W.: Public Bikesharing in North America: Early Operator Understanding and Emerging Trends. Transp. Res. Rec. J. Transp. Res. Board 2387, 83–92 (2013). https://doi.org/10.3141/2387-10
6. Parkes, S.D., Marsden, G., Shaheen, S.A., Cohen, A.P.: Understanding the diffusion of public Bikesharing systems: evidence from Europe and North America. J. Transp. Geogr., vol. 31, pp. 94–103, 2013. http://linkinghub.elsevier.com/retrieve/pii/S0966692313001130
7. Froehlich, J., Neumann, J., Oliver, N.: Sensing and predicting the pulse of the city through shared bicycling. In: IJCAI (2009)
8. Kaltenbrunner, A., Meza, R., Grivolla, J., Codina, J., Banchs, R.: Urban cycles and mobility patterns: exploring and predicting trends in a bicycle-based public transport system. Pervasive Mob. Comput. **6**(4), 455–466 (2010)
9. Vogel, P., Mattfeld, Dirk C.: Strategic and operational planning of bike-sharing systems by data mining – a case study. In: Böse, Jürgen W., Hu, H., Jahn, C., Shi, X., Stahlbock, R., Voß, S. (eds.) ICCL 2011. LNCS, vol. 6971, pp. 127–141. Springer, Heidelberg (2011). https://doi.org/10.1007/978-3-642-24264-9_10
10. Borgnat, P., Fleury, E., Robardet, C., Scherrer, A.: Spatial analysis of dynamic movements of Velo'v, Lyon's shared bicycle program. In: European Conference on Complex Systems (ECCS) (2009)
11. Li, Y., Zheng, Y., Zhang, H., Chen, L.: Traffic prediction in a bike sharing system. In: ACM SIGSPATIAL (2015)
12. Contardo, C., Morency, C., Rousseau, L. M.: Balancing a dynamic public bike-sharing system. Technical Report vol. 4. CIRRELT (2012)
13. O'Mahony, E., Shmoys, D.B.: Data analysis and optimization for (citi)bike sharing. In: Proceedings of the Twenty-Ninth AAAI Conference on Artificial Intelligence (AAAI 2015). pp. 687–694. AAAI Press (2015)
14. Schuijbroek, J., Hampshire, R.C., Van Hoeve, W.J.: Inventory rebalancing and vehicle routing in bike sharing systems. Eur. J. Oper. Res. **257**(3), 992–1004 (2017)

15. Chemla, D., Meunier, F., Pradeau, T., Calvo, R.W., Yahiaoui, H.: Self-service bike sharing systems: Simulation, repositioning, pricing (2013). https://hal.archives-ouvertes.fr/hal-00824078

16. Fricker, C., Gast, N.: Incentives and regulations in bike-sharing systems with stations of finite capacity. arXiv:12011178 (2012)

17. Pfrommer, J., Warrington, J., Schildbach, G., Morari, M.: Dynamic vehicle redistribution and online price incentives in shared mobility systems. IEEE Trans. Intell. Transp. Syst. **15**(4), 1567–1578 (2014)

18. Fernández, A., Timón, S., Ruiz, C., Cumplido, T., Billhardt, H., Dunkel, J.: A bike sharing system simulator. In: Bajo, J., et al. (eds.) PAAMS 2018. CCIS, vol. 887, pp. 428–440. Springer, Cham (2018). https://doi.org/10.1007/978-3-319-94779-2_37

Towards Distributed Real-Time Coordination of Shoppers' Routes in Smart Hypermarkets

Marin Lujak$^{(\boxtimes)}$ ⓘ and Arnaud Doniec ⓘ

IMT Lille Douai, Douai, France
{marin.lujak,arnaud.doniec}@imt-lille-douai.fr

Abstract. In this paper, we consider the problem of route guidance for shoppers in crowded hypermarkets equipped with smart space technologies. This is an actual and a highly computationally complex problem in peak hours due to dynamically changing congestion conditions, the size and complexity of hypermarkets, and the presence of a multitude of shoppers with different shopping constraints and preferences. High computational complexity of this problem requires a computationally efficient solution approach. We propose a shopper route guidance architecture in which a hypermarket is modelled as a network of communicating smart building agents, each one monitoring its exclusive physical area. Moreover, each shopper is represented by an agent installed on a shopper's app that, by interacting with other shoppers and smart building agents, dynamically updates its shopping route. Each shopper agent resolves the pick sequencing problem with congestion, i.e., given a shopper's list, the shopper's items' locations are sequenced in the route proposed to a shopper so that the overall traveling time is minimized considering congestion in real-time. We propose a (low computational complexity) greedy tour algorithm and a distributed TSP mathematical model solved in Cplex for this problem and compare their performance. The results show that the proposed architecture and methods scale well and provide efficient shoppers' routes.

Keywords: Route guidance · Pick sequencing · Multi-agent system · Hypermarket

1 Introduction

Commercial activities are crucial in terms of jobs and economic growth. For many years, supermarkets and hypermarkets have been in competition with their online counterparts. Compared to e-commerce, physical stores are more time consuming and less convenient: large open spaces with long aisles difficult to navigate with a multitude of products whose locations frequently change, and jammed at peak hours and on weekends. A considerable percentage of retail is lost when large hypermarkets get crowded, even when the attendance rate is

© Springer Nature Switzerland AG 2019
M. Lujak (Ed.): AT 2018, LNAI 11327, pp. 223–238, 2019.
https://doi.org/10.1007/978-3-030-17294-7_17

relatively low. This is due to the shoppers' tendency to decrease their purchases when they travel through congested aisles. Shoppers can feel time pressure in shopping in case of a too high crowdedness that can make them even leave the hypermarket too early.

To the best of our knowledge, literature on the shopping route optimization considering crowdedness is limited. This is due to the lack of indoor localization technologies and relatively recent massive adoption of smart phones in our everyday lives: the two basic means for inexpensive indoor route guidance. However, with the developments in smart space technologies and smartphones, we can provide intelligent solutions for improving shopping experience while lowering time spent in shopping. A prerequisite for avoiding crowdedness is a detailed information about the real-time position of all persons in the infrastructure. An overview of indoor ultrasonic positioning systems with related state of the art can be found in, e.g., [11,19]. Currently, mostly used technologies for indoor localization are Wi-Fi, RFID and bluetooth low energy (BLE). They use radio signal intensity to infer distance between a smartphone and other stationary devices (Wi-Fi router, RFID tags, BLE devices (iBeacon), etc.). To the best of our knowledge, localization with beacons is currently the best approach, e.g., [5,20].

Information about shoppers' position and their paths is needed to deduce about the crowdedness dynamics in a hypermarket. Such situational knowledge cannot be predefined and must be inferred by exploiting continuous real–time data streams provided by sensors. Situational knowledge can be considered as a dynamic knowledge with a high change frequency. We may use Complex Event Processing for filtering streams of events in real-time to achieve situation awareness (see, e.g., [8]).

In this paper, we study a distributed shoppers' route guidance in hypermarkets equipped with smart space technologies. We deal with the problem of minimizing a shopper's shopping time given a predefined shopping list of the items to purchase in a crowded hypermarket. A parameter strictly related to crowdedness is the design of a hypermarket and the aisle width. To improve the shopper's throughput in peak hours, it is essential to dispose of a scalable and dynamic method of coordination for the shoppers' routes that will consider people flow capacities of narrow aisles prone to congestion.

We propose a distributed multi-agent Shopping Route Guidance Architecture (SRGA) together with a mathematical model and a greedy heuristic algorithm for shopping route guidance, both of which consider crowdedness in real-time. The objective is to minimize the time in purchasing items in a given shopping list considering shoppers' preferences and real-time congestion. We tackle congestion by finding routes through aisles with sufficient free-flow capacity. We experiment the proposed approaches in simulations. The results show that they scale well and provide efficient shoppers' routes.

The paper is organized as follows. In Sect. 2, we describe the background and the state-of-the-art optimization models and algorithms related to shopping route guidance. In Sect. 3, we formally define the problem of route guidance for shoppers considering congestion. In Sect. 4, we explain the main features of the shopper's route guidance architecture. Section 5 presents our proposed mathematical model and a greedy tour algorithm for shopping route guidance. Our experiment setup description and results are presented in Sect. 6. We conclude the paper with the main conclusions and future work in Sect. 7.

2 Background and Related Work

The literature on shopping route guidance mostly covers qualitative aspects of shopping and shopper's experience. Li et al. in [15] proposed a social route recommender mechanism for store shopping support that recommends appropriate routes to first-time customers or those who are unfamiliar with a retailer's shopping space by extracting and analysing shopping information (shopping context, visiting trajectory) and social information (user's interest, friends' influence). They employed a clustering technique and a Markov chain model to generate appropriate routes for the target users. Similarly, in [4], a Markov decision process-based system is proposed for finding a next location to visit in a mall based on preferred products, current location and shopping done so far. The proposed approach does not consider congestion and it gives no guarantee that all preferred items will be purchased or that the route is the one of the minimum cost. Bajo et al. in [3] proposed a distributed multi-agent architecture composed of "lightweight" agents that can reside in mobile devices, such as phones, PDAs, etc. based on case-based planning for guidance and advising of users in shopping centers.

The problem of finding the shortest shopping route in a hypermarket through locations of items to purchase given in a shopping list can be represented by an undirected graph whose nodes represent items' locations and each arc a walkable way free of obstacles between a pair of two neighboring nodes. Then, we can model this problem as an order picking problem in warehouses with an arbitrary aisle configuration. The latter is a special type of the Travelling Salesman Problem (TSP) (see, e.g., [22]) defined as follows. Given is an order, i.e., a list of items demanded from a customer. A picker should leave the loading dock to pick up the items in the order and transport them back to the loading dock. We assume that the capacity of the picker's vehicle is sufficient to pick up all the items in the order. The objective is to find a minimum-cost tour by the picker, where the total cost is the sum of the travelled distances among the items in the tour. In the shopping route's cost minimization, any tour that includes a hypermarket entrance node and one of the cash-desk nodes while going through every item in the shopping list exactly once is a feasible solution with a given cost that cannot be smaller than the minimum cost tour.

Although TSP is an NP-hard problem and there is no efficient solution that scales and works on all graphs, some of its special formulations can be solved efficiently in polynomial time (e.g., [13]). These formulations in the CPLEX branch-and-bound solver can solve instances with over 200 nodes to proven optimality [14]. This is in contrast to the standard TSP, where sophisticated cutting-plane and branch-and-cut techniques are needed to solve instances with more than about 50 nodes (see, e.g., [2]). However, a disadvantage of exact algorithms is that they show a very strong variability in computation time between different TSP instances. Heuristic algorithms, on the other hand, construct feasible solutions, and thus upper bounds for the optimum value. Often, they have no quality guarantee as to how far off they may be from the optimal solution [10]. However, their complexity is generally low. For example, Lin-Kernighan-Helsgaun (LKH) TSP heuristic [9] is based on a series of $n - opt$ moves with $n \leq 5$, which are restricted by carefully chosen candidate sets. The latter are defined by a measure based on sensitivity analysis of minimum spanning trees, and are kept small but at the same time large enough to allow good solutions to be found.

In this paper, we focus on narrow and long aisle systems, in which the distance travelled crossing the aisle from one side to the other is negligible compared to the distance travelled along the centreline of the aisle. Exact approaches to this problem only exist for warehouses with at most 3 cross aisles. For other warehouse types, various heuristic approaches exist, e.g., [23]. Since such systems can get crowded, waiting time must be taken into account in the solution approach together with travel time and distance. Unlike optimal solutions, heuristics will (mostly) lead to non-optimal orderings but they offer feasible solutions and require virtually no time to get generated.

In this paper, we consider real-time congestion information to keep shopping routes updated up-to-the-minute and thus dynamically cope with congestion. Related to this is a dynamic traveling salesman problem (TSP), where the vertices and/or weights of the graph that represents the TSP are changed during the optimization process (see, e.g., [25]). In [26], Toriello et al. formally propose a dynamic TSP with stochastic arc costs and a lookahead price-directed policy implied by their cost-to-go approximation. In [21], Pan and Shih propose a throughput model for the determination of the picking operation performance for multiple-picker environments with congestion and validate it through a simulation experiment. They consider a trade-off between the picking distance and the blocking-caused delay for the storage assignment.

There is a limited number of works with the topic of multi-agent computation of TSP solution. For example, in [12], an ant colony optimization on a distributed architecture is proposed where each node of the graph is conceptualized and implemented as a software agent sending and receiving ants. A distributed multi-agent computation model for route guidance under congestion in vehicle traffic considering envy-freeness and fairness was proposed in [16,18]. It was shown by simulation experiments that by proposing routes that are envy-free and fair, the user equilibrium traffic assignment solution can be improved towards the system optimum. Since congestion (crowdedness) plays an important role in the shopping experience, we consider the problem of shopping route guidance under congestion in this paper and formulate it in the following.

3   Problem Formulation

In this section, we define the problem of dynamic shopping route guidance in smart hypermarkets considering congestion stated as follows: Given an arbitrary current location of a shopper and a set of hypermarket locations that still have to be visited, what route should the shopper follow in order to minimise the time travelled considering actual hypermarket crowdedness?

A hypermarket layout may be represented by an undirected graph $G = (N, A)$, where N is a set of nodes representing separate physical spaces of a hypermarket, and A the set of arcs connecting these spaces where each arc $a \in A$ has associated length d_a, people flow f_a, travel time t_a, and free-flow capacity u_a (a maximum sustainable people free flow up to which there is no congestion). Two space nodes are adjacent (i.e., connected by an arc) if it is possible to walk directly from the space represented by one node to another without passing through the spaces represented by other nodes. Moreover, let $O \subset N$ be a set of entrance nodes to the hypermarket and let $D \subset N$ be a set of cash desk nodes such that $O \cap D = \emptyset$. For each shopper $s \in S$, given is an unordered shopping list $L_s = \{l_s^1, l_s^2, \ldots, l_s^n\}$ made of m item location nodes to visit, where S is a set of shoppers. We assume that a shopping path of each shopper $s \in S$ starts at one of the entrance nodes $o \in O$, passing through the locations of items in L_s in some order, and terminates at one of exit nodes $d \in D$. Moreover, we assume that each shopper has a sufficient cart capacity for all the items in his/her shopping list.

For simplicity and without loss of generality, we assume that there is a dummy node $\hat{d}$ that is connected to entrance nodes $o \in O$ and cash desk nodes $d \in D$ by dummy arcs with a sufficiently high travel time and length and infinite capacity such that, in our model, each shopper starts his/her shopping path and terminates it at dummy node $\hat{d}$. We call such a path that starts and ends at the same node $\hat{d}$ a cycle. Requiring a shopper's route to be a cycle rather than an origin-destination path is not restricting because we can equivalently look for a cycle made of an origin-destination path plus a destination-origin path made of dummy arcs with zero length and travel time. Now, let an extended node set be $N' = N \cup \{\hat{d}\}$, and extended arc set $A' = A \cup A_{\hat{d}}$, where $A_{\hat{d}}$ is a set of dummy arcs with zero length and travel time adjacent to node $\hat{d}$. Then, let $R_s \subset N'$ be an unordered node subset such that $R_s = L_s \cup \{\hat{d}\}$, i.e., it contains all n item location nodes in L_s, as well as the dummy node $\hat{d}$. We consider graph $G' = (R_s, A')$, where arcs $a' \in A'$ connecting nodes in R_s are computed based on the shortest distance among the nodes in R_s on $G = (N, A)$.

To deal with uncertainty in our model, we consider estimated arcs' travel times $\hat{t}_a$ and people flow $\hat{f}_a$ instead of exact ones. They are computed based on the following assumptions: (i) estimated travel time $\hat{t}_a(d_a, \hat{f}_a(\tau), u_a)$ depends on arc's (positive) length $d_a \geq 0$, estimated people flow $\hat{f}_a(\tau)$ at each time period $\tau \in T$, and arc's capacity u_a; (ii) estimated people flow $\hat{f}_a(\tau)$ on each arc $a \in A$ changes dynamically and is a function of time $\tau \in T$; (iii) arcs are undirected so that both length, travel time, and people flow are symmetric, i.e., $d_{ij} = d_{ji}$,

$\hat{t}_{ij}(\tau) = \hat{t}_{ji}(\tau)$, and $\hat{f}_{ij}(\tau) = \hat{f}_{ji}(\tau)$, respectively. However, we could consider a directed graph in a model representing a physical layout with physical barriers that control the direction of people flow. In the generic case that we consider in this paper without physical barriers and explicit people flow control, we assume that the flow of shoppers in aisles self-organizes in terms of the lane formation, drifting, and synchronization, (see, e.g., [24]).

Estimated travel time $\hat{t}^{ij}(\tau)$ for each arc $(i, j) \in A$ and time period $\tau \in T$ is computed at the beginning of time period $\tau = 1$ and is updated in real-time during execution. The following formula is used:

$$\hat{t}^{ij}(\tau) = \min\left[max\left(\hat{t}^{ij}_{tr}(\tau), \Delta\hat{t}^{j}_{w}(\tau)\right)\right], \tag{1}$$

where $\Delta\hat{t}^{j}_{w}(\tau)$ is the estimated waiting time at node j due to a queue of shoppers (if any) on arc (i, j) who arrived before and have still not reached it at time $\tau \in T$, and $\hat{t}^{ij}_{tr}(\tau)$ is the estimated travel time from i to j considering estimated arc's flow $\hat{f}_{ij}(\tau)$ at time $\tau \in T$. Estimated travel time $\hat{t}^{ij}_{tr}(\tau)$ of each arc $(i, j) \in A$ can be seen as a volume delay function modeled as a modified Davidson's function, see, e.g., [1].

Since the congestion dynamics is uncertain further ahead we look, we update the shoppers' routes as they progress. By this approach, we follow the first come first served principle. Then, let $\hat{t}_s(\tau)$ be an estimated time of a shopping tour of shopper s at time $\tau \in T$ comprised of the following components: (i) Estimated total travel time $\hat{t}^{tr}_s(\tau)$, which is the sum of the travel times of arcs starting at dummy node $\hat{d}$, continuing through the nodes of items in shopping list L_s, and ending at dummy node $\hat{d}$, $\hat{t}^{tr}_s(\tau) = \sum_{(i,j)\in R^o_s} \hat{t}^{ij}(\tau)$, where R^o_s is a Hamiltonian tour minimizing the overall estimated travel time of the nodes in R_s and $\hat{t}^{ij}(\tau)$ is the estimated minimal travel time between the locations of items i and j considering estimated people flow at time $\tau \in T$; (ii) Estimated item search time $\hat{t}^{si}_s$ at the location of item $i \in R_s$; (iii) Estimated pick time $\hat{t}^{pi}_s$ for picking an item $i \in R_s$ from its storage location and placing it on a shopping basket or a shopping cart; (iv) Estimated set-up time $\hat{t}^{su}_s$ for searching for an empty shopping basket or a shopping cart after entering into the hypermarket, and emptying of a shopping basket or a shopping cart with the items in R_s at the cash-desk at the end of shopping.

The estimated overall shopping time for each shopper agent s at time period $\tau \in T$ is then:

$$\hat{t}_s(\tau) = \hat{t}^{tr}_s(\tau) + \sum_{i \in R_s}\left(\hat{t}^{si}_s + \hat{t}^{pi}_s\right) + \hat{t}^{su}_s. \tag{2}$$

Travelling is the most time consuming subtask of shopping in hypermarkets. For simplicity, search and pick times are assumed constant independently of the shopping tour composition, while setup time is assumed negligible. With these assumptions, we have:

$$\hat{t}_s(\tau) = \sum_{i,j \in R^o_s} \hat{t}^{ij}(\tau). \tag{3}$$

To support constant search and pick times, we can use, e.g., smart space LEDs to indicate the position of a wanted product on a shelf.

To facilitate scalability and lower the computational complexity, our approach to this problem is based on a multi-agent architecture made of building and shopper agents that compute their shopping routes in a distributed way as described in the following.

4   MAS Architecture for Hypermarket Shopping

In this section, we present the distributed architecture for parallel, asynchronous and decentralized shopping route computation considering congestion.

In order to provide a scalable and modular architecture robust to failures, our proposed solution follows a distributed multi-agent approach with two types of agents inspired by the distributed architecture for evacuation route computation presented in [17]: a set of Smart Building (SB) agents (implemented and located at a (static) set $N_{SB} \subset N$ of graph $G = (N, A)$) and a set of shopper agents SA moving in space (changing position over the nodes in N), both considered rational. While smart building agents are considered collaborative, each shopper agent installed in an app of a shopper's smartphone is considered self-concerned. An overview of this architecture is given in Fig. 1. The objective of the proposed shopping route guidance architecture (SRGA) is to provide personalized and optimal shopping route guidance considering congestion to shopper agents installed in an app on shoppers' smartphones.

Shopper Agents. Each shopper agent SA is associated with the application installed on the smartphone of a shopper (see Fig. 1). It manages and stores the information related to a specific shopper and informs the closest SB agent of it. Moreover, it computes and updates the shopper's route based on the filtered semantic map of the hypermarket including its layout and topology received from the closest SB agent.

In a hypermarket, global crowdedness situation is dynamically updated in real–time. Thus, each SA agent recalculates its shopping route each time significant changes on the route occur. To compute shopping routes, it is necessary to consider knowledge representation and reasoning regarding products' locations, shopper's requirements and preferences, and a shopping process. Before computing shopping routes, we first need to reason about semantic information and then transfer semantic data of the shopping list and the hypermarket contents to graph representation. The following components are used:

- Data regarding the building topology: Static information about physical elements in the building (e.g. rooms, corridors, floors, doors, etc.) and relation among them (e.g. the area of room A is 10 m^2; room A is next to room B and they are both at floor F). Topology knowledge is represented in such a way that it is sufficient to describe the building network by a graph with weights and tags on the constituent nodes and connecting arcs as described in Sect. 3. Nodes and arcs are described by their type, surface, area, inclination, etc.

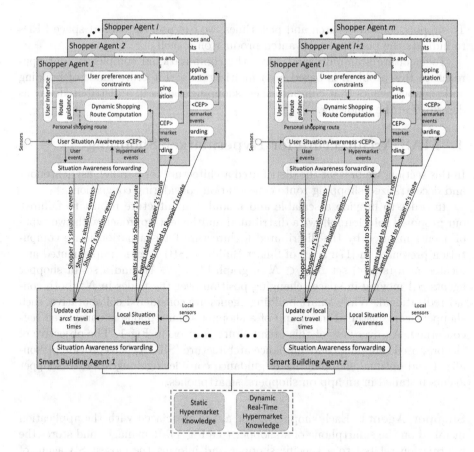

Fig. 1. Situation-aware real-time distributed shopping route guidance architecture.

- Shopping ontology: This ontology contains general knowledge about shopping in a hypermarket, e.g., facts that people with strong affiliate ties move together (for instance, families with children and persons with disability and their assistants), the appropriateness of short routes for people with limited mobility, and the influence of certain events like congestion, degustation, demonstration on the crowdedness level of a hypermarket.
- Real-time hypermarket situation: Current physical space situation awareness received from the closest SB agent.

Smart Building Agents. Each SB agent has a corresponding region (Voronoi cell) consisting of the hypermarket areas represented by the nodes of graph $G = (N, A)$ that are closer to that SB agent than to any other SB agent within the same space. It processes and senses its Voronoi cell over a strategically distributed network of sensors and communicates with the rest of SB agents and with the shopper agents that are momentarily within its cell. For processing of the sensing information, it contains a local space situation awareness module that perceives the crowdedness conditions of its physical space through combining and analysing the events provided by the environment sensors and the SAs in its area.

The local space situation awareness module functions in cycles. At the first phase, the local building sensor data is fused with the data received from the locally present shopper agents. Then, the normalized crowdedness value is deduced through Complex Event Processing (CEP) events. This data is sent to a blackboard or alike globally shared data structure containing the overall network safety values and visible to all SB agents. Thus, the global situational awareness of the building is accessible to every SB agent by accessing the blackboard.

The situation awareness and decision making are distributed in the network of SB agents such that each agent is responsible of the semantic reasoning concerning the crowdedness of its assigned physical space. Moreover, each SB agent is responsible of informing shopper agents in its physical area regarding the crowdedness dynamics on their shopping routes. An SB agent here is a link between the distributed SB agent network and an individual shopper (see Fig. 1). Subsequently, the SB agent updates the hypermarket map and sends it to all SAs in its physical area.

To relieve the communication load, each SB agent maintains a local copy of the hypermarket's network with the updated crowdedness conditions. CEP is used to filter irrelevant information and to generate higher level events. Individual user events are aggregated to detect events regarding groups of users, their distribution and density in the building.

5   Proposed Solution Approaches

In this Section, we present two approaches to shopping route optimization: a distributed mathematical programming model and a greedy heuristic algorithm.

5.1   TSP Mathematical Programming Model

In dynamically changing congestion conditions, we update travel time matrix $D_s(\tau)$ by calculating the minimum travel time between any two remaining locations to visit $i, j \in R_s$ (including the present one and the dummy node $\hat{d}$) whenever the travel times between the remaining locations to visit change above a given threshold. We apply a First Come First Reserved policy for controlling the congestion on arcs and when an arc's free-flow capacity is fully reserved, the arc is not available any more for passage at that time period. In $D_s(\tau)$, the travel time of arc (i, j) if $i = j$ is set to infinity. Calculating the set of least cost chains connecting all pairs of nodes in G is easily done in $|N|^3$ simple operations [7].

The result is a symmetric and dynamic travel time matrix $D_s(\tau)$ for each shopper $s \in S$ that depends on updated congestion conditions in real-time. With such a travel time matrix, any efficient approach for the static TSP can be used to solve the considered problem. In this way, the shopper is routed dynamically based on real-time aisle congestion information.

Next, we find for each shopper a minimum cost Hamiltonian tour R_s^o on a complete undirected graph $G_1 = (R_s, A_s)$, i.e., an optimal sequence of nodes to be visited by solving a symmetric version of a dynamic TSP in G_1, where estimated travel times $\hat{t}_a(\tau)$ are not known with certainty in advance, and the Hamiltonian tour is found a priori and is updated every time there is a significant change in the travel times of the constituent arcs of the Hamiltonian tour.

To minimize the computational complexity of the approach, we apply the conventional TSP formulation, or sub-tour elimination formulation of the TSP, due to Dantzig, Fulerkson, and Johnson [6]. For this scope, we define a binary variable x_{ij} associated with each arc (i, j), which indicates whether the arc is part of the tour, and its cost (travel time) t_{ij}.

Then, each shopping agent solves a TSP that can be formulated as the following mixed integer linear programming problem with n^2 zero-one variables and $n - 1$ continuous variables as follows:

$$\min \sum_{i=0}^{n} \sum_{j \neq i, j=0}^{n} t_{ij} x_{ij} \tag{4}$$

s.t.

$$\sum_{i=0, i \neq j}^{n} x_{ij} = 1, \quad j = 0, \dots, n \tag{5}$$

$$\sum_{j=0, j \neq i}^{n} x_{ij} = 1, \quad i = 0, \dots, n \tag{6}$$

$$u_i - u_j + n x_{ij} \leq n - 1, \quad i, j = 1, \dots, n; \; i \neq j \tag{7}$$

$$u_i \in \mathbf{Z}, \quad i = 0, \dots, n \tag{8}$$

$$x_{ij} \in \{0, 1\}, \quad i, j = 0, \dots, n \tag{9}$$

The objective function (4) minimizes the total shopping travel time of each shopper $s \in S$. Constraints (5) are degree constraints that ensure that the shopper comes from exactly one other item at each item. Constraints (6) ensure that a shopper leaves an item departing to exactly one other item. Moreover, constraints (8) ensure that, if the shopper travels from i to j, then the position of node j is one more than that of node i. Here, u_i is a dummy variable. Together with the bounds (7), they ensure that each non-dummy node is in a unique position. These constraints forbid subtours and enforce that there is only a single tour covering all items, and not two or more disjoint tours that only collectively cover all items. Movement restrictions are not imposed since they will be followed due to the values in the travel time matrix D_s.

MILP problem (4)–(9) will give us the shopping path with the minimal travel time. Hence, a shopper faces this problem whenever the congestion change influences his/her shopping path.

5.2 A Distributed Greedy Heuristic Approach

By using our proposed heuristic solution approach, each shopper agent builds incrementally the trajectory in real- time as he/she moves through a hypermarket. The approach is fully distributed as each shopper agent computes individually and autonomously the trajectory by interacting with other shopper and smart building agents. We follow a First Come Fist Served principle: a first shopper that declares its intention to pass through a node or an arc reserves its passage in time and space and the capacity of the node/arc decreases respectively.

The heuristic operates in iterations as follows. Given is an unordered list of shopping items' nodes to visit and a store entrance node as a starting point of each shopper. In each iteration, the heuristic chooses the closest item in the list to the momentary shopper's node to which the shortest path does not contain any nodes or arcs whose occupancy rate is higher than a given threshold. The shortest paths are computed based on estimated travel times between each two nodes in the path. When the shopper agent confirms the trajectory, it sends to the closest smart building agent this estimated time so that the latter can update its occupancy map and communicate it to other infrastructure and shopper agents.

Algorithm 1 gives a programmatic overview of the heuristic. We consider the following procedures:

- RECEIVEMAPOCCUPANCYFROMINFRASTRUCTUREAGENT allows a shopper agent to receive the hypermarket occupancy map;
- NODEOF returns the node of an item since each item is associated to a node;
- DISTANCETO calculates the distance (following the shortest path) between the current position of a shopper and the next item node to visit;
- ISJAMMED? returns "True" when a node is jammed with people;
- SENDNEXTNODETOVISITTOINFRASTRUCTUREAGENT allows a shopper agent to send, the next node to visit, to the closest smart building agent that updates its hypermarket occupancy map.
- COMPUTESHORTESTPATH returns the shortest path between two nodes (here any classical algorithm from literature can be used).

Clearly, this heuristic is not optimal for several reasons. Firstly, it operates asynchronously. So, when a shopper agent receives the occupancy map, potentially this map may be already obsolete. Secondly, since the closest nodes are favoured for next visit, there is no guarantee to obtain the shortest path among all item nodes. Finally, there is no real negotiation between shopper agents but rather a common agreement to follow a first come first serve principle. Nevertheless, this heuristic is sufficiently sophisticated to be used for shoppers' guidance in hypermarkets with congestion as this is a problem with high computational complexity and fast solution time is of utmost importance.

Algorithm 1. Simple heuristic for shoppers' route guidance

1: **procedure** ROUTEGUIDANCE($S(a)$: the list of items to buy, currentPosition: Node)
2:     **local variables:** d: Integer, nextNodeToVisit: Node, path: list of Node
3:     **while** $S(A) \neq$ **do**
4:         $d \leftarrow +\infty$
5:         RECEIVEMAPOCCUPANCYFROMAGENTBUILDING( )
6:         **for** $i \in S(a)$ **do**
7:             **if** DISTANCETO(NODEOF(i)) $<$ d **and not** ISFULL?(NODEOF(i)) **then**
8:                 nextNodeToVisit $\leftarrow$ NODEOF(i)
9:             **end if**
10:        **end for**
11:        SENDNEXTNODETOVISITTOAGENTBUILDING( )
12:        path $\leftarrow$ COMPUTESHORTESTPATH(currentPosition, NextNodeToVisit)
13:        MOVE(currentPosition, path)
14:    **end while**
15: **end procedure**

---

6 Experiment

We consider a narrow-aisle hypermarket layout graph with a (horizontal) front, intermediate and back aisle and multiple (vertical) lateral aisles, as seen in Fig. 2. The graph is composed of 952 nodes distributed in 18 rows and 64 columns and connected to their neighboring nodes.

The entrance is positioned at the lowest right node $(18, 64)$ connected by dummy arcs (of weight 0) with 20 cash desks that are positioned in row 18 and columns: 4, 7, 10, 13, 16, 19, 22, 25, 28, 31, 34, 37, 40, 43, 46, 49, 52, 55, 58, and 61. Given is weight for each other arc of the graph, $3m$. For the sake of simplicity, we consider that pick time, search time, set-up time and cash-desk waiting times are fixed.

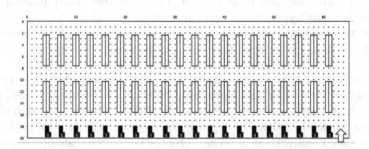

Fig. 2. Use-case hypermarket layout graph with 952 communicating SB agent nodes

A set of 10 predefined shopping lists composed of 50 item nodes has been generated randomly and considered to compare the two approaches proposed in the paper. A shopper starts at the entrance node with one of these shopping lists and ends the shopping at one of the cash-desks with a minimum travel time. The objective of our two approaches is to propose the path to a shopper at his/her current position based on the real-time congestion taking into account the remaining items to buy. We assume that shoppers move one node per time period (from their current node to one of their 4-neighboring nodes, excluding diagonal movements).

Application of the TSP Mathematical Programming Approach. Each shopper agent finds the shortest paths for each pair of its shopping list item nodes by using a variant of the Floyd–Warshall algorithm. In the case there are various paths to reach one node from an actual position, the minimum cost path considering congestion is found. A path capacity of 1 is reserved in time and space by assuming the estimated arrival time based on the momentary crowdedness in the graph's nodes. In the case there are multiple such paths, a path is chosen arbitrarily among the shortest paths.

Then, each shopper agent solves individually the TSP problem (4)–(9) in graph $G_1 = (R_s, A_s)$. This graph is updated as the shopping proceeds and once a node has been reached and surpassed, it is excluded from the graph together with its related arcs.

Application of the Greedy Approach. Similarly to the TSP approach, each agent finds the shortest path between two nodes of the shopping list using a classical algorithm (Dijkstra) (line 12 of the Algorithm 1). A capacity is defined for each node of the graph; this one is then used by the algorithm to choose the next targeted node for the shopper. For the experiment, this capacity is set arbitrary to 15 persons.

In the following, we present the results of the TSP mathematical model run in CPLEX in comparison to our greedy algorithm, in terms of the total distance traveled and the computational time.

Results. Table 1 presents the performance[1] of the two approaches regarding two metrics: the computational time and the traveled distance. The maximum run time of the CPLEX solver was 60 s. The best found solution up to this time is presented in the Table. An optimal solution was found when the computational time was lower than 60 s.

We observe that globally the CPLEX-based TSP mathematical programming model outperforms the greedy approach. On average, the solutions obtained are 22% better, which represents almost 200 m of walking difference in the considered scenario. This result has to be put in perspective with the total length of the store, which is equal to 195 m: therefore, the TSP-based approach allows the user to save a full trip from one end of the store to the other. Then, the larger the

---

[1] Simulation experiments were performed on HP ProBook with Intel Core i5-6200U CPU at 2.30 Ghz with 16 Gb RAM memory.

hypermarket is, the more the use of TSP is justified. Concerning the computational time, the greedy heuristic runs significantly faster, with an average largely inferior to 1 s. Consequently, the greedy algorithm is more appropriate for small and crowded hypermarkets which require to recompute quickly the paths of the shoppers while moving from one item to another.

Table 1. Comparison between the TSP mathematical model solved by CPLEX and the greedy heuristic approach

	Computational time		Cost (traveled distance)		
	Greedy heuristic	TSP	Greedy heuristic	TSP	Gap (in %)
List of items 1	0.697	60	987	708	28.26
List of items 2	0.585	60	846	708	16.31
List of items 3	0.683	60	972	681	29.93
List of items 4	0.689	47	1032	699	32.26
List of items 5	0.775	60	912	717	21.29
List of items 6	0.65	3.94	885	747	15.59
List of items 7	0.702	60	981	756	22.93
List of items 8	0.633	0.92	858	714	16.78
List of items 9	0.671	1.44	936	705	24.67
List of items 10	0.778	60	951	753	20.82
Mean	0.6863	60	951	753	22.88

7 Conclusions

In this paper, we proposed a distributed shopping route guidance architecture and a shopping route computation mechanism for hypermarkets equipped with smart space technologies with the objective to minimize the time spent in shopping given a shopping list. In our proposed approach, a hypermarket is modelled as a graph on which each person is seen as a particle of network flow. Each node of the graph represents a part of the hypermarket where a set of items are located with a given capacity to accommodate people around them. Similarly, an arc connects two nodes and has the capacity that corresponds to the maximum flow of people on an unobstructed walk way it presents.

In the proposed architecture, we modelled smart hypermarket as a network of rational and collaborating smart building agents and each shopper as a rational self-concerned agent with a given list of items to buy. We assumed that the choosing and picking time are constant for all shoppers and products. However, this time is influenced by multiple factors: visibility, type of a shopper, type of a product, crowdedness, a part of the day, etc. In our future work, for simplification purposes, we will investigate a modelling assumption of an estimated pickup time depending on a type of a product and a shopper. Since shopping is not only a purchasing, but also a social experience, the shoppers' personality and preferences play an important role. In our future work, we will also work on the extension of the proposed approach to include shopping lists that are more loosely defined, as e.g., shopping for fun with a qualitative item descriptions and preferences regarding broad product categories open to marketing suggestions.

To simplify path computation considering congestion, which is a computationally hard problem, we used a first come first served principle. We assumed that people follow the suggested routes. The users that do not use the app and therefore do not share the information are seen as a white noise to the system. In case a shopper does not follow the suggested route or he/she deviates significantly from the route, we may introduce penalties. We will deal with this topic in future work.

By updating estimated travel times of the network in real-time during execution, we can accommodate future shoppers that want to minimize the time of their shopping by choosing an interval of the day for their shopping and consider congestion in this interval. This topic will also be a possible part of future work.

References

1. Akcelik, R.: Travel time functions for transport planning purposes: Davidson's function, its time dependent form and alternative travel time function. Aust. Road Res. **21**(3) (1991)
2. Applegate, D.L., Bixby, R.E., Chvatal, V., Cook, W.J.: The Traveling Salesman Problem: A Computational Study. Princeton University Press, Princeton (2011)
3. Bajo, J., Corchado, J.M., De Paz, Y., et al.: SHOMAS: intelligent guidance and suggestions in shopping centres. Appl. Soft Comput. **9**(2), 851–862 (2009)
4. Bohnenberger, T., Jameson, A., Krüger, A., Butz, A.: Location-aware shopping assistance: evaluation of a decision-theoretic approach. In: Paternò, F. (ed.) Mobile HCI 2002. LNCS, vol. 2411, pp. 155–169. Springer, Heidelberg (2002). https://doi.org/10.1007/3-540-45756-9_13
5. Cho, H., Ji, J., Chen, Z., Park, H., Lee, W.: Measuring a distance between things with improved accuracy. Proc. Comput. Sci. **52**, 1083–1088 (2015)
6. Dantzig, G., Fulkerson, R., Johnson, S.: Solution of a large-scale traveling-salesman problem. J. Oper. Res. Soc. Am. **2**(4), 393–410 (1954)
7. Deo, N., Pang, C.Y.: Shortest-path algorithms: taxonomy and annotation. Networks **14**(2), 275–323 (1984)
8. Dunkel, J., Fernández, A., Ortiz, R., Ossowski, S.: Event-driven architecture for decision support in traffic management systems. Expert. Syst. Appl. **38**(6), 6530–6539 (2011)
9. Helsgaun, K.: An effective implementation of the Lin-Kernighan traveling salesman heuristic. Eur. J. Oper. Res. **126**(1), 106–130 (2000)
10. Hoffman, K.L., Padberg, M., Rinaldi, G.: Traveling salesman problem. In: Gass, S.I., Fu, M.C. (eds.) Encyclopedia of Operations Research and Management Science, pp. 1573–1578. Springer, Boston (2013). https://doi.org/10.1007/978-1-4419-1153-7
11. Ijaz, F., Yang, H.K., Ahmad, A.W., Lee, C.: Indoor positioning: a review of indoor ultrasonic positioning systems. In: 2013 15th International Conference on Advanced Communication Technology (ICACT), pp. 1146–1150. IEEE (2013)

12. Ilie, S., Bădică, C.: Distributed multi-agent system for solving traveling salesman problem using ant colony optimization. In: Essaaidi, M., Malgeri, M., Badica,C. (eds.) Intelligent Distributed Computing IV, vol. 315, pp. 119–129. Springer, Heidelberg (2010). https://doi.org/10.1007/978-3-642-15211-5_13

13. Kabadi, S.N.: Polynomially Solvable Cases of the TSP, pp. 489–583. Springer, Boston (2007). https://doi.org/10.1007/0-306-48213-4_11

14. Letchford, A.N., Nasiri, S.D., Theis, D.O.: Compact formulations of the Steiner traveling salesman problem and related problems. Eur. J. Oper. Res. **228**(1), 83–92 (2013)

15. Li, Y.M., Lin, L.F., Ho, C.C.: A social route recommender mechanism for store shopping support. Decis. Support. Syst. **94**, 97–108 (2017)

16. Lujak, M., Giordani, S., Ossowski, S.: Fair route guidance: bridging system and user optimization. In: 17th International IEEE Conference on Intelligent Transportation Systems (ITSC), pp. 1415–1422, October 2014

17. Lujak, M., Billhardt, H., Dunkel, J., Fernández, A., Hermoso, R., Ossowski, S.: A distributed architecture for real-time evacuation guidance in large smart buildings. Comput. Sci. Inf. Syst. **14**(1), 257–282 (2017)

18. Lujak, M., Giordani, S., Ossowski, S.: Route guidance: bridging system and user optimization in traffic assignment. Neurocomputing **151**, 449–460 (2015)

19. Lymberopoulos, D., Liu, J., Yang, X., Choudhury, R.R., Handziski, V., Sen, S.: A realistic evaluation and comparison of indoor location technologies: experiences and lessons learned. In: Proceedings of the 14th International Conference on Information Processing in Sensor Networks, pp. 178–189. ACM (2015)

20. Ng, T.M.: From "where I am" to "here I am": accuracy study on location-based services with IBeacon technology. HKIE Trans. **22**(1), 23–31 (2015)

21. Pan, J.C.H., Shih, P.H.: Evaluation of the throughput of a multiple-picker order picking system with congestion consideration. Comput. Ind. Eng. **55**(2), 379–389 (2008)

22. Pan, J.C.H., Wu, M.H.: Throughput analysis for order picking system with multiple pickers and aisle congestion considerations. Comput. Oper. Res. **39**(7), 1661–1672 (2012)

23. Theys, C., Bräysy, O., Dullaert, W., Raa, B.: Using a *tsp* heuristic for routing order pickers in warehouses. Eur. J. Oper. Res. **200**(3), 755–763 (2010). https://doi.org/10.1016/j.ejor.2009.01.036

24. Timmermans, H.: Pedestrian Behavior: Models, Data Collection and Applications. Emerald Group Publishing Limited, London (2009)

25. Tinós, R.: Analysis of the dynamic traveling salesman problem with weight changes. In: 2015 Latin America Congress on Computational Intelligence (LA-CCI), pp. 1–6. IEEE (2015)

26. Toriello, A., Haskell, W.B., Poremba, M.: A dynamic traveling salesman problem with stochastic arc costs. Oper. Res. **62**(5), 1107–1125 (2014)

Author Index